TORTS

Fifth Edition

by

Lawrence C. Levine
Professor of Law
University of the Pacific,
McGeorge School of Law

QUICK REVIEW SERIES®

Mat #41372004

Sum & Substance Quick Review Series is a Publication of West Academic Publishing.

© West, a Thomson business, 2000
© 2009 Thomson Reuters
© 2014 LEG, Inc. d/b/a West Academic
    444 Cedar Street, Suite 700
    St. Paul, MN 55101
    1-877-888-1330

Printed in the United States of America

ISBN: 978-0-314-28640-6

TABLE OF CONTENTS

TABLE OF CONTENTS

CHAPTER I

BASIC INTENTIONAL TORTS

A. IN GENERAL. [§ 1]

The key focus of intentional torts is on the **mental state** of the defendant; intentional torts are generally committed by a **purposeful** or **knowing** (but not always evil) wrongdoer. Indeed, in many situations the intentionally tortious conduct at issue could also constitute a crime under the state penal code statute (e.g., assault and battery). The criminal law aspects are irrelevant here, however. Focus on the mental state and the other required elements for each intentional tort. See overview chart on page 3.

B. STUDY APPROACH. [§ 2]

The primary focus for the study of intentional torts is on the meaning of "intent" and on the **elements** of each specific intentional tort (e.g., false imprisonment). Understanding the meaning of "intent" is crucial in order to distinguish fact patterns raising intentional tort issues from those that do not. As discussed below, the meaning of intent actually varies somewhat depending on the tort in issue.

1. Exam Hint. [§ 3]

> Some professors test intentional torts heavily, providing the student with a complex (and often bizarre) fact pattern teeming with possible intentional torts. In such a "Name That Tort" type of question, the task is to **be creative** and to identify as many possible intentional torts and defenses as possible. It's not always as easy as it may seem.

> **Example. [§ 4]** Dex throws a rock through Polly's glass front window, hoping to hit Polly on the head with the rock. Polly is asleep at the time. The rock grazes Polly's head. Polly does not wake. As discussed below, there is likely a battery here. However, there is also a conversion of Polly's window.

C. INTENT. [§ 5]

1. The Meaning of Intent. [§ 6]

Normally, the term "intent" means that the defendant had the act or result either as her goal **or** that she was **aware that it was substantially certain** to occur. In other words, although intent is surely satisfied by finding a **conscious desire** on the part of the defendant, proof that the defendant **knew** the act or result was practically certain will suffice for "intent" as well. **Beware:** "Practically" certain does not mean likely, possible or even probable; it is a level of greater definiteness.

> **a. Example of Purposeful Intent. [§ 7]** Dan saw his archrival Pol across the wide street. Aware that his chances for success were slim because he had lousy aim, Dan picked up a stone and hurled it at Pol hoping to hit Pol with the stone. To Dan's great surprise, the stone hit Pol. Because Dan's conscious object was to hit Pol with the stone, Dan has the intent to commit the tort (here the tort of battery).

> **b. Example of Knowing Intent. [§ 8]** Deb, a department store owner, was in a great hurry to close the store. Although she knew that typically customers could be found in the store at 5:00 p.m., she locked the doors exactly at 5:00 p.m. anyway, figuring that the security guards would let anyone out when they arrived at 5:30 p.m. Pam was locked in against her will. Although Deb did not desire to confine Pam nor was she positive that anyone was inside the store when she locked it, she had the intent to falsely imprison Pam because she knew that it was **substantially certain** that someone would be locked in against her will.

2. Intent as to Act or Consequences. [§ 9]

It is important to recognize that "intent" means different things for different intentional torts. For some of these torts (trespass to land, trespass to chattels, and conversion) all that is required is that the defendant **intended to do the act** which resulted in the plaintiff's injury. However, in the case of those intentional torts against the person—assault, battery, false imprisonment, and intentional infliction of emotional distress—there is no liability unless the defendant was purposeful or knowing as to the **consequences of the act**.

INTENTIONAL TORTS TO PERSONS

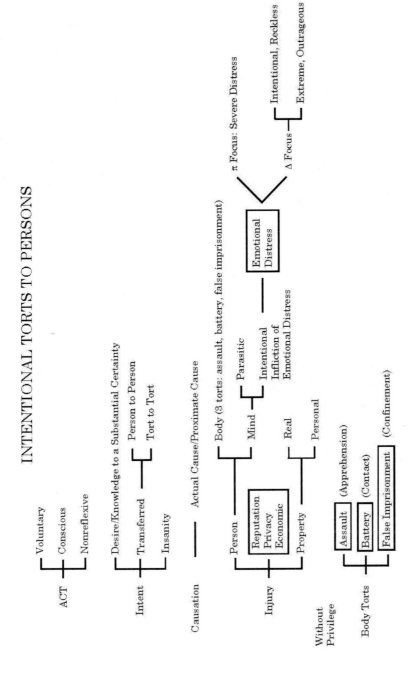

a. **Example.** **[§ 10]** Patsy enters Doc's Gunshop to purchase a pistol. When Doc picks up a gun to demonstrate the safety features of the weapon, Patsy is frightened because she thinks that Doc is going to shoot her. While Doc's act of displaying the weapon was intentional, he did not intend to cause Patsy to be apprehensive of being shot (the basis of an assault cause of action). That is, he neither had the purpose of causing her fright nor was he substantially certain that his acts would engender such fear. Accordingly, there was no "intent."

b. **Example.** **[§ 11]** Darryl, one dark night, walked out on a dock which he believed that he owned. The dock actually belonged to Penelope, and Darryl's identical dock was next door. Darryl has the "intent" required for the intentional tort of trespass to land because Darryl intended to walk onto the dock. His mistaken belief that the dock was his is irrelevant for purposes of finding intent here.

3. Transferred Intent. [§ 12]

The doctrine of **transferred intent** permits a defendant to be held liable for an intentional tort even if he was neither purposeful nor knowing. It takes two basic forms: where there is the wrong victim or where there is the "wrong" tort.

a. Transferred Intent Between Victims. [§ 13]

It is clear that knowledge of the identity of the victim is not essential for the defendant to be liable for an intentional tort.

(1) Example: Unintended Victim. [§ 14] Del wanted to injure Xavier, who was standing on a crowded street corner, by throwing a rock at him. The rock missed Xavier, but struck Pete, who was standing behind Xavier. Even though Del had no conscious desire to harm Pete, nor was he substantially certain that Pete would be hurt, his intent to injure Xavier will be transferred (i.e., be held sufficiently blameworthy) to render him liable to Pete. Del had the purpose to make contact, and he did so. That the victim was not the one intended will not relieve Del of liability.

(2) Example: Mistaken Identity. [§ 15] Diana wished to play a practical joke on her brother, Apollo. She followed Apollo into a restaurant and waited outside the restroom door when Apollo went in to wash his hands. When the door opened, Diana hurled a cream pie into the face of Perseus, who had exited the restroom before Apollo. Diana's mistake as to the identity of the person struck is irrelevant to her liability to Perseus since she clearly intended to inflict a nonconsensual touching upon someone.

b.   Transferred Intent Between Torts. [§ 16]

Just as intent can transfer between victims, a blameworthy defendant may be liable in tort if his intentional conduct causes an injury of a different type than originally contemplated. The most common application of this rule relates to assault and battery.

> **(1) Example. [§ 17]** Don intends to frighten Peg by throwing a firecracker near her. The firecracker accidentally explodes in Peg's eye. Under the doctrine of transferred intent, Don will be deemed to have the requisite intent for the battery even though he did not intend to cause a harmful or offensive touching. His intent to commit an assault will be enough.

c.   Dimensions of This Form of Transferred Intent. [§ 18]

This branch of transferred intent historically applied whenever the plaintiff had the desire to commit any of the five torts redressed at early common law by the "writ of trespass" (**assault, battery, false imprisonment, trespass to land,** and **trespass to chattels**). The trend, however, is toward limiting this type of transferred intent to the intentional torts of assault, battery and false imprisonment.

4.   Insane and Immature Persons May Have Intent. [§ 19]

Neither insanity nor infancy typically will shield the defendant from responsibility for her intentional torts.

a.   Children Are Liable for Their Intentional Torts. [§ 20]

As long as the child is capable of forming the intent required for the tort, she is legally responsible for her intentional torts.

> **(1) Example. [§ 21]** Brian, age five, was visiting Ruth, an adult. When Ruth started to sit down, Brian yanked the chair from where it had been and sat down on it himself. Ruth broke her hip when she missed the chair and fell to the ground. Brian is liable for the intentional tort of battery regardless of whether he could understand the wrongfulness or seriousness of his act so long as he was substantially certain that his movement of the chair would cause Ruth to fall (*Garratt v. Dailey, 279 P.2d 1091 (Wash. 1955)*).

> **(a) Note:** **[§ 22]** Absent a statute to the contrary, parents are not vicariously liable for their child's intentional torts. This means that, using the prior example, Brian's parents are not liable to Ruth for their son's tortious act due to their status as his parents. Parents can be liable for their own tortious conduct, however, as when they negligently fail to supervise their minor child.

b. Insane Persons Are Liable for Their Intentional Torts. [§ 23]

Unlike the criminal law, a lack of moral blameworthiness is irrelevant provided the defendant understood the consequences of her volitional act. The exceptions are those intentional torts which require "especially" culpable mental states such as "malice."

> **(1) Example.** **[§ 24]** Don, because of a mental disease, believes Pru is Adolph Hitler. Don picks up a knife and throws it hoping to hurt "Adolph Hitler." Don has the intent for battery despite his delusional thinking.

5. Intent Need Not Be Hostile. [§ 25]

As a general rule, the intent need not be hostile, malicious, or otherwise improperly motivated. A practical joker who has no hatred for her victim nor desire to injure her victim may nevertheless have sufficient intent to be liable for an intentional tort. Thus, intent should be distinguished from "motive," the latter going to the defendant's reason for engaging in the tortious conduct.

D. CAUSATION. [§ 26]

All torts require the defendant's act to have a causal nexus to the plaintiff's harm (i.e., to be a **"cause-in-fact"** of the injury). Further, while the intentional tortfeasor is generally liable for all extended consequences of her action, there is some outer limit where the defendant will no longer be liable for the consequences of her intentional act (**"proximate cause"**). For example, would any court have held the man who assassinated Archduke Ferdinand, thus precipitating World War I, liable in tort for all the death and destruction of that war? Since causation problems tend to be taught in the context of **negligence analysis,** however, this topic will be discussed there.

E. INTENTIONAL TORTS TO THE PERSON. [§ 27]

1. Battery. [§ 28]

Battery is an intentional harmful or offensive contact with the plaintiff's person, or something closely attached thereto. The tort of **battery** thus requires (a) an **affirmative act** by the defendant (b) with the **intent to touch another** (c) resulting in a **harmful** or **offensive contact** (d) with a person or something closely connected to the person. The tort of battery protects a person's bodily integrity.

a. Act. [§ 29]

To be liable for battery, the defendant must do some volitional act which causes an offensive or harmful touching of the plaintiff.

(1) Personal Touching Not Required. [§ 30]

It is not necessary that the defendant personally touch the plaintiff as long as the defendant sets the touching instrumentality into motion. For example, Dot can be liable for battery if she throws a rock at Pip that hits him, or causes her dog to attack and bite Pip.

b. Intent. [§ 31]

In order to be liable for battery, the defendant must have acted with the intent to inflict the unwanted touching (i.e., intent with regard to the consequences). The ultimate test is whether the defendant desired to make contact or intended to do an act which she knew was substantially certain to result in contact. It probably does not matter that the defendant thought the contact would be neither harmful nor offensive. As long as there is intentional contact which proves to be harmful or offensive, there is a battery in most jurisdictions.

(1) Single versus Dual Intent. [§ 32]

In most jurisdictions, it is sufficient for the plaintiff to prove that the defendant intended contact that turned out to be harmful or offensive. A minority of jurisdictions, however, have adopted a dual intent requirement for battery that requires the plaintiff to prove that the defendant not only intended contact but that he also intended that the contact be harmful or offensive. Thus, if Dino believed that he was so handsome that he would share his love by patting passersby on their behinds as they passed him on a busy street, in most jurisdictions,

Dino would be liable for battery because he intended contact that would be offensive to a reasonable person. Seemingly, he would not commit battery in a dual intent jurisdiction: although he has the intent for the contact he does not intend that it be offensive.

(2) Intent to Assault Sufficient. [§ 33]

As mentioned above in the discussion of transferred intent, if a harmful or offensive touching results from an action which was actually intended to cause the plaintiff to be apprehensive of receiving a battery (an assault), the intent to frighten will be sufficient to maintain an action for battery.

> **(a) Example. [§ 34]** Druxel, standing behind Prav unbeknownst to Prav, hopes to scare Prav by throwing a knife near Prav's right ear. The knife accidentally hits and cuts Prav's right ear. Under the transferred intent doctrine, the intent for the assault will satisfy the intent element for the battery and Druxel will be liable for a battery.

(3) Consider Negligence as Alternative Basis of Liability. [§ 35]

When the intent for battery is lacking or cannot be proved, the defendant may nevertheless be liable under the tort of "negligence," in which the focus is on whether the defendant's conduct created such foreseeable risks of harm that a reasonably prudent person in the defendant's position would not have acted as the defendant did. Unlike a plaintiff in a battery action, a plaintiff in a negligence action must prove damages in order to recover.

c. Injury: Harmful or Offensive Touching. [§ 36]

The tort of battery is not complete unless there is **actual contact** with the person of the plaintiff **or** with something **closely and physically associated with her.**

(1) Physical Invasion of Sphere of Personality. [§ 37]

The defendant's act need not necessarily cause a touching of the plaintiff's person—the touching of **something closely associated** with her may constitute a physical invasion of her person. Thus, if Dora intentionally strikes Patrick's cane or knocks off his hat, there is a clear battery. On the other hand, if Dora strikes the fender of Patrick's car with her hand, there is less likelihood of finding a battery as the car is probably not so intimately associated with Patrick so as to make Dora's action an invasion of Patrick's sphere of personality.

(2) Awareness of Touching Not Required. [§ 38]

The civil wrong of battery is based upon an actual touching of the plaintiff's person. Thus, unlike for assault, the plaintiff need not be aware of the contact at the time it occurs.

> **(a) Example. [§ 39]** If Dwight, finding Polly asleep, secretly kisses her under circumstances where he has no right to do so, Dwight is liable for battery even if the kiss is so light that Polly was not awakened by it. Polly's lack of knowledge at the time of the touching makes the touching no less offensive.

(3) Nature of Injury. [§ 40]

No particular injury must be proven as part of the plaintiff's prima facie case so long as the contact was either harmful or offensive.

(a) Is Touching Offensive?: Normally an Objective Standard. [§ 41]

Whether a touching is **offensive** is generally determined by **whether an ordinary person, not unduly sensitive as to her dignity, would be offended by the contact.** However, if the defendant is **aware** that a certain type of touching is peculiarly offensive to a particular person and causes such a touching, she may be liable for battery even if such a touching would not offend ordinary persons.

> **(i) Example. [§ 42]** Diego and Percy are delegates at a convention of the Benevolent Order of Buffaloes, a fraternal organization. Diego walks up to Percy and grabs his hand in a vigorous handshake. While most persons would not find such conduct offensive under the circumstances, Percy has an abnormal fear of being touched and is extremely upset. So long as Diego was not aware of Percy's unusual sensibilities, he is not liable for battery because this contact is not objectively offensive. If, however, Diego was aware of Percy's aversion to being touched and shook Percy's hand anyway, Diego would be liable for battery.

(b) Harmful Touching: Eggshell Skull Rule. [§ 43]

In the case of a **harmful** touching (one which causes physical injury), the defendant will be responsible for all direct consequences of her wrongful conduct, even if the injury is surprisingly severe due to the unknown and unforeseeable susceptibilities of the plaintiff. This doctrine, typically and charmingly called the **eggshell skull rule,** expresses the notion that, **in cases of physical injury,** the tortious wrongdoer "**takes the plaintiff as she finds him.**"

> **(i) Example. [§ 44]** Desdemona intentionally hits Portia on the forehead. While most persons would not have been injured by the contact, Portia has an unusually thin skull and suffers a serious brain injury. Desdemona will be liable for all of the damages caused to Portia even if she could not have reasonably foreseen the extent of the damages resulting from her act.

(4) Proof of Damages Not Required. [§ 45]

Where the plaintiff establishes the prima facie elements of battery, she may recover substantial damages (as the jury sees fit) without specific proof of loss. Thus, the person kissed against her will while asleep will recover compensatory damages for the unconsented, offensive contact in the amount that the jury sees fit. If the plaintiff suffers physical harm, she may recover for that too, along with damages for the invasion of her bodily integrity. Further, punitive damages may be appropriate where the defendant has a particularly culpable mental state.

d. Defenses. [§ 46]

Defenses to battery are discussed below [§ 102].

2. Assault. [§ 47]

The tort of **assault** is committed when the defendant's (a) affirmative **intentional** act (b) places the plaintiff in **apprehension** (c) of an **imminent** (d) **harmful or offensive touching.** Assault was the first tort that recognized interference with mental tranquility as a legally cognizable harm. No contact occurs in the context of assault.

a. Act. [§ 48]

The tort of assault requires some **affirmative** intentional act by the defendant. Courts (and others) often state that "an assault cannot be committed by words." This is not really accurate. While normally words alone are not sufficient to constitute an assault because they do not create a reasonable apprehension of an **immediate** battery, there are times when words are clearly sufficient.

> **(1) Example. [§ 49]** Po is walking down an alley one night. From behind he hears a voice commanding: "Stop where you are. I've got a gun pointed at your head and am about to blow your brains out." It turns out that the voice came from Dixie, who didn't even have a gun. Po could bring an action for assault against Dixie though the tort was completely committed by words.

b. Intent. [§ 50]

As with battery, the intent of the defendant must relate to the **consequences** of the defendant's act. That is, it must be the subjective intent of the defendant to induce apprehension of a harmful or offensive touching in the mind of the plaintiff or the defendant must know it is substantially certain that the plaintiff will suffer such apprehension.

(1) Intent to Batter Sufficient. [§ 51]

As noted earlier, an assault will be found if the defendant had the requisite intent to commit a battery (an unwanted touching) regardless of any intent with regard to any apprehension of such a contact. This result follows from the doctrine of transferred intent (See §§ 12–18)

> **(a) Example. [§ 52]** Dork, trying to hit Port with a snowball, misses when Port ducks to avoid getting hit. Dork, who intended a battery, is liable for an assault.

(2) Assault and Battery. [§ 53]

A layperson often speaks of "assault and battery" as if they are inseparable concepts. It is true that they often arise in the same factual situation, as where Donna throws a knife at Paco and Paco sees the knife coming toward him and then gets stabbed with the knife. The pre-impact fear is the "assault" and the harmful contact is the "battery." Because there is no "merger doctrine" for intentional torts, the defendant can be liable for both an assault and a battery. However, clever law professors can easily create a situation where there is one without the other (e.g., a sleeping victim who gets kissed against her will; a thrown knife that comes close but misses the victim, etc.).

> **(a) Example. [§ 54]** Dumont sneaks up on Porky from behind and strikes him in the back with a club. Dumont is liable for battery but not assault. Prior to the touching Porky was not put in any apprehension of being struck. The combination of assault and battery applies only when the victim was in reasonable apprehension of the touching and was in fact subsequently touched.

c. Injury: Apprehension of Imminent Touching. [§ 55]

The defendant's acts must create a reasonable apprehension of a harmful or offensive touching in the mind of the plaintiff. Obviously, the plaintiff must be aware of the threatened harm, since without such awareness he could not be under any apprehension.

(1) Reasonableness of Apprehension. [§ 56]

Similar to the rule relating to the offensive touching, the defendant's act must be sufficient to cause apprehension in the mind of a **reasonable person of ordinary sensibilities** (unless the defendant **knows** of this particular plaintiff's special susceptibilities). It is **not** necessary that the plaintiff be in fear, however, only that he reasonably apprehend that the defendant will commit an immediate battery.

(2) Special Problems of Threats. [§ 57]

Difficult assault problems arise when no direct action toward touching the plaintiff has occurred but rather there is only a threat of future injury.

(a) Words Must Be Accompanied by Some Act. [§ 58]

As noted in § 46, words alone usually will not constitute an assault because they do not create a threat of an imminent touching. An action for assault may lie, however, when such words are accompanied by acts or gestures, such as the pointing of a gun or walking toward the plaintiff while shaking one's fist.

(b) Defendant's Intent or Ability to Carry Out Threat Irrelevant. [§ 59]

It is normally held that the defendant's actual intent to physically touch the plaintiff in the manner threatened or even his actual ability to do so (as when the defendant threatens to shoot the plaintiff with a gun that is in fact unloaded) is irrelevant for civil liability for assault. All that is required is that the defendant intends that the plaintiff be apprehensive of the contact and that the plaintiff reasonably believes that the threat will be carried out.

(c) Conditional Threats. [§ 60]

Whether a conditional threat may constitute an assault depends upon whether it would reasonably cause the plaintiff to be apprehensive of a touching.

> **(i) Example 1. [§ 61]** Duck shakes his fist at Pigeon and says, "If you weren't so small already, I'd break you in half." Since Pigeon is not likely to grow in the next few seconds, there was no assault since there is no threat of imminent injury.

> **(ii) Example 2. [§ 62]** Doris moves toward Peaches and says "If I ever catch you near my husband again, I'll scratch your eyes out." This, too, is not an assault because the threat is not immediate.

> **(iii) Example 3. [§ 63]** Devlin points his gun at Pock and says "Your money or your life." Although no harm is **immediately** threatened and even though Pock could theoretically avoid injury by complying with Devlin's demand, a lack of any justification to impose such a condition would reasonably cause Pock to be fearful of an imminent injury. An assault results.

(3) Proof of Damage Not Required. [§ 64]

It is unnecessary to the plaintiff's prima facie case to allege or prove damages. **Damages are assumed to result from any intentional invasion of one's person.** A jury may award substantial amounts for actual pain and suffering as well as for any other harm that follows from the intentional tort. Also, punitive damages may be appropriate in many cases of intentional torts.

d.   **Defenses. [§ 65]**

Defenses to assault are the same as those for battery and are discussed below [§ 102].

3.   **False Imprisonment. [§ 66]**

The essence of the tort of **false imprisonment** is the unlawful detention of a person in such a way as to deprive that person of her liberty. The tort requires: (a) an **act or omission by the defendant (b) with the intent to confine** someone (c) resulting in **actual confinement** of the plaintiff and (d) either **awareness of the confinement or injury resulting therefrom.** The tort of false imprisonment protects a person's freedom of movement.

a.   **Act or Omission. [§ 67]**

False imprisonment requires some act or omission by the defendant which has the effect of detaining the plaintiff or confining her to any particular area. The defendant need not personally confine the plaintiff as long as he instigated and caused the restraint of liberty.

(1)   **Physical Restraint. [§ 68]**

False imprisonment typically results from constructing physical barriers.

(2)   **Threats. [§ 69]**

False imprisonment may also be accomplished by the intentional use of threats for the purpose of confining and restraining the plaintiff. As with assault, however, the threat must be of **imminent injury** and it must be sufficient to **overbear the will of the ordinary, reasonable person** (unless the defendant knew of this particular plaintiff's unusual sensibilities).

> **(a) Example. [§ 70]** Dopey informs Popeye that Dopey will shoot him if Popeye tries to leave the room. This is enough for false imprisonment (as well as possibly an assault).

(b)   **Kinds of Threats. [§ 71]**

Traditionally, only threats of physical violence to plaintiff or plaintiff's family constituted sufficient intimidation to amount to a confinement. More recent cases, however, have held that threats directed at the plaintiff's valuable property ("If you go, I'll push your car off of the cliff") may also give rise to liability for false imprisonment if the plaintiff in fact stays due to the threat. Threats of reputational harm are not sufficient, however. Thus, if the plaintiff stayed because of the defendant's threat to tell their friends that the plaintiff cheated on the torts midterm, this would not be a basis for a false imprisonment claim.

(3) Omission: Duty to Release. [§ 72]

When the defendant has a special duty to release someone validly confined, failure to do so is false imprisonment. For example, the intentional failure of a jailer to release a prisoner when her sentence has been completed is false imprisonment.

b. Intent. [§ 73]

The defendant's acts must be purposeful or knowing with regard to the consequences of the confinement of a person. Thus, the defendant's intent to confine need not be directed toward the specific plaintiff or any particular individual or group.

c. Result: Actual Confinement. [§ 74]

It is not necessary that the plaintiff be confined by four walls or to a very small area—even confinement to a particular city has been held to be false imprisonment. All that is required is that there be substantial interference with the plaintiff's freedom to leave.

(1) Blocking Way or Locking Out Distinguished. [§ 75]

It is not false imprisonment merely to block a person's way so long as reasonable alternatives are available.

(a) Example. [§ 76] Professor Dread locks the classroom door to exclude latecomers. Pava arrives to class late and cannot get into the room. Pava has no false imprisonment claim. Pon, another student, tries to leave the classroom but cannot because the door is locked, Pon has a claim for false imprisonment.

---

(2) Time Period Irrelevant. [§ 77]

The length of the confinement is not a material element of false imprisonment—even a detention of a few seconds is actionable. Of course, the time period of the confinement is relevant to establishing the amount of damages to be awarded.

(3) Reasonable Means of Escape. [§ 78]

In spite of the defendant's intent, the plaintiff has no action for false imprisonment if she could have escaped the confinement by reasonable means **of which she knew.**

(a) Dangerous or Embarrassing Escape. [§ 79]

Any method which is dangerous or unduly embarrassing is not a "reasonable" means of escape. Thus, if Pernicious steals all of Dundee's clothes while he is in the shower, requiring him to run naked to a neighbor's house to get something to wear, or locks Dundee in a third-story room with a trellis outside the window as his only means of escape, Dundee has been confined despite the technical availability of a means of escape since a reasonable person in his position would have remained where he was.

(b) Leaving Property. [§ 80]

Since a reasonable person would not leave her valuable property behind, an offered release conditioned upon such an act does not preclude liability for false imprisonment (e.g., "you can go if you want, but your suitcase stays here").

d. Knowledge or Actual Harm. [§ 81]

Traditionally, no action lies for false imprisonment unless the plaintiff **knew** that she was confined at the time (note how this is similar to assault). However, such knowledge is not required when the plaintiff suffers some actual injury due to the confinement (e.g., a newborn baby suffers physical injury from three days of confinement).

---

(1) Example. [§ 82] Darth kidnaps Pablum, a two-month old baby, and locks Pablum in a closet for two hours. Pablum would not be able to recover for false imprisonment unless she suffered physical harm as a result of that confinement.

---

e. Defenses. [§ 83]

In addition to the usual defenses to intentional torts to person (discussed starting in § 102) the following defenses typically arising in the false imprisonment context exist.

(1) Arrests by Police Officers. [§ 84]

A police officer acting upon a warrant which is valid on its face may physically restrain a person and is not liable for false imprisonment even if the warrant is ultimately determined to be invalid. Moreover, the officer has no duty to inquire beyond the face of the warrant.

(a) Arrests without Warrants. [§ 85]

A police officer may arrest a person without a warrant if she reasonably believes that a **felony** has been committed and she reasonably believes that the person arrested is the perpetrator. An officer may arrest a person for a **misdemeanor** if she has probable cause to believe (i.e., it is more likely than not) that the arrested person committed the crime in her presence. If there is probable cause, the officer is not liable for false imprisonment even if the person arrested did not commit the crime in question.

(2) Citizen's Arrests. [§ 86]

A private person may lawfully arrest another for a felony if the felony has, in fact, been committed and she reasonably believes that the person arrested committed the felony. It is not necessary that the felony has been committed in the private person's presence, however.

(a) Misdemeanor Arrest. [§ 87]

As to misdemeanors, the rule is more restrictive. A private person may arrest another for a misdemeanor only if it was committed in her presence and constituted or threatened a breach of the peace. The defendant acts at her peril both as to whether a misdemeanor has occurred and whether the person arrested is guilty (i.e., any mistake, however reasonable, defeats this privilege).

(3) Shopkeeper's Privilege. [§ 88]

All states, by statute or case law, grant immunity to a shopkeeper if the merchant or her agent had **probable cause** for believing that the plaintiff was shoplifting. Note, however, that the shopkeeper's actions must not extend beyond that which would be reasonably permissible under the circumstances as to both the length of the detention and the manner of the detention. In other words, if a store owner has reasonable suspicion that a patron is shoplifting, she may detain the patron for a reasonable time to conduct a reasonable investigation without fear of liability for false imprisonment and other intentional torts.

(a) Example. [§ 89] Plaintiff Mrs. Bonkowski was leaving defendant's store one evening when she was stopped by the store detective. He said that because someone inside the store had told him that Mrs. Bonkowski was observed taking some jewelry she needed to empty out her purse. When Mrs. Bonkowski produced receipts showing she had paid for the jewelry, the store detective permitted her to leave the store. A jury awarded the plaintiff substantial damages for false imprisonment. The appellate court reversed the jury verdict for a new trial because if the store detective reasonably believed that the plaintiff had wrongly taken the items from the store, he was privileged to detain her for a reasonable time for a reasonable investigation. *Bonkowski v. Arlan's* Department Store, 162 N.W.2d 347 (Mich. App. 1968).

(b) Consent. [§ 90]

There is no false imprisonment where the plaintiff consents. Thus, if DunCo.'s security guard informs Pam that she is suspected of shoplifting and asks her to wait in a back room for the police to arrive and Pam goes to the back room stating that she looks forward to the arrival of the police so that she can clear her "good name," there is probably no false imprisonment due to Pam's consent to be detained.

4. Intentional Infliction of Emotional Distress. [§ 91]

Despite the absence of physical injury, the plaintiff may recover for emotional injuries caused intentionally (or recklessly) by the defendant. This relatively new tort action requires: (a) an **extreme and outrageous act** by the defendant with (b) the **intent to cause serious emotional distress** or **recklessness** with regard to such injuries (c) resulting in **severe emotional distress.**

a. Act: Extreme and Outrageous Conduct. [§ 92]

The conduct must be **extreme and outrageous.** It is not sufficient that the conduct would not be done by a reasonable person or that the conduct is unprivileged. The threshold is a high one; many courts require that **the conduct exceeds all notions of common decency.**

(1) Words May Be Sufficient. [§ 93]

Words can be sufficient to support a cause of action for intentional infliction of emotional distress. However, mere insults are typically insufficient. Look for the defendant abusing a position of authority and using particularly offensive language (e.g., racist epithets).

(2) Special Standards. [§ 94]

Those who owe special duties to the public (i.e., **common carriers, innkeepers,** and **public utilities**) will be held to a different standard of conduct than other persons or businesses. The plaintiff must, of course, be dealing with the defendant in a business capacity as opposed to merely being lawfully on the defendant's premises. Thus, if the conductor for DrekTrack Railroad uses abusive language causing Paula emotional distress, Paula may recover if she was a paying customer but not if she was merely walking through the railway station as a short cut to her home. Paula does not have to show that the conduct was "extreme and outrageous"; proof that the defendant's conduct was reasonably calculated to cause emotional distress is enough.

(3) Special Susceptibilities of Plaintiff. [§ 95]

As with other intentional torts relating to psychological injury (non-injurious battery, assault, and false imprisonment), the defendant is not responsible for the special susceptibilities of the plaintiff unless she had actual knowledge of them. Absent such knowledge, the act must be so outrageous as to cause injury to an ordinary, reasonable person.

> **(a)   Example. [§ 96]** To upset Pam, who Deville knows is highly superstitious, Deville sends Pam a box of broken mirrors. Because Deville knew of Pam's particular susceptibility, Deville's conduct will be deemed extreme and outrageous.

b.   Intent. [§ 97]

THE MENTAL STATE FOR THIS TORT DIFFERS FROM OTHER INTENTIONAL TORTS. In addition to the usual "intent," whereby the defendant must be **purposeful or knowing** with regard to severe emotional distress, it is sufficient if the defendant is **reckless** with regard to the likelihood of causing such distress. Since liability is imposed only for conduct exceeding all tolerable bounds, a finding of recklessness is often easy to make once it is concluded that the defendant's conduct was in fact extreme and outrageous.

(1) Recklessness. [§ 98]

Recklessness is found if the defendant consciously disregards a significant risk of harm. [Rest. 2d. § 500] "Recklessness" suggests more culpability than negligence—there must be a consciousness on the part of the defendant. On the other hand, the standard requires less than "intent" as the defendant does not have to be aware of a substantial certainty. Thus, the mental state for intentional infliction of emotional distress is satisfied if the defendant consciously disregards a significant risk that her conduct will cause the plaintiff severe emotional distress.

(2) Intent Need Not Be Malicious. [§ 99]

Although spite or ill will is commonly found in cases of intentional infliction of emotional distress, such a morally reprehensible motive is not required so long as the act is extreme or outrageous. Thus, a tasteless practical joker may be liable for this tort even if she acted in the name of fun.

(3) No Transferred Intent. [§ 100]

Unlike other intentional torts, neither of the two forms of transferred intent (discussed in §§ 12–18) will apply. Thus, if Dastardly falsely tells Anxious that her husband has just been hit by a train, Anxious may collect, though Priscilla, her daughter who was present in the next room and heard the remark, could not collect unless Dastardly knew of her presence and intended or was **reckless** about whether she would suffer severe emotional distress as a result of hearing these words. Because recklessness—requiring the conscious disregard of a substantial risk—is an acceptable mental state for this tort, Dastardly could be liable even if he did not intend Priscilla to suffer emotional distress.

c. Injury: Severe Emotional Distress. [§ 101]

Despite the defendant's intent, an action for the intentional infliction of emotional distress cannot succeed unless the plaintiff actually suffers **severe** mental or emotional distress. While it is impossible to quantify how serious the distress must be, courts look to the **intensity and the duration** of the emotional distress. It is clear that the plaintiff's mere annoyance is not enough. **In any case, there is no requirement that any physical injury be shown.**

F. DEFENSES TO INTENTIONAL TORTS TO PERSONS. [§ 102]

1. Consent. [§ 103]

Consent is a defense to all intentional torts. Because most consent issues arise in the battery context, the focus here is on consent in that context. For example, if the defendant proves that the plaintiff consented to a particular act that results in a harmful or injurious touching, she may not recover for battery.

a. Actual Consent. [§ 104]

Actual consent is defined as words or conduct that are intended by the plaintiff to express a willingness to submit to the touching and which are understood as consent by the person accused of invading the interest.

b. Apparent Consent. [§ 105]

A plaintiff may be deemed to have consented to what would otherwise be battery without expressly saying so. Any words or conduct which would lead a reasonable person to believe that there was consent to a particular touching and which are understood by the defendant as permission can amount to **apparent consent.** The issue is **not** what the plaintiff subjectively intended, but whether the defendant **reasonably believed** there was consent.

> **(1) Example. [§ 106]** Pax, a newcomer to the neighborhood, likes to play basketball. Pax notices that the games at the local playground are quite rough, but he nevertheless joins in a game. Pax suffers two broken ribs when he is struck by Dax's elbow while going for a rebound. By participating in a game in which physical contact is inevitable, Pax will be deemed to have consented to Dax's contact under the doctrine of apparent consent. Note, however, that he would not be deemed to have consented to extraordinary harmful conduct far outside the realm of "acceptable" rule violations.

c. Implied Consent. [§ 107]

In addition to actual and apparent consent, under certain circumstances, the law will **imply** consent.

(1) Contact as Part of Living in a Society. [§ 108]

A technical battery will be excused if the touching was committed as part of the inherent contact arising from living in a populous world (e.g., the jostling received in a crowd or the tap on the shoulder to get the plaintiff's attention).

(2) Emergency Aid. [§ 109]

As a matter of public policy, there is no battery when a person renders emergency aid to an unconscious victim. Of course, **negligent** care in such circumstances may be actionable subject to the special rules relating to emergencies and "Good Samaritan Statutes" (discussed in the Negligence portion of this summary).

d. Informed Consent. [§ 110]

The validity of consent may well depend upon the information available to the consenting person at the time of her consent. Under certain circumstances, a lack of an informed consent may negate consent, because valid consent may require that the consenting party understand that to which she is consenting.

> **(1) Example. [§ 111]** Pete, a former 98-pound weakling, is proud of his newly well-developed body. At a party, he boasts "I can take any punch." Doreen, who is unknown to Pete, a tremendously powerful karate expert despite her diminutive size, strikes Pete, breaking his collar bone. Pete did not consent to being so injured.

e. Scope of Consent. [§ 112]

Permission to accept one sort of contact for a certain purpose is not the equivalent of consenting to all types of touching. Any contact **beyond the scope of consent** is not privileged.

> **(1) Example. [§ 113]** Pele consents to Doreen's demonstration of a karate chop on his person having seen her "pull her punches" in prior similar situations. Pele reasonably assumes that Doreen will "pull her punch" this time as well. If Doreen strikes Pele with an uninhibited blow, breaking one of Pele's bones, Doreen may not properly invoke the defense of consent.

f. Medical Situations. [§ 114]

Informed consent issues often arise in the context of the practice of medicine. Although these problems are now **usually** treated under the law of negligence (as part of medical malpractice), originally the importance of informed consent was as a defense to the tort of battery.

(1) Failure to Warn of Inherent Risks. [§ 115]

A doctor may commit malpractice by failing to disclose information to a patient. At times, this failure to disclose can give rise to a battery claim by the patient. Because these cases mostly are negligence claims now, the topic is discussed in the negligence chapter.

(2) Need for Additional or Separate Treatment. [§ 116]

In medical situations, when a surgeon with authority to perform a particular operation discovers a compelling need for an additional or separate surgical treatment, difficulty arises as to the scope of the consent granted by the patient to the surgeon. While this is generally handled by having the patient sign a general waiver form allowing the surgeon to use her best professional judgment in such an event, in the absence of express consent, the following rules apply:

(a) Immediate Need. [§ 117]

The surgeon may go beyond the bounds of the express authority given by the patient only if she reasonably believes that the added surgical treatment **could not be postponed** without causing serious additional risks, **and** she knows that a **reasonable person would consent** to the operation if he knew of the conditions that had been discovered.

(b) Related to Original Cure or Life Saving. [§ 118]

The surgeon must be seeking either to save the patient's life or to accomplish the cure originally desired when the plaintiff consented to the operation.

(c) Patient's Wishes Paramount. [§ 119]

If the doctor **knew** that even under all the conditions the patient would not have consented to performance of the additional procedures, there will be a battery even if a reasonable person would have consented.

(3) Gross Deviations from Initial Consent. [§ 120]

Even today, a physician's gross deviation from the patient's consent gives rise to a battery action as where the plaintiff consents to an appendectomy and the doctor amputates the patient's foot.

g. Consent to Illegal Force. [§ 121]

Generally, one may consent to a battery even though the defendant's conduct violates the criminal law.

---

(1) Example. [§ 122] Pyg asks his friend, Diane, to help Pyg keep his diet by jabbing him with a knife whenever Pyg is about to succumb to the temptation of sweets. Just as Pyg is about to shove a cookie into his mouth, Diane grabs a knife and cuts Pyg's arm. Pyg's battery action against Diane will fail due to his consent, even though Diane could be criminally prosecuted for assault with a deadly weapon or criminal battery.

---

(2) Mutual Combat. [§ 123]

A majority of courts, for largely historical reasons, permit the participants in a street fight to recover from each other on the ground that each one's conduct is an illegal breach of the peace. (With set-off, in effect, the loser collects the difference between his damage and the winner's damage.) A large minority of courts hold that both participants in a street fight are barred from recovery on grounds of consent and pari delicto (in equal fault).

(3) Alternative Defenses. [§ 124]

In cases involving mutual combat or arguably illegal conduct, self-defense and similar defenses might also be successfully interposed as justification for otherwise tortious conduct.

h. Consent Vitiated. [§ 125]

Even "actual" consent will fail as a defense if the plaintiff was incapable of giving consent or the consent is invalidated by fraud or duress.

(1) Incapacity. [§ 126]

A young child or mentally incompetent person who consents to a certain type of contact, the serious nature of which he could not be considered to appreciate, has given no effective consent for purposes of tort law. Thus, a doctor who performs an operation based upon an incompetent person's consent would be liable for battery. The consent of a properly appointed guardian is required.

(2) Duress or Fraud. [§ 127]

Consent given under threats or pressures constituting duress will not provide a defense to a civil action. Similarly, consent obtained on the basis of a fraudulent misrepresentation may not be used as a defense.

(3) Insufficient Threats. [§ 128]

It should be noted, however, that threats of **future** violence or of some future economic deprivation do not constitute legal duress. Thus, an insurance company's threat to cut off disability benefits unless the insured submits to certain reasonable surgical treatments would not vitiate the insured's consent to the operation on the theory of duress.

2. Self-Defense. [§ 129]

As in criminal law, a person is privileged to use force in self-defense if the other person acts so as to lead her to know, or reasonably believe, that the other intends to inflict harm upon her.

a. Aggressor Limitation. [§ 130]

The defendant is not entitled to raise the defense of self-defense if she was the **initial aggressor** (i.e., the one who first used or threatened unprivileged force) and the person she attacked has used reasonable force in responding to the attack.

b. Reasonable Belief that Force Is Necessary. [§ 131]

To assert successfully a claim of self-defense, the defendant must **reasonably believe** that the use of force is necessary to prevent the plaintiff from inflicting an offensive contact or bodily harm upon her.

(1) Threat Must Reasonably Be Believed to Persist. [§ 132]

Note that the use of force is not privileged after the aggressor is disarmed or helpless, or after the danger **has** clearly passed.

c. Only Reasonable Amount of Force May Be Used. [§ 133]

The privilege of self-defense is limited to that amount of force which reasonably appears to be necessary under the full circumstances of the case. Thus, if the only harm that Pluto threatens to inflict on Demeter is a slap, Demeter is **not** privileged to shoot Pluto in self-defense. If lesser force would not prevent Pluto's advances, Demeter is required to accept the contact and sue for battery.

(1) Deadly Force: Duty to Retreat. [§ 134]

In a majority of jurisdictions, a party acting in self-defense need not retreat, even when contemplating using deadly force. However, a substantial minority of American jurisdictions impose a duty upon a person attacked to retreat **prior to the use of deadly force** (i.e., force calculated to cause death or which raises the substantial likelihood of causing death or great bodily harm). This rule does not apply, however, unless the defendant knew that she could retreat in full safety; nor is retreat required if the defendant is in her own home. This concept is normally taught in greater depth as part of the course in Criminal Law.

3. Defense of Other Persons. [§ 135]

Virtually all jurisdictions allow the use of reasonable force to protect a third person from an attack. The courts differ, however, as to what the consequences are if the defendant erroneously uses force.

a. Mistake as to Justification. [§ 136]

The major problem in this area arises when the person defended had no right to use the type of force utilized by his "defender." For example, suppose that Darnell punched Paul in the nose in an effort to prevent what Darnell believed to be a robbery of Fred by Paul. In fact, Fred and Paul were simply "horsing around" (or, alternatively, Fred had in fact robbed Paul, and Paul was trying to regain his wallet).

(1) Traditional View. [§ 137]

In such cases, the traditional view is that Darnell, the person asserting the privilege of defense of another, **stands in the shoes** of the person he sought to defend (Fred). Since in either variation of the above hypothetical Fred was not privileged to use force against Paul, Darnell was not privileged to strike Paul.

(2) Minority View. [§ 138]

A growing number of states, supported by the Restatement (Second) have abandoned the traditional view and would allow Darnell to successfully defend a suit by Paul so long as Darnell **reasonably believed** that the person defended

(Fred) had the right of self-defense even if this belief was erroneous.

4. Defense of Property. [§ 139]

A person may use whatever **non-deadly** force is reasonably necessary under the circumstances to defend her land or personal property.

> **a. Example of Excessive Force: Spring Guns and Similar Devices. [§ 140]** Briney set a spring gun to protect an abandoned farm building on his property. It was set in such a manner that a shotgun would shoot anyone entering a certain door. Katko entered the building to steal some fruit jars and was shot in the leg. In Katko's suit against Briney, the Iowa Supreme Court disallowed the defense of property since Briney had used deadly force. The same rule would seem to apply to booby traps and even vicious dogs, at least assuming that there was no adequate warning. *Katko v. Briney,* 183 N.W.2d 657 (Iowa 1971).

5. Recapture of Chattels: Retrieval of Personal Property in Hot Pursuit. [§ 141]

A property owner has the right to use non-deadly force to repossess property which was, **at that moment**, taken from him by another. While he will be given reasonable latitude if in "hot pursuit" to pursue the taker of his property, there is a strong preference that the owner use peaceful, lawful means (i.e., the legal process) to regain possession.

a. Prior Demand Required. [§ 142]

Before using force to protect property or to eject a trespasser, there must be a request to cease and/or depart **or** the circumstances must be such that a request would be futile.

b. Mistake Destroys Defense. [§ 143]

The privilege to use force in protection of property is defeated by any mistake, however reasonable, as to key elements of the defense. Thus, if Lisa, David's wife, gives David's old overcoat to Pete, David is not privileged to use force to regain possession of the coat even if David had no way of knowing that Lisa had given the coat away.

PRIVILEGES TO INTENTIONAL TORTS

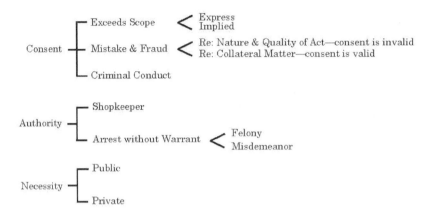

DEFENSE OF	HOW MUCH FORCE?	MISTAKE OK?	ANY LIMITS?
SELF	Reasonable → Deadly	Yes	Retreat < major / minor No retaliation
OTHERS	Reasonable → Deadly	Split	Stand/Shoes v. Reasonable Belief
PROPERTY	Reasonable Non-Deadly	No	Demand first No delay Claim of Right

Recapture of
Chattels

REVIEW PROBLEM—INTENTIONAL TORTS TO THE PERSON

Duke is walking down a street when he hears the following conversation from around the corner: "Give me your wallet and valuables or I'll kill you." Duke rushes around the corner and sees Count cowering against a building with Prince standing over him. Actually, Count and Prince are friends, practicing their parts for the school play. Duke jumps Prince from behind and injures Prince's back. Prince has an exceptionally fragile back from a previous injury and wears a brace constantly.

Count runs into a nearby store to get help and Baron, the shopkeeper, alarmed at Count's frantic entry and appearance, hits an electronic system which is supposed to lock all entrances. In fact, the front entrance is not locked, as the device is defective. As Lady, a customer, attempts to leave, Baron says, "That door has been electronically sealed. No one may leave until I say so." Lady is petrified and is sleepless for months afterward. Prince sues Duke for battery and Lady sues Baron for false imprisonment and intentional infliction of emotional distress. Are they liable?

> **Answer:** Prince can establish the prima facie elements of battery (i.e., those elements the plaintiff must prove to establish the tort) because Duke had the purpose to make harmful contact with Prince's body and did so. The fact that Prince's injuries were more extensive than would be typical due to his prior injury does not matter as Duke will be liable for all of the harm he caused. Duke, however, will assert defense of others. Based on the wording of the conversation he overheard, which sounded like a threat of harm to Count made by Prince, Duke reasonably believed he was acting to prevent imminent harm to Count (and he used proportionate force—non-deadly force was met with non-deadly force). In some jurisdictions, Duke would not be liable for the battery based on the defense of others. However, in jurisdictions that limit the defense and hold that the person asserting the defense of others stands in the shoes of the person aided, Duke would be liable for battery because Count was not really at risk of harm and would not have been permitted to batter Prince because it was just play acting.

> As for Lady's claim for false imprisonment against Baron, she would likely be successfully as Baron intended to confine her against her will in the store and Lady was aware of the confinement. The fact that the door did not actually lock does not change the result because Lady reasonably believed she was confined and did not know of a reasonable means of escape. The shopkeeper's privilege defense would likely not apply here because there does not seem to be a reasonable basis for Baron to assert it based on Count's behavior and it would not apply to Lady in any event. It is unlikely that Lady will recover for intentional infliction of emotional distress because, while she may be able to prove that Baron's conduct caused her extreme emotional distress, it is unlikely to be bad enough to be extreme and outrageous. Also, it would be hard to prove that Baron was intentional or reckless as he acted very quickly and seemingly without any thought about Lady's reaction to his conduct.

Multiple Choice Questions 1–3 are based on the following fact situation.

Ten-year-old Pon was new to the neighborhood. Drew, a neighbor of the same age, decided to see if Pon was a "good sport." The next day when Drew saw Pon riding his bicycle down the sidewalk, Drew stood in front of the bicycle, stopping Pon. Drew told Pon that if he continued an inch further down the road, Drew would break Pon's leg. As Drew with a raised fist took a step toward Pon, Pon turned his bicycle around and pedaled as quickly as possible in the opposite direction. As Pon was pedaling away, Drew started throwing stones at the fleeing Pon. One stone missed Pon and accidentally hit the letter carrier, Maria. Another stone hit Pon's bicycle, knocking Pon off the bicycle and onto the ground. Pon did not realize that Drew was throwing stones at him.

1. In Pon's initial interaction on the sidewalk with Drew which of the following intentional torts did Drew commit?

   (A) Assault

   (B) Battery

   (C) False imprisonment

   (D) None, because Drew is only 10 years old.

2. If Maria sues Drew for battery she will

   (A) recover.

   (B) not recover because Drew was aiming at Pon.

   (C) not recover because Drew as a ten-year-old is not liable for his torts.

   (D) not recover because Drew did not intend to hurt anyone.

3. Is Drew liable for the harm Pon suffered when Pon fell off the bicycle?

   (A) Yes, Drew is liable for false imprisonment.

   (B) No, because Drew only hit the bicycle.

   (C) Yes, because the stone hit the bicycle.

   (D) No, if Drew only was hoping to scare Pon.

G. INTENTIONAL TORTS TO PROPERTY. [§ 144]

1. Trespass to Land. [§ 145]

A **trespass to land** consists of (a) an **affirmative act** (b) with intent by the defendant which (c) **invades the plaintiff's possessory interest** (d) in **land.**

a. Act. [§ 146]

In order to be liable in trespass, the defendant must perform some volitional act which brings about a physical invasion of the plaintiff's possessory rights in land.

(1) Defendant Need Not Personally Trespass. [§ 147]

It is not required that the defendant actually enter the land herself as long as she causes any person or instrumentality to invade the exclusive possessory right of the plaintiff. Thus, trespass may occur if the defendant builds a fence on the plaintiff's land; if the defendant shoots a gun across the plaintiff's land; if the defendant floods the plaintiff's land; if the defendant chases third persons on the plaintiff's land; or if the defendant deposits some object on the plaintiff's land, such as throwing a ball onto the plaintiff's land.

b. Possessory Interest. [§ 148]

The plaintiff must have a **possessory** interest in the land at the time of the invasion since the tort is premised on an interference with the plaintiff's possessory interest in the land. Ownership is not the relevant focus. Thus, the fee owner may have no cause of action for trespass if the land is leased to another and she may in fact be guilty of trespass herself if she enters the property without the consent of the tenant.

c. Definition of "Land." [§ 149]

The common law notion that plaintiff's property extended upward to infinity and downward to the center of the earth has been discarded by modern cases. Instead, a common sense test is applied on a case-by-case basis.

(1) Above the Surface. [§ 150]

The extent to which the plaintiff has a possessory interest in **airspace** above the surface of the land is subject to wide dispute. Normally, a trespass is committed only if the defendant's conduct is a reasonable distance above the land.

(2) Below the Surface. [§ 151]

The question of what is reasonable use of land below the surface is again a question of fact. Thus, a utility company commits no trespass in installing a pipeline 50 feet below the plaintiff's residential property, though the same act would be trespass if the land was being used for mining.

d. Intent with Regard to Act. [§ 152]

THE INTENT ISSUE IS DIFFERENT HERE THAN FOR TORTS TO THE PERSON. Unlike the intentional torts discussed above, the defendant **need not** be purposeful, knowing, or even negligent with regard to the **consequences** of her acts. All that is required is the **act** which causes the trespass be done intentionally. The defendant is liable if the plaintiff proves the defendant desired to enter the land or knew entry was substantially certain.

(1) Mistake No Defense. [§ 153]

Since the defendant needs only the intent to enter the land, not any wrongful intent, the defendant's mistake as to ownership, consent, or even as to where the defendant is, is no defense.

> **(a) Example. [§ 154]** Irene directs Dan to take a shortcut across "her" property. Dan drives across what he believes to be Irene's property. The land actually belongs to Pax. Pax can recover for trespass to land because Dan had the intent to enter the land.

(2) Recklessness or Negligence Not Enough. [§ 155]

On the other hand, reckless or negligent entry is not enough for trespass. Thus, if Damon, while driving negligently, loses control of his car, which ends up on the land of Pythius, there is no trespass since Damon did not intentionally enter the land owned by Pythius.

e. Injury: Invasion of Interest. [§ 156]

Nominal damages are presumed upon a showing of the intentional act resulting in an entry onto the plaintiff's land. In addition, once a trespass is proven, the defendant is **strictly liable** for all damages caused to the plaintiff's land or chattels **regardless of foreseeability.** Punitive damages may be awarded where defendant is particularly culpable, as where the plaintiff has repeatedly ordered the defendant off the plaintiff's property.

> **(1) Example. [§ 157]** De intentionally drives onto Poe's land without permission. Due to Poe's negligence in maintaining the driveway, the driveway cracks under the weight of De's car, and injures the leg of one of Poe's cows. De is liable for the damage to Poe's driveway and to the cow.

f. Nuisance Compared. [§ 158]

Trespass must be accomplished by something with a particulate nature. Where the invasion is brought about by something wholly intangible (such as noise), consider Nuisance. Nuisance is discussed in Chapter VI A., *infra.*

g. Defenses. [§ 159]

While all battery defenses could apply in appropriate circumstances, the typical defenses to trespass to land are:

(1) Consent. [§ 160]

If the defendant has the consent from the **rightful possessor** to enter realty, he has a complete defense to a charge of trespass even against one who may be in **actual** possession of the realty at the time of entry. However, only a person with the right of present possession may consent.

(2) Privilege to Reclaim Property. [§ 161]

If the defendant's property has somehow entered the plaintiff's land (as when the defendant's sheep break through the fence separating the defendant's property from the plaintiff's), the defendant will be entitled to enter the plaintiff's land to reclaim the property.

(a) Prior Request. [§ 162]

The defendant must normally make a reasonable request of the land possessor for return of the property or permission to enter before entering the land. However, if the facts demonstrate that such a request for return would have been futile, no such request will be required.

(b) Normally, a Limited Privilege. [§ 163]

Normally, the privilege to enter another's land in order to reclaim property is a **limited privilege;** although the defendant will not be liable in trespass, he normally will be liable for any actual damages caused by his entry (e.g., damages to the plaintiff's crops).

(c) Complete Privilege if Plaintiff Acted Wrongfully. [§ 164]

If the defendant's property is on the plaintiff's land through the plaintiff's wrongful act, the defendant will be privileged to enter to recapture his property, and he will not be liable for any harm done as long as he does not unreasonably exercise the privilege.

(3) Entry under Necessity. [§ 165]

Necessity arises where the defendant asserts that the defendant's decision to commit an intentional tort is appropriate in light of the interest the defendant is seeking to protect.

(a) Public Necessity. [§ 166]

A person is privileged to go upon another's property if it reasonably appears to be necessary to prevent a public disaster.

(b) Private Necessity. [§ 167]

Under certain circumstances, an entry on another's property may be justified by a private necessity if the entry is made for the purpose of saving life or for the protection of property. As with the privilege to reclaim property which is on the plaintiff's land through no fault of the plaintiff, the defendant's privilege to enter land under a private necessity is a limited privilege which only excuses liability for the trespass itself; **the defendant will still be liable for all actual damages caused by her entry.**

> **(i) Example. [§ 168]** Deb and her family are rowing in a small boat when a thunderstorm suddenly erupts. To protect herself and her family, Deb rows to the nearest shore and ties the boat to Paco's dock. If Paco sues Deb for trespass to land, Deb may assert a privilege of necessity. If her boat damages Paco's dock, Deb will be liable for those damages, however. See *Vincent v. Lake Erie Transportation Co.*, 124 N.W. 221 (Minn. 1910).

(4) Entry to Abate Nuisance. [§ 169]

(a) Public Nuisance. [§ 170]

Under certain circumstances, public officials may enter private property to abate **a public nuisance.**

(b) Private Nuisance. [§ 171]

If a nuisance on the plaintiff's land causes damages only to the land of a specific landowner, that person may be privileged to enter the plaintiff's land to abate the nuisance only if: (a) she has made a demand and has been refused; (b) she has a possessory right in the damaged land; (c) she has used reasonable means prior to entering the plaintiff's land in order to avoid the injuries caused by the nuisance; and (d) she has used no force causing personal injury or constituting a breach of the peace. Of course, persons should generally seek relief from the judicial system rather than engaging in self-help remedies.

2. **Trespass to Chattels. [§ 172]**

Trespass to chattels prevents another from the wrongful exercise of control over, interference with, or possession of chattels lawfully possessed by the plaintiff. Trespass to chattels requires: (a) an **affirmative, intentional act** by the defendant that (b) **interferes with the plaintiff's possessory interest** (c) in **movable personal property** (d) **resulting in injury.**

a. **Act. [§ 173]**

In order to be liable for trespass to chattels, the defendant must have acted **intentionally.**

b. **Possessory Interest. [§ 174]**

The act must interfere with the plaintiff's **possessory** rights (the right to presently use and enjoy the chattel). As a condition precedent to an action, the plaintiff must show that her interest in the chattel immediately before the act complained of was one of actual possession or the right to immediate possession.

c. **Forms of Interference. [§ 175]**

(1) **Dispossession. [§ 176]**

The act may consist of taking possession of the chattel from the plaintiff, including the defendant's assertion of a **proprietary interest** in the chattel as against the rights of the true owner.

(2) **Intermeddling. [§ 177]**

Trespass may also be accomplished by **intermeddling,** which is the mere interference with the property rights in the chattel without any intent to assert ownership over it (e.g., joyriding).

d. **Intent with Regard to Act. [§ 178]**

As in trespass to land, the defendant must intend to do the act which results in the interference with the plaintiff's right of possession in the chattel, but she need **not** intend **wrongfully** to interfere with the possession (i.e., she is liable even if she is acting under a mistake or a claim of right).

> **(1) Example. [§ 179]** Darla takes what she believes to be her denim jacket from a coatrack. The jacket, which is identical to Darla's jacket, really belongs to Pol. Darla has the intent required for trespass to chattels.

e. Injury. [§ 180]

Unlike trespass to land (and assault, battery, and false imprisonment), the plaintiff's exclusive right to control the chattel must cause some **actual** injury or no recovery is allowed whatsoever.

(1) Measure of Damages. [§ 181]

In an action for trespass to chattels, the plaintiff is always entitled to recover for any injury to the chattel itself. In addition, the defendant is liable for the plaintiff's loss of the use of the chattel.

f. Defenses. [§ 182]

Consent is the most common defense to an action for trespass to chattels, but all defenses to intentional torts to persons might be applicable in appropriate circumstances.

3. Conversion of Chattels. [§ 183]

Conversion consists of (a) an **act or omission** by the defendant (b) with the **intent to assert dominion and control over a chattel** (c) which **in fact belongs to the plaintiff** (d) resulting in **substantial injury** to the chattel or significant dispossession to the plaintiff.

a. Act. [§ 184]

In order to be liable for conversion, the defendant must do an act (or refrain from acting) which amounts to a **claim of ownership** in the plaintiff's chattel (i.e., the defendant must assert dominion and control over the chattel which is inconsistent with the rights of the true owner).

b. Forms of Conversion. [§ 185]

The assertion of a right of ownership may be found if there has been any (a) **destruction** of the chattel, (b) **alteration** of the chattel, (c) **unauthorized use** of the chattel, (d) **unauthorized sale** with the intent to pass title to the chattel, or (e) **refusal to surrender** the chattel on demand when the plaintiff has the right to possession at the time of the demand.

c. **Intent with Regard to Act. [§ 186]**

In order to create liability for conversion, the defendant's assertion and control over the chattel must be intentional (negligence alone cannot be a basis for an action in conversion), but it **need not be <u>wrongful</u>** (that is, he need not have the desire to interfere with the true owner's rights). Thus, a mistake, however reasonable, is no defense; **even an innocent purchaser of stolen property is still a converter.** It is the intent to exercise dominion and control that gives rise to liability.

d. **Several Persons May Be Liable. [§ 187]**

While the plaintiff may recover her damages only once, she may sue several tortfeasors regarding the same property.

> **(1) Example. [§ 188]** Larry steals goods from Shemp and sells them to Moe, who sells them to Curley. Curley refuses to return them on demand of Shemp. Larry, Moe, and Curley are all converters. Shemp may collect from any of them, but he is only entitled to one recovery.

e. **Injury: Substantial Interference Required. [§ 189]**

In order for an action in conversion to lie, the defendant's interference with the possessory rights of the plaintiff must be **substantial.** There is no conversion action for insubstantial violations of property interests.

f. **Ownership Interest. [§ 190]**

Unlike trespass, the conversion plaintiff may recover if she has a **present or future** right of lawful possession. Of course, a converter will not have to pay for the same injury twice, but she may not raise the superior rights of someone else as a defense against a lawful possessor. Procedurally, the converter may protect herself by proper joinder of all possible plaintiffs.

g. **Remedy: Forced Purchase. [§ 191]**

When the defendant has converted the plaintiff's property, **she may be required to pay the full fair value of the property at the time it was converted.** In essence, the converter is required to "purchase" the personal property involved. While the plaintiff may also have the right to repossess the property (as opposed to the value thereof) by an action in replevin, detinue, or claim and delivery, she is not required to accept the return of the item even if the defendant is willing to return it in an undamaged condition.

h. Defenses. [§ 192]

In addition to the defenses to intentional torts to persons, if the defendant has appropriated or destroyed the plaintiff's property under **necessity** (whether public or private), she is not a converter, although she may still be liable for trespass to chattels (and thus liable for actual damages, but not for the full value of the chattel).

i. Trespass to Chattels Distinguished. [§ 193]

(1) In General. [§ 194]

In reality, the torts of conversion and trespass to chattels usually overlap. Indeed, every conversion is a trespass, although not every trespass is a conversion since every interference with the owner's interest is not necessarily an assertion of ownership by the tortfeasor.

Multiple Choice Questions 4–5 are based on the following fact situation.

Pete was sailing on a public lake when an unexpected storm arose. Pete barely made his way to the shore and tied his boat to Owen's dock. Owen objected to Pete's boat being tied to his dock and told Pete to get in his boat and shove off as the boat was damaging the dock. Pete offered to pay for the damages but Owen would not listen to him and Owen untied the boat.

Pete then said that Owen should at least drive Pete home as the only way for Pete to get home was to take a three mile walk which, because of the storm, was very dangerous, or to take a twenty mile walk along the shore of the lake. Owen refused.

Pete waited for the storm to end. Finding that his boat had sunk, Pete then took the three mile walk home.

4. If Pete sues Owen for the loss of his boat, Owen is most likely to be held

   (A) not liable because Pete was a trespasser.

   (B) not liable because the storm was an act of God.

   (C) not liable because he gave Pete an opportunity to take his boat and leave.

   (D) liable.

5. By refusing to drive Pete home, Owen is liable for

   (A) infliction of emotional distress.

   (B) false imprisonment.

(C) battery.

(D) none of the above.

INTENTIONAL TORTS TO REAL PROPERTY

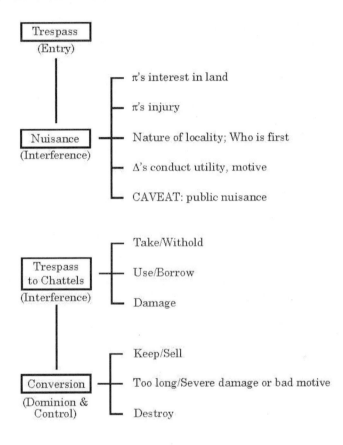

ANSWERS TO THE MULTIPLE CHOICE QUESTIONS

Answer to Question 1.

(A) is the best answer.

By stepping toward Pon in a hostile manner, Pon was in reasonable apprehension of an imminent battery. Drew's actions and language indicate that he may well have known it was substantially certain that Pon would be in such apprehension. (D) is wrong because children are liable for their intentional torts provided they can form the intent. (B) is wrong because there was no contact made at that time so there cannot be a battery. (C) is not the best answer because just blocking someone's way is not confinement. Thus, there was no false imprisonment.

Answer to Question 2.

(A) is correct.

B is wrong since transferred intent applies. C is wrong since even young children are capable of the limited intent associated with battery. D is wrong since battery requires no intent to harm.

Answer to Question 3.

(C) is the best answer.

Drew either intended to scare or hit Pon with the stones. Because contact was made with the bicycle and because Pon was on the bicycle making it closely connected to his body, here was a battery. Choice (D) ignores the potential application of transferred intent. And (B) ignores that the bicycle was closely connected to Pon's body here. (A) is not the best answer because Pon was not confined.

Answer to Question 4.

(D) is correct.

Pete has a privilege to trespass based on private necessity which is sufficient to rebut any privilege on Owen's part to eject him or his boat. A is true, but ignores the privilege. B and C raise arguments lacking in legal significance.

Answer to Question 5.

(D) is correct.

Note that the question asks whether failure to drive Pete home was, by itself, tortious. Certainly there was no imprisonment because Owen did not restrict Pete's freedom of movement. Thus, B is incorrect. Further, C is incorrect because there is no basis for Pete to claim a battery due to the absence of a harmful or offensive touching. Nor is A the best answer because it is unlikely that there was extreme and outrageous conduct when Owen refused to do what Owen had no legal obligation to do.

CHAPTER II

NEGLIGENCE

A. NEGLIGENCE OVERVIEW. [§ 195]

Negligence is the most important and most heavily tested cause of action studied in torts. While the elements of this tort can be easily stated, as they were for the intentional torts, each negligence element is capable of great complexity. Thus, just listing the elements of a negligence action will rarely score any credit. The key is to understand each of the elements of the negligence cause of action and their interrelationship.

B. NEGLIGENCE ELEMENTS. [§ 196]

In order to recover in a negligence action, the plaintiff must prove each of the following elements by a preponderance of the evidence (i.e., by more than 50%): 1) that there is a legally recognized relationship between Defendant and Plaintiff—**duty;** 2) that Defendant failed to comport with the legal measure of appropriate conduct—**breaching** the duty owed by falling below the **standard of care**; 3) that there is a causal nexus between Defendant's breach of duty and the injury suffered by Plaintiff—**causation in fact** or actual cause; 4) that there are no policy reasons to exculpate Defendant from liability notwithstanding the fact that Defendant breached a duty owed to Plaintiff and that this breach caused Plaintiff's harm—**proximate cause** or legal cause; and 5) that Plaintiff suffered a legally cognizable injury—**damages**. Once proven, Defendant will try to assert any possible **defenses** against Plaintiff. Although there is considerable overlap among these elements, each of them—duty, standard of care, breach of duty, cause in fact, proximate cause, damages and defenses—will be considered in turn.

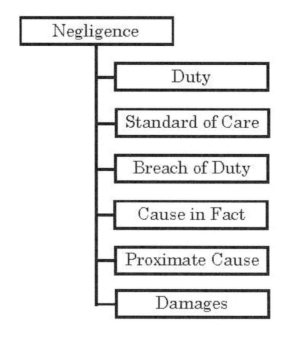

C. EXAM HINT. [§ 197]

Scholars, of course, disagree about the relationship and the parameters of the negligence elements as well as about the proper terminology. Obviously, you should employ the terms and mode of analysis taught in class, as with any other topic in this outline. Further, though you should keep the above elements in mind any time you are analyzing a negligence question, don't assume that all elements need lengthy analysis in every exam problem. Be careful to discuss quickly those elements that are clear, while spending greater time on those elements open to serious debate. In making the sometimes tough decision of what is a key issue, let the facts be your guide. If there are many facts applicable to a given element, it is likely that that element is significant. Remember, though law professors are sometimes perceived as sadistic, it is highly unlikely that your professor expects an exhaustive analysis of every element in a negligence action in the limited time in which most exams are taken. Avoid lengthy dissertations about the state of the law, and get to analyzing those issues that are open to the greatest debate. Finally, when analyzing a negligence question, do not speak in generalities, but rather focus on the specifics of the question. Doing so will lead you to issues that you might otherwise miss.

D. THE DUTY ISSUE. [§ 198]

Duty focuses on the **legal relationship** between the parties—whether the law obligates the defendant to act (or not act) in a certain way vis-à-vis the plaintiff. As a question of law, duty issues are determined by judges, not juries. Normally, the law imposes upon everyone a duty to use due care whenever he is engaging in any conduct which creates a risk of harm to others. As a general proposition, there is an obligation in law to avoid acting in a manner that creates foreseeable risks of harm to foreseeable plaintiffs. Thus, in the vast majority of tort cases, the duty issue presents no problem whatsoever. For example, if Dap's careless driving leads him to collide into Pam, another motorist on the road, there is no question that the law will find a duty [to use reasonable care] to other motorists, such as Pam. However, the debate about who is a foreseeable plaintiff for purposes of duty has engendered serious debate.

1. Duty Pointer. [§ 199]

Duty is rarely a key issue where the defendant affirmatively acts in a manner that causes the plaintiff personal injury or property damage. Conversely, duty is usually a major issue where the plaintiff suffers harm other than personal injury or property damage, where the defendant is a land possessor or a government entity, or where the plaintiff is basing her claim on the defendant's failure to intervene for the plaintiff's benefit. Duty issues may also arise where it is unforeseeable that the plaintiff would have been injured by the defendant's conduct.

2. The Unforeseeable Plaintiff Problem. [§ 200]

a. *Palsgraf v. Long Island Railroad.* [§ 201]

In *Palsgraf v. Long Island Railroad*, 162 N.E. 99 (N.Y. 1928), an employee of the railroad tried to help a passenger who was attempting to board a moving train and, in so doing, dislodged a package from the passenger's arms. The package contained fireworks which exploded, knocking down some scales approximately 30 feet away, which fell on Mrs. Palsgraf. While it was conceded that the employee was negligent with regard to the passenger, the great debate was whether there was negligence toward Mrs. Palsgraf.

(1) Cardozo View: No Duty if Outside Zone of Risk. [§ 202]

Justice Cardozo, for the majority, stated that there is no duty owed to one who is not within the **zone of risk.** Thus, the railroad was not liable to Mrs. Palsgraf because the conduct of its agent, even though negligent, created no foreseeable risk of injury or harm to her. **Zone of risk is an issue of place and time that depends on the nature of the defendant's negligent act;** the plaintiff's safety must be foreseeably threatened or there is no duty owed to her.

(2) Andrews View: "Negligence in the Air." [§ 203]

Justice Andrews, dissenting, stated that the defendant owes a duty of care **to society,** not just to specific individuals. Thus, in his view, if the defendant is negligent toward **anyone,** he owes a duty to the injured plaintiff.

(3) Modern Interpretation of *Palsgraf.* [§ 204]

While *Palsgraf* is often discussed in torts classes and is often cited by attorneys and judges who find themselves lacking better authority, be careful about relying too heavily on the case. Modern tort principles have gone far beyond the views expressed in *Palsgraf.*

(4) Proximate Cause Remains a Separate Issue. [§ 205]

Note that Cardozo and Andrews disagreed about the scope of **duty.** A separate basis for potentially limiting liability is **proximate cause.** Thus, policy considerations may result in a finding of no liability even if a duty is owed. Proximate cause is fully discussed in §§ 423–461.

b. The Rescuer Doctrine. [§ 206]

Public policy requires that potential rescuers be included in the class of foreseeable plaintiffs. Thus, a person injured coming to the aid of a person harmed by the defendant's negligence will be owed a duty by that negligent party. This has resulted in the maxim **"danger invites rescue."** This rule has also been applied to situations where the plaintiff was injured while attempting to rescue the defendant from her own negligence. Accordingly, a duty will be found owing to the injured rescuer.

c. Injuries to an Unborn Child. [§ 207]

At common law, a **child could not recover for injuries sustained prior to birth,** the rationale being that an unborn child has no legal existence apart from its mother (and therefore could not possibly be a foreseeable plaintiff). However, a majority of jurisdictions has departed from this rule, holding that where a child is **viable** (i.e., capable of life apart from its mother at the time of injury) it can recover for its **prenatal injuries.** Some states have gone further and allowed recovery to an infant even before it is viable.

3. Nonfeasance and Special Duty Problems. [§ 208]

A key distinction is made between affirmative acts— **misfeasance**—and the failure to act—**nonfeasance.** As a general rule, a failure to act (including a failure to rescue another who is in a position of peril) will be **insufficient** to impose liability on a defendant for injury caused thereby. As the Third Restatement puts it: "An actor whose conduct has not created a risk of physical harm has no duty of care to the other unless [an exception applies.]."

a. Duty to Rescue. [§ 209]

This distinction is most visible in the well-settled rule that Defendant has no obligation to rescue Plaintiff, even though Defendant could do so easily and with no risk to herself.

> **(1) Example. [§ 210]** Darth spots a child, Par, caught on the railroad tracks. In the distance Darth notes an oncoming train. Though Darth could have rescued Par without any threat to himself, Darth sits under a nearby tree and watches the train run over Par. If Par sued Darth for Par's serious injuries which Darth could easily have prevented by pulling Par from the tracks, most courts would find no duty, characterizing Darth's conduct as nonfeasance.

(2) Exceptions. [§ 211]

Not surprisingly, there has been discomfort with this no duty rule. Thus there are a growing number of exceptions to the no duty to rescue rule. These exceptions include requiring the defendant to rescue when the need for rescue is brought about by the defendant's conduct, where there is special relationship, and where the defendant has undertaken to act.

b. Alleviating Consequences of Prior Conduct. [§ 212]

(1) Prior Negligent Conduct. [§ 213]

If the defendant's negligence injures the plaintiff (or threatens her safety), the defendant must make reasonable efforts to prevent further injury. This duty to take affirmative action has been recognized even when the plaintiff would have been barred from recovery for the original injury by contributory negligence.

> **(a) Example. [§ 214]** If in the above hypo, Darth had negligently dropped nails on the train track, and it was these nails that led to Par falling onto the tracks, then Darth would have to act to rescue Par.

(2) Prior Non-Negligent Conduct. [§ 215]

The trend in the law, though still clearly a minority position, is to impose a duty on a defendant to alleviate foreseeable risks of harm threatened by even **non-negligent** conduct.

(a) Example. [§ 216] Dubois was driving carefully when Poindexter, a child who lived in the neighborhood, suddenly ran into the street. Dubois collided into Poindexter, leaving him unconscious. So long as Dubois was not negligent with regard to the incident, the common law would allow him to ignore Poindexter's condition and drive on. This developing minority approach would require Dubois to render necessary assistance to the child.

---

c. **Special Relationship. [§ 217]**

Where there is a "special relationship" between the defendant and the plaintiff, the defendant must make reasonable efforts to rescue the plaintiff.

(1) **Traditional Special Relationships—Innkeepers and Common Carriers. [§ 218]**

The common law has long recognized that an innkeeper/guest and a common carrier/passenger had a special relationship obligating the former to act to aid the latter. Thus, innkeepers and common carriers are often held liable for injuries caused or aggravated by their failure to render prompt assistance to a stricken guest or passenger.

(2) **Extension of Theory. [§ 219]**

This theory has been expanded in recent years to impose a similar obligation to act in the context of other **special relationships.** Thus, a school must take affirmative steps to protect its pupils, a hospital must assist its patient, and jailers must render aid to their prisoners. The **trend** seems to be toward imposing a duty on all commercial establishments to make reasonable efforts to aid their customers. The Restatement (Second) suggests that a relationship of trust or dependence may give rise to a special relationship. One court went so far as to characterize social co-adventurers ("drinking buddies") to be a special relationship obligating one to act to aid the other. See *Farwell v. Keaton*, 240 N.W.2d 217 (Mich. 1976).

d. **"Undertaking" to Act. [§ 220]**

Even when no duty existed at the outset, according to the traditional view, **one who undertakes to act may not** discontinue assistance if he has, in some way, put the plaintiff in a worse condition than he would have been in if nothing had been done. The modern position provides that once the defendant has voluntarily chosen to act, she must act reasonably.

> **(1) Example 1. [§ 221]** Desi finds Pepper injured on a main highway and starts to take her to a doctor. If Desi changes his mind and lets Pepper off in a deserted area he has breached his duty to Pepper, as he has left her in a worse position.

> **(2) Example 2. [§ 222]** Dora, a prize-winning Olympic swimmer, spots Pal drowning in the distance. Except for Dora and Pal, the beach is totally deserted. Dora swims to Pal, brings Pal slightly toward shore, and then, for no reason, decides to leave Pal. Under the traditional view, there would be no liability because Dora did not leave Pal in a worse position. Under the more modern position, Dora would be liable because, once undertaking to act, she did not act reasonably.

(3) Act Undertaken Must Be Done Reasonably. [§ 223]

Quite aside from liability for wrongful discontinuation, a person is liable if **affirmative acts** undertaken are done in a negligent manner (e.g., Pepper's arm is carelessly broken during Desi's rescue). Many jurisdictions, however, have "Good Samaritan" statutes that protect a rescuer from liability for acts of negligence in effecting the rescue.

e. Statute. [§ 224]

Under traditional analysis, a statute at most defines a standard of reasonable conduct which is more certain than the open-ended reasonable person standard. (See §§ 310–325). However, certain statutes designed to protect people like the plaintiff will create a **civil duty** to act. An example is the automobile hit-and-run statute, which has been influential in convincing many courts that even a non-negligent motorist has a duty to aid injured persons. Further, a few states (e.g., Vermont) have enacted statutes with **criminal penalties** imposed on those who fail to come to the aid of another when it would be safe to do so. Such criminal statutes seemingly create tort liability.

f. Duty to Control Third Parties. [§ 225]

Because of the nonfeasance no duty rule, there is no duty imposed upon a defendant to control third persons who may harm others. This is so even where the harm to the specific plaintiff is highly foreseeable.

---

(1) Example. [§ 226] Don and Rita begin a conversation as they sit side by side drinking at a bar. Rita tells Don that she is waiting for her husband, Paul, to pick her up and that, when he does, she intends to shoot him. Paul enters the bar and joins Don and Rita at the bar. Rita leaves them alone briefly and then leaves with Paul, shooting him soon after exiting the bar. Paul learns of what transpired and sues Don for failing to warn him about his wife's plans. Paul's actions would be dismissed because he had no legal obligation to control Rita or to warn Paul.

---

(2) Exceptions. [§ 227]

Where the defendant "takes charge" of a defendant who he knows is dangerous to others, a duty may arise. An example would be a jailor who negligently permits a dangerous criminal to escape thereby injuring a third party.

In *Tarasoff v. Regents of the University of California*, 551 P.2d 334 (Cal. 1976), the California Supreme Court held that a psychotherapist who determines, or pursuant to the standards of her profession should determine, that her patient presents serious danger of violence to another has an affirmative obligation to use reasonable care to warn the intended victim. The court based such an obligation on the special relationship existing between a psychotherapist and her patient. Most jurisdictions have adopted the *Tarasoff* rationale. Some jurisdictions require, however, that the psychotherapist warn all foreseeable victims, while others (like California) have limited the scope to "readily identifiable" victims. The extent to which the duty to warn/control applies to other contexts is open to debate.

g. Duty to Protect Against Third Party Harm. [§ 228]

Because it is nonfeasance, there is typically no legal obligation for a person to protect another from foreseeable third party criminal harm.

(1) Special Relationship Exception. [§ 229]

A special relationship might give rise to a duty to protect provided other factors are present. For example, in *Kline v. 1500 Massachusetts Ave. Apartment Corp.*, 439 F.2d 477 (D.C. Cir. 1970), the court found that the landlord owed a duty to a tenant who was assaulted in a common hallway of the apartment building.

(2) Special Foreseeability Rules. [§ 230]

Jurisdictions are divided about how much foreseeability of criminal conduct must be shown for a judge to find a duty. Some jurisdictions require that the plaintiff show that there were prior similar incidents before a duty could be found. Although there is debate about what is a prior similar incident, this approach has been criticized because the first victim/plaintiff will typically lose even if criminal conduct was generally foreseeable. Some jurisdictions permit the plaintiff to proceed to the jury upon proof that third party criminal harm was foreseeable under the "totality of the circumstances." Finally, some jurisdictions have adopted a middle ground under which the judge balances the foreseeability against the burden on the defendant. See *Posecai v. Wal-Mart Stores, Inc.*, 752 So.2d 762 (La. 1999).

(3) Public Policy. [§ 231]

There are major public policy issues underlying the determination of whether a duty to protect should be permitted. Indeed, duty is often determined by public policy which explains in part why the issue is left to judges to decide. All jurisdictions have duty factors that a judge considers when deciding difficult duty issues. An example would be the *Rowland* duty factors created by the California Supreme Court (*Rowland v. Christian*, 443 P.2d 561 (Cal. 1968)), which have been used by courts outside of California as well. These factors are: (1) the foreseeability of harm to the plaintiff, (2) the degree of certainty that the plaintiff suffered injury, (3) the closeness of the connection between the defendant's conduct and the injury suffered, (4) the moral blame attached to the defendant's conduct, (5) the policy of preventing future harm, (6) the extent of the burden to the defendant and consequences to the community of imposing a duty, and (7) the availability, cost, and prevalence of insurance for the risk involved.

h. "No Duty" Situations Based on Other Public Policy. [§ 232]

Duty (along with the element of proximate cause) is often used as a basis to place limits on the potentially unlimited liability flowing from Defendant's unreasonable conduct.

(1) Waterworks Case. [§ 233]

In most cases, water companies have been held **not** liable to the property owner whose home has been destroyed by fire, even when the company has been negligent in not providing water to fight the fire. This is so even though the case seems to fit squarely within the "undertaking" exception—the company has undertaken to supply water, and the situation has been made worse by reliance on the company as the sole source of water. One possible explanation of the result is that most urban property is covered by fire insurance, which is a superior mechanism for distributing fire losses. Further, there is a great interest in keeping the cost of water low. Courts have similarly limited the class of potential plaintiffs where the defendant is a public utility, such as a provider of electricity.

(2) Failure of a Municipality to Provide Police Services. [§ 234]

Even where sovereign immunity has been waived, governmental entities (such as cities) have generally not been held liable for failure to provide adequate police service. This reluctance to impose liability is based on the view that public policy precludes the confusion and violation of the separation of powers concept, which would result if the courts second-guessed administrative decisions concerning the allocation of scarce police resources. Accordingly, the general rule is that the police owe a duty to the public at large, but not to any individual member of the community. (See *Riss v. City of New York*, 240 N.E.2d 860 (N.Y.1968))

(a) Exceptions. [§ 235]

Courts have found a growing number of exceptions to the police no-duty rule. If the police have created reliance in an individual with promises of action or if the police undertook to act and left the plaintiff in a worse position, a duty may be found.

i. Liability of Supplier of Liquor—Common Law. [§ 236]

At common law, one who furnished intoxicants was not responsible for an intoxicated person's act, even when the seller was negligent—the intoxicated person was barred by contributory negligence and innocent third parties were barred by the intoxicated person's "independent intervening act" which prevented the seller from being the proximate cause of the third party's injuries.

(1) Dram Shop Acts. [§ 237]

Many states have dram shop acts which impose **civil liability** upon the seller of liquor when the sale results in injury to the interests of a third person because of the intoxication of the buyer. Also, most states make it **illegal** to sell liquor to minors or to persons who are **perceptibly intoxicated** and apply these criminal statutes to impose a civil duty of care. **Statutes of both types are generally inapplicable to private persons furnishing liquor.**

j. Adjunct Issue: Consider Cause in Fact. [§ 238]

In virtually every case where liability is premised on an omission, there will also be a substantial issue of **cause in fact.** This is because the plaintiff must prove by a preponderance of the evidence that the injury would not have occurred if the defendant had acted, something which requires some degree of clairvoyance.

4. Duty Limited by the Kind of Harm Suffered. [§ 239]

Just as duty has traditionally been limited in the context of nonfeasance or where there are other public policy reasons justifying the restriction of duty, duty has been traditionally limited where the harm suffered by the plaintiff is other than personal injury or property damage. In other words, where the plaintiff suffered pure economic harm (e.g., lost profits) or pure emotional distress, courts have traditionally restricted the element of duty.

a. Pure Economic Injury. [§ 240]

As a general rule, the plaintiff cannot recover in negligence for pure economic injury not resulting from personal injury or injury to property. Though readily measurable, the concern is with the potentially crushing liability flowing from the defendant's negligent act.

> **(1) Example. [§ 241]** Davis negligently burned down a factory. Most (if not all) courts hold that Davis is not liable to the workers in the factory for economic losses they may incur by reason of being unable to work until the factory is rebuilt.

> **(2) Example. [§ 242]** Dax negligently collided into Pak's store, destroying the plate glass window. While the window was being repaired, the business was closed and Pak suffered lost profits. Because there was property damage, followed by economic loss, Dax is liable for all of these damages.

(3) Negligent Misrepresentation. [§ 243]

A duty, albeit a limited one, is recognized in the context of negligent misrepresentation when a defendant (a) in the business of supplying information, (b) negligently gives erroneous information to a plaintiff who (c) justifiably and (d) detrimentally relies upon the information supplied; (e) and there was some form of particular foreseeability of harm by that plaintiff (e.g., the "end and aim" of the transaction was known by the defendant to be used by this plaintiff).

(4) Professional Advisers. [§ 244]

One who is in the business of supplying information to others must exercise due care in assuring that the information he dispenses is accurate. This includes attorneys, accountants, credit agencies, and any other person or business which knows or should foresee that others will rely upon information supplied by them. However, most jurisdictions require more than just foreseeability for a plaintiff not in privity of contract to recover from the negligent defendant. As noted above, in order to keep potential liability in check, most jurisdictions require that the plaintiff be particularly foreseeable.

(5) Actual Injury. [§ 245]

The plaintiff's reliance must cause actual economic injury.

b. Pure Emotional Injury: "Negligent Infliction of Emotional Distress." [§ 246]

If the plaintiff suffers any physical injuries to his person, there is no question that the defendant will also be liable for pain, suffering, and any other psychological injuries. These injuries are generally characterized as "pain and suffering." While one often hears of **"negligent infliction of emotional distress"** spoken of as if it were a separate tort, in fact, that label is simply a short hand method of referring to a negligence problem where there are **emotional injuries that do not follow from physical harm.** Thus, all of the normal rules of negligence must be considered in addition to the special rules discussed below.

(1) Direct Actions: Redefining "Physical Harm"—From Impact to Foreseeability. [§ 247]

Because emotional injuries are easy to allege and hard to disprove, damages for such harm were originally allowed only when such injury was incident to physical harm. Courts have gradually retreated from the requirement of significant physical injury as a precondition to giving relief for emotional suffering caused by negligent conduct. Since different jurisdictions have stopped at various places along the continuum, a **brief** discussion of the history of that development is necessary. As always, you should discuss all splits of authority if the jurisdiction is not provided.

(a) Impact. [§ 248]

At the end of the nineteenth century, the courts considered **impact** of an instrumentality negligently put in motion by the defendant with the person of the plaintiff as the line dividing non-compensable emotional injuries from recoverable damages. Once there was "impact," the plaintiff could recover for emotional harm followed by physical manifestations. Note that the impact itself did not have to cause any physical injury to the plaintiff.

> **(i) Example. [§ 249]** Andrews negligently allowed his bull to escape its pen. Bosley came across the animal, and was chased by the animal, nearly getting gored. Although the bull never touched Bosley, she suffered severe emotional injury from the incident. Recovery was denied because there was no impact. *Bosley v. Andrews*, 142 A.2d 263 (Pa. 1958). Had there been **any** contact, then recovery would have been permitted.

(b) "Zone of Danger." [§ 250]

Dissatisfaction with the impact rule (as well as absurd applications of that doctrine to include such things as dust in the eye and smoke in the lungs as impact) have led virtually all states to abandon that requirement of impact entirely. The test in many jurisdictions is whether there was a "near miss"—that the instrumentality came close enough to the plaintiff that she feared for her own physical safety. The zone of danger is the area in which the plaintiff was at risk of suffering physical harm due to the defendant's negligence.

> **(i) Example. [§ 251]** Doris negligently drives her car so that it jumps the curb and almost runs over Purt. Purt has a heart attack due to the fright of almost being run over. Purt would be owed a duty in most jurisdictions and, thus, could recover for his emotional (and subsequent physical) harm because he was in the "zone of danger."

(c) Pre-existing Duty Approach. [§ 252]

Some jurisdictions permit a plaintiff to state a cause of action even where she is not in the zone of danger if the defendant already owed her a duty. (See *Marlene F. v. Affiliated Psychiatric Medical Clinic, Inc.*, 770 P.2d 278 (Cal. 1989)).

> **(i) Example [§ 253]** Due to the negligence of the defendant hospital, Paula's newborn baby is kidnapped. Paula seeks to recover for her emotional distress. Most jurisdictions would deny her recovery because she was never threatened with physical harm, thus falling outside the zone of danger. (See *Johnson v. Jamaica Hospital*, 467 N.E.2d 502 (N.Y.1984)). In some jurisdictions, however, a duty would be owed because the hospital already owed a duty to Paula as its patient. Note that Paula's husband would **not** recover for his emotional distress.

(d) Foreseeability and Serious Emotional Distress. [§ 254]

A few jurisdictions have suggested that recovery for direct emotional distress extends well beyond near-miss situations. These jurisdictions have suggested recovery is appropriate where the plaintiff is foreseeable and where the plaintiff has suffered "severe emotional distress," defined as the sort of emotional harm with which a reasonable person, normally constituted, would be unable to cope.

(e) Physical Manifestations of Emotion or "Distress." [§ 255]

In most jurisdictions, in addition to a "near miss," The plaintiff must prove that there were **physical manifestations** of the disturbance (e.g., a heart attack) such that there is some certainty that the alleged injury is not merely feigned. Once physical manifestations are required, the issue becomes whether such things as sleeplessness, headaches, and "shock to the nervous system" constitute the requisite "physical injury."

(i) Special Situations. [§ 256]

In many jurisdictions two groups of special cases have allowed recovery for mental distress caused by negligent conduct even where the plaintiff is not in the zone of danger and in the absence of any physical manifestation of the emotional distress. These situations are considered so horrible that there is no concern about the genuineness of the plaintiff's claim for emotional harm.

(i-a) Telegraph Companies. [§ 257]

A number of cases have held **telegraph companies** liable for negligent transmission of messages announcing death or similar misfortune due to the special likelihood that emotional injury would be caused thereby. It is assumed the exception applies to more modern methods of communication (e.g., e-mail).

(i-b) Mishandling of Corpse. [§ 258]

Similarly, many cases have allowed recovery to relatives for pure mental upset caused by the **mishandling of the corpse** (e.g., negligent embalming, loss of a body in shipment, or internment in the wrong grave).

(f) Minority View. [§ 259]

Some jurisdictions do not require proof of physical manifestations.

(2) Bystander Recovery. [§ 260]

Another controversial area for emotional distress is whether a plaintiff can recover against a negligent defendant where the plaintiff has suffered emotional distress because of physical injury to another. Most jurisdictions recognize the propriety of such a bystander action for negligent infliction of emotional distress. In order to keep limits on the potential class of plaintiffs, however, courts have employed a variety of tests.

(a) Zone of Danger. [§ 261]

Fearing the tremendous scope of liability for emotional injuries if no limitation is employed, most courts allow recovery only for those plaintiffs within the **zone of danger.** The "zone of danger" is that area in which the plaintiff fears for **her own physical safety.** In addition to a potential direct action, recovery is being sought for the emotional distress suffered from witnessing harm to a close family relative (as when the plaintiff could have been struck by the defendant's negligent driving but, in fact, his emotional distress arose from observing the physical injuries suffered by the plaintiff's child). Most jurisdictions require physical manifestations of the emotional distress.

(b) Witnessing Accident. [§ 262]

Many jurisdictions have allowed recovery for emotional injuries suffered by persons **witnessing injuries to close relatives even though they fall outside the zone of danger** (e.g., a mother who looks out her window and sees her child being struck on the sidewalk by a negligent driver). These jurisdictions permit recovery by plaintiffs who **observe** the harm—causing event and who are closely related to the victim. A recent trend has been to limit the class of potential plaintiffs by rigidifying the prerequisites to recovery. *Thing v. La Chusa*, 771 P.2d 814 (Cal. 1989).

> **(i) Example. [§ 263]** Dad is walking with his young child, Xena, when Dor's negligently driven car jumps the curb and runs over Xena. Mom witnesses this from across the street. In many jurisdictions, a bystander emotional distress duty would be owed only to Dad because he was in an area where he could have suffered physical harm. Mom will be owed a duty only in those jurisdictions that permit a bystander action by one who witnesses the harm—causing event though not in the zone of danger.

(c) Furthest Extension. [§ 264]

Under the furthest extension, a few courts have abandoned all artificial guidelines and judge the **duty** issue as an ordinary matter of foreseeability (under which a person is obviously a foreseeable plaintiff whenever his child or spouse is injured), leaving the primary issue of liability to be determined by the jury.

(d) Abolishing the Requirement of Physical Manifestations. [§ 265]

A minority of jurisdictions no longer require that the plaintiff prove physical manifestations of her emotional distress as a prerequisite to success of recovery. Such physical manifestations remain relevant, of course, as they buttress the plaintiff's case.

(e) Bystander Action Is a Derivative Action. [§ 266]

In most jurisdictions, the action of a bystander suing for emotional distress from witnessing harm to a close relative is **derivative**—meaning that the action depends on the success of the underlying action. Accordingly, the underlying action of the victim must be established before the derivative plaintiff can recover for her emotional distress. Further, the negligence of the victim and of the derivative plaintiff will affect the derivative action.

> **(i) Example. [§ 267]** Mom watches Son run into street and get seriously injured by car driven by Defendant. Mom suffers severe emotional distress as a result. In order to recover for her emotional harm, Mom must establish that Son could recover against Defendant for Defendant's negligence. If Son was negligent, or if Mom was negligent, Mom's cause of action would be barred in a contributory negligence jurisdiction and reduced in a comparative fault jurisdiction.

c. Wrongful Conception—Wrongful Birth—Wrongful Life. [§ 268]

A separate duty issue arises when a physician's negligent conduct leads to the birth of a child. When a parent is suing due to the birth of an unhealthy child, this is a "wrongful birth" action. An action by the unhealthy child is called a "wrongful life" action. The parents action for the birth of a healthy, but unwanted, child is called "wrongful conception."

---

(1) Example. [§ 269] Because he and his wife, Wendy, cannot afford more children, Pierre goes to Dr. Dest for a vasectomy. Due to Dr. Dest's negligence the vasectomy fails and another child is born. Most jurisdictions would permit some recovery in Pierre and Wendy's wrongful conception action, limiting damages to damages associated with childbirth. Costs of raising the child and the emotional upset of having an additional child are not recoverable generally because these injuries are viewed as outweighed by the joy of having a child. No jurisdiction would permit the child to sue in a "wrongful life" action.

---

(2) Example. [§ 270] Pete and Wendy have given birth to one child who is deaf. They are tested by Dr. Donna to see if there is a hereditary problem that may render their next child deaf as well. Dr. Donna negligently informs them that there is no risk of deafness and they give birth to Joy, who is born deaf. Some jurisdictions would permit the parents to recover in a "wrongful birth" action for expenses associated with Joy's deafness. Currently, no jurisditction will permit Joy a "wrongful life" action. Because of the difficulty in measuring damages (the harm of being born) and of the discomfort courts have in suggesting non-life could be preferable to life, recovery for wrongful birth and wrongful life has been quite limited and remains controversial.

---

d. Loss of Consortium. [§ 271]

A loss of consortium action is brought by a person who suffers such things as loss of comfort and companionship because the defendant negligently injured a close relative. The key area of dispute is about who may bring an action for loss of consortium.

(1) Husband's and Wife's Recovery. [§ 272]

At common law, a **husband** had the right to recover, **in his own action**, an amount for the loss of **services**, loss of **consortium**, and the **expenses** for his wife's care incurred as a result of the tortious act of a third person. At common law, the **wife's** recovery was not permitted. Now one spouse is entitled to seek damages for loss of consortium against a defendant who has injured the other spouse. Damages include interference with conjugal affection.

(2) Parent's and Child's Recovery. [§ 273]

Most jurisdictions have limited the action for loss of consortium to spouses. Neither parents (whose child has been negligently harmed) or children (whose parent has been negligently harmed) are permitted a loss of consortium action in most jurisdictions. Courts are concerned about excessive liability flowing from a negligent act. A growing minority of jurisdictions, however, permit actions by parents and children for loss of consortium.

(3) Derivative Action. [§ 274]

Most jurisdictions treat loss of consortium as a derivative action.

e. Wrongful Death. [§ 275]

The common law denied actions for wrongful death in civil suits. Today, however, every state allows recovery for wrongful death by statute, permitting an action to recover monetary damages for **the loss suffered by the persons who might have expected to receive support or assistance from the decedent** (e.g., the decedent's spouse, children, and other dependents). The state's wrongful death statute identifies who may recover damages for wrongful death.

(1) Derivative Action. [§ 276]

Most jurisdictions treat the wrongful death cause of action as derivative so that the **claimant's own negligence** will bar or reduce his claim. Further, though the **decedent's** negligence should be irrelevant, most jurisdictions with wrongful death statutes also allow the defendant to raise any defenses that she might have had against the decedent.

(2) Damages. [§ 277]

In some jurisdictions, wrongful death damages are limited to the **pecuniary** loss of the claimants (i.e., loss of financial support, services, and contributions). A growing number of states permit recovery for the loss of companionship. There is **no recovery** for the **mental suffering** of the survivors.

f. Survival of Actions. [§ 278]

(1) Common Law. [§ 279]

At common law, tort actions did **not** survive the death of either party and no recovery could be had by the injured parties' estate or personal representative.

(2) Modern View. [§ 280]

By statute, states today hold that **most actions based on tort survive the death of either party.** If the **victim** dies, the action can be commenced or continued by his personal representative. If the **tortfeasor** dies, the action may be brought against his estate (or if he dies during the pendency of an action, it can be continued against his estate). Statutes vary in their terms, however.

(3) Defenses. [§ 281]

Since the survival action is merely a continuation of the decedent's cause of action, **any defense that the defendant could have raised against the decedent may be asserted against the estate.** Conversely, the negligence of the **personal representative** of the decedent or of the ultimate beneficiary of the action is **irrelevant**.

(4) Damages. [§ 282]

In most jurisdictions, the estate may recover for the decedent's pain and suffering, medical expenses, and loss of earnings between the time of injury and the time of death.

---

g. Example. [§ 283] Dahl negligently injures Len, who languishes in a hospital for a month before dying of his injuries. Len is married to Wendy and has an eleven-year-old son, Saul. In a survival action brought by a representative of Len's estate, the damages Len amassed between his injury and death (e.g., medical expenses) will be recoverable from Dahl. Wendy will be permitted to pursue a loss of consortium claim for that month period as well in every jurisdiction. Some jurisdictions would permit Saul to bring a loss of consortium claim too. Both Wendy and Saul will be permitted to bring a wrongful death action for the economic and possibly intangible losses they suffered due to Len's death.

NEGLIGENCE

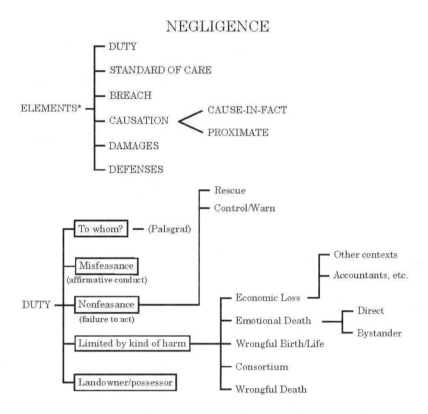

* All of these elements, *except* duty, are questions for jury determination.

E. STANDARDS OF CARE. [§ 284]

Once it is determined that there is a legal obligation owed by the defendant to the plaintiff, it is necessary to determine the measure of that duty. In other words, did the defendant comport to the standard imposed by law or did he fall below it? This question is dependent upon applying the appropriate **standard of care** to evaluate the conduct. Happily, there are only several possible standards of care. You should understand the context in which each standard of care may apply. Once you identify the appropriate standard of care, the appropriate breach analysis will follow.

STANDARD OF CARE	BREACH ANALYSIS
1. Reasonably prudent person	Burden < Probability x Magnitude; Custom
2. Child—unless engaged in adult activity	Failure to act like other children of same age, experience, and intelligence
3. Professional—*custom* is the standard of care	Deviation from custom; expert witness usually required
4. Statues—terms of statute may become the standard of care	Violation of statute [negligence *per se*]

1. Usual Test: The Reasonable Person Standard. [§ 285]

The test normally used to determine whether the defendant is negligent is to ask if he acted as would a **reasonable person under the same or similar circumstances.**

a. Emergency. [§ 286]

Many tort cases involve situations where the defendant is confronted with an **emergency**. The emergency becomes part of the "circumstances." When the defendant **did not** create the emergency, the lack of time for reflection **may** be considered by the trier of fact in evaluating his conduct. However, if the defendant's own intentional or negligent conduct created the situation, courts will not permit him to argue that his conduct should be considered in light of the emergency circumstances.

> **(1) Example. [§ 287]** Dole, traveling at a very high rate of speed, collides with and injures Parth. If Dole is doing so because he is taking a critically ill child to a hospital, a jury may conclude he was not negligent, as a reasonable person may well engage in such conduct because of the emergency. On the other hand, if Dole's object in speeding was to avoid being late to work, his conduct most likely would be deemed to be negligent. Thus, in evaluating whether Dole has breached the duty of due care, one must consider the object to be gained and weigh it against the risks Dole is creating.

b. Objective Test. [§ 288]

The reasonable person test is an objective standard; the specific defendant is being compared to the external standard of a reasonably prudent person. The reasonable person is a mythical representation of the appropriate community standard.

> **(1) Example. [§ 289]** Delores is an adult who just received her driver's license. On her first day as a licensed driver, she collides into Porter's car. The fact that Delores is a new driver will be irrelevant in determining her liability. Instead, she will be expected to possess the skills of the reasonably prudent driver (who has been driving for an average period of time).

c. Defendant's Special Knowledge. [§ 290]

A person will be held to use all information that he or she **actually knows**, whether or not it is knowledge commonly held in the community. This does **not** change the standard of care. Rather, a reasonable person is expected to use her special knowledge or expertise.

d. Occasional Relevance of Subjective Factors. [§ 291]

In **rare** situations, however, some subjectivity is injected into the analysis.

(1) Mental Characteristics Ignored. [§ 292]

Generally, the **mental deficiencies** of an adult defendant are irrelevant, even if the deficiency renders him legally insane. This rule is justified by the tremendous difficulties, even with modern advances in psychiatry, in proving actual mental state or capacity, and is due to the belief that the harm-causing defendant should still pay for the harm caused to the innocent plaintiff. Some modern authorities question the logic of this well-settled rule, however.

(2) Physical Characteristics Relevant. [§ 293]

On the other hand, **physical deficiencies** of a defendant are relatively easy to prove with an adequate degree of certainty and thus they generally are considered as part of the circumstances to be taken into account (e.g., "the reasonably prudent blind person" standard). Physical infirmity may cut both ways, however (e.g., Defendant's poor eyesight may show that he was not negligent in failing to see Plaintiff **but it may also show** that he was unreasonable because he should not have driven at all).

2. Standard of Care for Children. [§ 294]

Under the majority view, a child's age, intelligence, and experience may be taken into account as part of the circumstances in which the negligence determination is to be made. This is partially a subjective standard since some of the focus is on the specific child defendant's intelligence and experience, and partially an objective standard since he is being compared to an external standard of other similar children.

a. Minority View: Presumptions. [§ 295]

A minority of jurisdictions have adopted the common law rules relating to a child's capacity to commit a crime in a negligence context. In these states, (a) a child under 7 is **conclusively** presumed incapable of negligence, (b) a child between the ages of 7 and 14 is rebuttably presumed incapable of negligence, and (c) a child over 14 but under the age of majority is rebuttably presumed to be governed by an adult standard of care.

b. Exception: Adult or Inherently Dangerous Activities. [§ 296]

Children are normally held to an adult standard when they are engaged in **adult activities** (e.g., driving an automobile or flying an airplane). Some jurisdictions use an "inherently dangerous" test instead of an "adult activity test."

(1) Exam Hint. [§ 297]

What constitutes an adult or inherently dangerous activity is often debatable so that an analysis under an adult standard and under a child standard may both be appropriate.

3. Malpractice: Standard of Care for Professionals. [§ 298]

The customary standards of behavior of those in "the learned professions" (i.e., doctors, lawyers, architects, engineers, etc.) are given much greater weight than in other negligence cases. This is because the courts are reluctant to subject these professions to the judgment of laypersons who may be incapable of understanding the complexities involved in a given specialized discipline. Thus, the deference given by the courts allows the professional standard to virtually displace the typical standard of care.

a. Basic Standard. [§ 299]

The propriety of a professional's care is measured against the **minimum common skill of members in good standing of the profession.** Note that this does **not** require a defendant professional to do what is in fact correct according to the learning of her profession. All that is required is that the defendant professional act in accordance with the minimal level of competency of the profession. What is done by most others (or even a respectable minority) is deemed acceptable conduct. **Accordingly, unlike other negligence cases, the custom of the profession becomes the standard of care.**

(1) Caveat. [§ 300]

This professional standard of care only applies in situations where the defendant is called upon to use her professional judgment. A doctor driving her car without paying attention will be held to a reasonably prudent person standard of care in the evaluation of the reasonableness of her conduct.

b. Expert Testimony. [§ 301]

Since the issue in malpractice cases is what other professionals would have done in the same circumstances, expert testimony is normally required to establish the relevant standard of care and that the defendant has deviated from that standard (thus proving the standard of care and breach of duty). However, expert testimony will not be necessary with reference to acts that do not require professional expertise to judge (e.g., when the defendant surgeon amputates the wrong leg or a defendant attorney allows the statute of limitations to run).

c. Special Considerations for Medical Profession. [§ 302]

(1) General Practitioners: Locality Rule. [§ 303]

At one time a rule was rigidly followed that expert testimony in medical cases must relate to conduct of physicians in the **same or similar locality**, so that small town doctors were held to a different standard of care than doctors practicing in large cities. This rule was based on the theory that small town doctors did not have the same access to modern techniques and other medical advances or the broad range of experience of large city doctors. Obviously, this distinction is no longer entirely justified given modern communication and educational technology.

(2) Specialists: National Standards. [§ 304]

The locality rule has generally been abandoned with regard to persons who hold themselves out as **specialists.** Such board-certified specialists are generally compared to others in the same specialty on a **nationwide** basis.

(3) "Good Samaritan Acts" for Emergency Actions. [§ 305]

Many states have passed "Good Samaritan Acts" which protect **doctors or nurses** who in **good faith** render assistance in an **emergency situation** at the scene of an accident (or at any other place where there are no proper medical facilities) when no prior medical relationship existed between the medical person and the injured party. **Under such circumstances, the attending medical person will be liable only for gross negligence or willful and wanton misconduct.**

d. **Failure to Obtain Informed Consent. [§ 306]**

As mentioned in the battery discussion (See § 110), the issue of **informed consent** is now commonly treated as a negligence problem. Thus, the issue is whether a physician is liable in negligence for injuries resulting from the unavoidable risks of treatment where the physician failed to inform the patient of these inherent risks. Some courts use the usual professional standard here and hold that a doctor is liable for nondisclosure where the custom of doctors would be to warn of such risks. The **modern trend** rejects this focus, noting that the patient is the party entitled to determine whether he wishes to accept certain risks. These jurisdictions require that the doctor inform the patient of all "**material risks**" of a given procedure— material risks being those to which a reasonable person would attach importance in determining whether to undergo a certain procedure.

> **(1) Example. [§ 307]** Patient Cobbs was to undergo an operation for a gastric ulcer. An inherent risk of this procedure is internal bleeding, which could require significantly extended hospitalization. Dr. Grant chose not to tell Cobbs of this risk. Cobbs suffered from internal bleeding after the operation due to no fault of Dr. Grant. Dr. Grant is liable for medical malpractice if the risk of internal bleeding is a "material risk," and if Cobbs would have declined the operation had he been told of the risk. *Cobbs v. Grant*, 502 P.2d 1 (Cal. 1972).

(2) Risk of Refusing Procedure and Alternatives. [§ 308]

In addition to divulging material risks, the physician must **disclose alternative treatments,** as well as the risks involved in **refusing** to undergo the suggested procedure in many jurisdictions.

e. **Legal Malpractice. [§ 309]**

Legal malpractice is just another form of professional negligence. Thus, the custom of the profession sets the standard of care, breach is deviation from custom, and expert testimony is routinely required. There is an additional hurdle for legal malpractice plaintiffs: cause-in-fact. Legal malpractice plaintiffs must show as part of their prima facie case that they would probably have prevailed in the action in which the defendant committed malpractice had their attorney complied with the customary practice of the profession. This can be a substantial hurdle.

4.   Civil and Criminal Statutes. [§ 310]

A statute, ordinance or regulation may replace the usual standard of care of a reasonably prudent person. If the defendant violates a statute which, by its terms, purports to establish **civil liability** if violated, that statute clearly supplants the ordinary standard of care. Such a civil statute is a rarity, however. More common is a statute which makes certain conduct **criminal,** creating the issue of whether a court should adopt the **criminal** statute as establishing the standard of care to be used in evaluating the **civil** consequences of defendant's conduct.

a.   General Rule. [§ 311]

As a general rule, in most jurisdictions, a court will adopt a criminal statute as the standard of care in a negligence action where it is applicable because it represents a pronouncement of a legislative body of what should constitute reasonable conduct in a given situation. The judge, however, has considerable leeway in deciding whether the statute should supplant the usual standard of care.

b.   Test. [§ 312]

In order for a court to adopt a criminal statute as establishing a civil standard of care, the plaintiff must show that (a) he was in the **class of persons** the statute was intended to protect and (b) the statute was designed to protect the class against the **type of harm the plaintiff actually suffered.**

> **(1) Example. [§ 313]** The "Contagious Disease Act" imposed criminal fines for failing to build pens to keep groups of sheep separate when being transported. Dumbo failed to do so and Porky's sheep were washed overboard. The court refused to use this statute in the negligence action Plaintiff brought against Defendant because the purpose of the statute was to protect animals from contracting disease, not to guard them from being washed overboard. *Gorris v. Scott*, L.R. 9 Ex. 125 Eng. (1874).

c. **Exam Hint. [§ 314]**

> Like most things, the parties may disagree about the proper purpose of a statute. Be careful about being too quick to conclude that a statute does or does not apply. **CONSIDER ALL ARGUMENTS.** Further, not only formal statutes may be adopted by a judge as the standard of care; look for other deliberative decisions such as municipal ordinances, school board regulations, and the like that could be used as the standard of care since they represent a specific determination of reasonableness in a narrow context.

d. **Effect if Statute Not Adopted. [§ 315]**

If a judge decides that the proffered statute, regulation or ordinance is not appropriate to set the standard of care (because it is too general, because the plaintiff is not in the protected class, or because the harm the plaintiff suffered was not the type of harm the law was designed to protect against), the plaintiff has not necessarily lost her negligence case. **The case may proceed on an alternative standard of care, typically that of the reasonable prudent person.**

e. **Effect of Violation of Statute. [§ 316]**

There are three views as to the effect of a violation of a relevant statute: (a) The majority view is that violation of a relevant statute is **negligence per se;** (b) A minority of states holds that violation of a relevant statute creates a **presumption of negligence;** (c) Some courts hold that violation of a relevant statute is merely **some evidence of negligence.**

(1) **"Negligence Per Se" Jurisdictions. [§ 317]**

In a jurisdiction which holds that the violation of a relevant statute establishing a standard of care amounts to negligence per se, the defendant may **not** argue that her conduct was reasonable—the jury will be instructed that she was negligent as a matter of law if she violated the statute.

(a) **Defenses and Excuse. [§ 318]**

In negligence per se jurisdictions the only arguments available to rebut breach of duty are: (a) that the statute should not be adopted as the standard of care; (b) that the defendant did not in fact violate the statute, or (c) that the circumstances surrounding her conduct create an excuse for the violation of the statute.

(2) "Presumption-of-Negligence" and "Evidence-of-Negligence" Jurisdictions. [§ 319]

In jurisdictions which consider a statutory violation to be either a rebuttable presumption of negligence or some evidence of negligence, the defendant is free to argue that his conduct in violation of the statute was, nevertheless, reasonable under the circumstances. (A key difference between these views is that, where there is a rebuttable presumption, the defendant must persuade the jury that he was not negligent, whereas in a some evidence jurisdiction, the violation of the statute only helps the plaintiff to establish negligence.)

> **(a) Example. [§ 320]** A criminal statute requires bicycle riders to ride on the right-hand side of the road. Because both automotive and pedestrian traffic was extremely heavy on the right side of the street, Derek rode his bike on the left side of the street. Derek lost control of his bicycle and struck and injured Peg, a pedestrian, who was walking on the left side of the road. In **any** jurisdiction, Derek could defend his action on the ground that the statute was irrelevant (that it was not designed to protect pedestrians from being hit by bicyclists) or that there was an implied exception to the statute when heavy traffic would make it unreasonably dangerous to ride on the right-hand side of the road. In jurisdictions which reject the majority negligence per se rule, Derek could present to the jury the issue of whether his conduct was reasonable, given the risks of harm to himself, motorists, and pedestrians caused by the heavy traffic on the right-hand side of the road.

f. Conformity to Statute. [§ 321]

Generally, compliance with a statute will **not** itself establish due care, though it may be evidence of the defendant's reasonable conduct. A relevant statutory provision merely represents the minimum standard necessary to hold the defendant morally culpable; a party may still have been negligent in failing to take additional precautions even though he complied with the statute.

> **(1) Example. [§ 322]** A statute requires hotels to keep a lifeguard on duty between certain hours. Drake Hotel complies and yet a child swimming during that time drowns due to the failure of the lifeguard to rescue. Here, Drake's compliance with the statute is evidence of due care but is not conclusive (e.g., the lifeguard may have been incompetent, negligently inattentive, or negligently trained).

g. **Licensing Statutes. [§ 323]**

Licensing statutes are not used as the standard of care. The lack of a license does not establish by itself the unreasonableness of the conduct. Accordingly, the plaintiff still must show that the unlicensed defendant failed to use due care.

> **(1) Example. [§ 324]** A statute in the State of Ennui makes it illegal for a person to drive an automobile without a valid driver's license. Dexter never obtained a driver's license but was driving with utmost care when Pinky ran in front of his car and was injured. Dexter's violation of such a statute will not itself make him liable to Pinky since it had nothing to do with the accident (i.e., Pinky would have been just as injured even if Dexter had had a license).

h. **Other Elements of Negligence Must Still Be Proven. [§ 325]**

The violation of a statute is only relevant to the issues of duty, standard of care, and breach of duty. In order for such violation to give rise to civil liability, the violation must also be the **cause in fact and proximate cause** of the plaintiff's injury, and there must be **damages** compensable in negligence.

> **(1) Example. [§ 326]** In violation of a criminal statute, Daisy was driving without headlights. Daisy struck and injured Paula. Paula must prove that, had Daisy been using her headlights, Daisy would have seen Paula and been able to avoid the collision.

5. **Owners and Occupiers of Land. [§ 327] (See Chart on page 78, *infra*)**

Due to the great importance placed on land ownership, the common law developed many hard and fast rules defining a landowner's obligations to persons entering her land. Originally, the law was loathe to impose obligations on those owning land. As will be seen, many exceptions developed to lessen the harsh effects of these rules. Ultimately, some jurisdictions have abolished the special protections given to land owners and occupiers, requiring instead that the landowner adhere to the usual obligation of reasonable care. Because some duty (albeit often a highly limited one) is typically owed in the land possessor context, the topic is being discussed in the context of standards of care.

a. **The Common Law Approach. [§ 328]**

The traditional rules represent a **hierarchy of duties,** ranging from ordinary care to virtually no duty at all, depending on the **status of the actual land entrant plaintiff**. Accordingly, under the common law approach, the key is to identify the status of the plaintiff—classifying her as either a trespasser, a licensee, or an invitee.

(1) Adult Trespassers. [§ 329]

The general rule is that the landowner has no obligation to make his premises safe for trespassers, the landowner simply must not inflict willful or wanton harm. A trespasser is a person on the defendant's land without the express or implied permission of the landowner. The exceptions to this rule follow.

(a) Due Care in Affirmative Acts. [§ 330]

If the landowner **knows** that trespassers are **likely to be** present on his land, he must use due care when engaging in **affirmative conduct.** For example, if Dart is shooting a bow and arrow on his land and perceives Patches trespassing, Dart has an obligation to use due care toward Patches in shooting his arrows.

(b) Dangerous Condition of Premises. [§ 331]

Traditionally, the landowner had no duty to trespassers with regard to **conditions** (e.g., quicksand). The Restatement, however, takes the position that the landowner must **warn** of dangerous conditions which might not otherwise be noticed if he knows or has reason to know that trespassers will be on the land. Note that the landowner has no obligation to investigate whether trespassers may be present under this standard.

(c) Trespass Incident to Use of Public Way. [§ 332]

Those who stray a few feet onto the landowner's land incident to the use of a public way often have not been treated as trespassers (e.g., Plaintiff steps into a doorway to tie his shoelace; Plaintiff uses a board on Defendant's land to dive into a public river). The obligation owed to such persons is identical to that owed to any person outside the premises (See § 347).

(d) Defendants Who Are Not Landowners. [§ 333]

Licensees, invitees, and those holding easements in the land of another are required by a majority of

71

courts to use due care to protect trespassers on the land (e.g., a power company stringing wires over X's land with X's permission is liable to a trespasser injured by negligently maintained wires). Those working for or acting on behalf of the landowner (e.g., a contractor hired to improve the land) are subject to the same liability, and entitled to the same immunities, as the landowner.

(2) Child Trespassers. [§ 334]

An important exception to the general limited obligation owing to a trespasser exists when that trespasser is a child and several conditions are present. This exception for child trespassers is often referred to as the "attractive nuisance" doctrine. Under Section 339 of the Restatement (Second), a landowner is liable to **trespassing children** if five conditions are met: (1) the place is one where the possessor knows or has reason to know that **children are likely to trespass**; (2) the condition is one which the landowner knows or should know creates a **risk of serious injury** to such children; (3) the children, because of their youth, **do not realize** the risk of the condition; (4) the **utility** to the landowner of maintaining the condition and the **burden of eliminating the danger are slight compared** to the risk to children; and (5) the landowner **fails to exercise reasonable care** to eliminate the danger or otherwise protect the children.

(a) Children Likely to Trespass. [§ 335]

Given the well-known propensity of children to trespass, it is not necessary to establish that the landowner had actual knowledge of the presence of these trespassers. It is generally sufficient that the landowner was aware that children are frequently in the general area of his land.

(b) Very Dangerous. [§ 336]

Since children can injure themselves in many ways, the **Restatement** limits liability to situations where the condition creates a risk of **death or serious bodily harm** (i.e., a risk of minor cuts and bruises does not alter the standard of care). Risks of property damage are insufficient.

(c) Unawareness by the Child. [§ 337]

A child trespasser can recover under this theory only if she is too young to appreciate the risk of the particular danger on the land. Since many such dangers are reasonably obvious, most recoveries have been limited to under 13 years old. Nonetheless, consider the possibility of an attractive nuisance whenever there is a minor injured while on the defendant's property.

(d) Unreasonable Danger. [§ 338]

The defendant is not liable merely because the condition is **dangerous** to children; it must be **unreasonably dangerous.** One must always balance the cost of making the structure safe against the risk of danger. Thus, the more difficult it is to insure that children will not be injured (e.g., the defendant can protect children only by posting 24-hour guards), the less likely that the defendant will be held to owe a duty.

(e) Lack of Reasonable Care. [§ 339]

If a duty is created by the existence of the factors discussed above, the landowner must take reasonable steps to protect the children who might trespass onto her land. In essence, the trespassing child is transformed into an invitee.

(f) Artificial Conditions. [§ 340]

The **Restatement** rule, by its terms, applies only to the case of dangerous **artificial conditions** (e.g., swimming pools or construction sites), although a caveat to Section 339 indicates that, in appropriate circumstances, the same rules should apply to **natural conditions** (such as lakes or rock piles). Many cases have indeed done so, but since the dangers of such natural conditions are normally quite obvious and the costs of protecting children from such risks are often unduly burdensome, recovery is far less likely in such cases.

(g) Implied Invitation No Longer Required. [§ 341]

Under **the theory of "attractive nuisance,"** earlier cases involving trespassing children required that the child be **lured onto the premises** by the dangerous condition. This meant that the child could not recover if he became a trespasser before he could view the condition. Under the influence of the **Restatement,** most courts permitting recovery by trespassing children have rejected this requirement.

(h) Children Who Are Licensees. [§ 342]

The rules stated above with regard to child trespassers may be relevant to children who are not trespassers, if these rules would produce a more favorable result than the ordinary rules concerning liability to **adult** licensees. Accordingly, children who would be classified as licensees may receive the more favorable treatment given to invitees if they establish attractive nuisance. Thus, it is most appropriate to call this the "child land entrant doctrine."

(3) Licensees. [§ 343]

(a) Definition of Licensee. [§ 344]

A **licensee** is a person privileged to enter the land because the possessor gave permission to enter, such as a social guest, other household visitor (including an uninvited salesperson), official visitor (including a firefighter and police officer). Put another way, a licensee is any non-trespasser who lacks the special status of an invitee.

> **NOTE:** Under this definition, someone who has been invited socially is classified as a licensee.

(b) Duty Owed to Licensee: Warn of Known Danger. [§ 345]

The basic obligation owed to a licensee is to **warn of known non-obvious dangers.** There is no obligation for the landowner to examine the premises to ensure that they are safe.

(c) **Example.** **[§ 346]** Darla invites Pron to dinner at her home. Unbeknownst to Darla, there is chipped marble on the faucet handle in the guest bathroom. Pron cuts his hand on the faucet handle and sues Darla, claiming that she should have, at a minimum, warned him about the danger. Because Pron is a licensee, Darla will prevail as she has no obligation to warn about risks of which she was unaware. Nor is Darla obligated to inspect the property in search of dangers in preparation for the arrival of a licensee.

(4) Invitees. [§ 347]

(a) Definition of Invitee. [§ 348]

An **invitee** is one invited to enter land generally **open to the public** (referred to as a **"public invitee"**) or a person who is invited onto the land for purposes directly or indirectly **related to the possessor's business** (called a "**business** invitee").

(b) Public Invitees. [§ 349]

Included in the definition of **public invitees** are persons entering **public buildings** such as churches or museums **regardless of whether admission is charged** or other economic benefit is provided to the landowner. The key is that the land is held open to the public at large.

(c) Business Invitees. [§ 350]

The concept of **business visitors** focuses upon those who **may** provide economic benefit to the landowner, but also includes "window shoppers" as well as the **friends** and **children** of customers or shoppers.

(d) Persons Exceeding Invitation. [§ 351]

Since the consent of the landowner defines the status of the person coming onto the land, a person who **exceeds the invitation** by remaining after hours or entering areas of the property clearly not open to the public (e.g., a stockroom of a store) may be treated as a trespasser.

(e) Duties Owed to Invitees: Inspect, and Warn or Fix. [§ 352]

The duty owed to an invitee goes beyond the duty to warn of known dangers (the duty owed to a licensee).

The landowner owes an invitee a duty of reasonable care. What constitutes reasonable care depends on the circumstances—it might require the defendant to discover non-obvious dangers and to either warn or repair those dangers.

> **(i) Example. [§ 353]** Pong is shopping at Dacy's Department Store when he slips on a broken floor tile near the cosmetics counter. Even if the employees of Dacy were unaware of the broken tile, Dacy is liable to Pong if a reasonable inspection of the premises would have discovered the danger.

b. Minority Rule—The Unitary Standard. [§ 354]

In *Rowland v. Christian*, 443 P.2d 561 (Cal. 1968), California became the first state to decide that the traditional rules relating to landowner liability should be **replaced with "ordinary principles of negligence."** New York and many other states have followed suit. **Under this strong minority rule, a duty will be owed regardless of the status of the land entrant plaintiff. The key issue, rather than one of duty, will be one of breach of duty—whether the defendant acted as a reasonably prudent person.** Accordingly, the child trespasser doctrine is no longer relevant. The major change heralded by this new approach is to leave the key debate to the jury in its determination of breach, rather than to the judge in her decision whether a duty is owed. Accordingly, many more cases go to a jury for final resolution.

> **(1) Example. [§ 355]** Prat is cutting across Dawn's land when she trips over a sprinkler head hidden by tall grass. Even though Prat is a trespasser, she will be owed a duty of due care. Her status as a trespasser could be relevant to whether Dawn acted reasonably, however.

c. Minority Rule—Combining Invitee and Licensee Categories. [§ 356]

Some jurisdictions have embraced a middle position under which they combine the invitee and licensee categories so that a duty of reasonable care is owed to either. But trespassers are still owed a limited duty.

d. Exam Hint. [§ 357]

> On most exams the jurisdiction is not stated. Accordingly, one should not presume that the jurisdiction is a common law status jurisdiction, or a modern *Rowland*-type jurisdiction. **You should analyze the problem using both approaches unless directed to do otherwise!**

e. Duty Owed to Those Outside the Land. [§ 358]

The landowner or occupier is required to exercise reasonable care, both as to **his activities** and **artificial conditions on his premises,** to protect those **outside** the land. According to the **Restatement, there is no affirmative obligation to remedy dangerous natural conditions** (except as to unreasonable risks of physical harm arising from trees on urban land near a public highway). Thus, under the traditional view, a landowner owes no duty to persons outside the land injured by a natural condition on the defendant's land.

(1) Modern Approach. [§ 359]

As with the case of land possessor liability to those injured on the land, however, it has been argued that the artificial condition/natural condition distinction makes no sense as a hard and fast rule, and this distinction, as well as the urban/rural dichotomy, ought to be left as factors to be considered by the fact finder in determining the reasonableness of the defendants' conduct. Indeed, some jurisdictions (e.g., California) do just this and no longer distinguish between natural and artificial conditions, requiring instead that the landowner employ reasonable care in both of these situations. (See *Sprecher v. Adamson Companies*, 636 P.2d 1121 (Cal. 1981)).

CHAPTER II

DUTY OF LANDOWNER Traditional: Status of π
                   Modern: Reasonableness

WHO IS π	PERSON OFF Δ'S LAND	TRESPASSERS*		LICENSEE	INVITEES
		UNKNOWN	KNOWN OR FREQUENT		
Δ'S ACTIVITIES	Duty of Due Care	No Duty	Duty of Due Care	Duty of Due Care	Duty of Due Care
Δ'S NATURAL CONDITIONS	No Duty except trees in urban areas	No Duty	No Duty	Warn or make safe (known dangers)	Warn or make safe and inspect
Δ'S ARTIFICIAL CONDITIONS	Duty of Due Care	No Duty	Warn or make safe	Warn or make safe (known dangers)	Warn or make safe and inspect

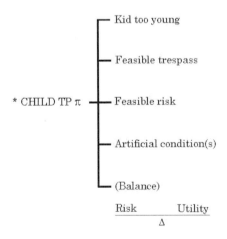

* CHILD TP π
- Kid too young
- Feasible trespass
- Feasible risk
- Artificial condition(s)
- (Balance)

$$\frac{Risk \quad Utility}{\Delta}$$

6. **Standard of Care Owed to Automotive Guests. [§ 360]**

a. **Common Law. [§ 361]**

At common law, a host owed guests in her automobile a duty of due care in the operation of the vehicle (although the guest's action might be barred by assumption of risk when the guest was aware of characteristics which made the host more dangerous than the average driver—e.g., the driver is a novice or drunk).

b. **Condition of Vehicle. [§ 362]**

By analogy to the rule for social guests in the home, the traditional view is that the host's only obligation insofar as the condition of the vehicle is concerned is to **warn of any known defects.** Many recent decisions, however, have imposed an obligation of reasonable inspection of the vehicle.

c. **Guest Statutes. [§ 363]**

At one time, roughly half of the states substantially reduced the duty of care owed to automotive guests by so-called "guest statutes." Under a typical guest statute, a driver is liable for injuries to his guest only if he was **grossly negligent** or if his actions amount to **willful and wanton misconduct** (perhaps including drunk driving).

d. **Who Is a Guest. [§ 364]**

Generally, a passenger is a "guest" within the meaning of a guest statute only if he confers **no pecuniary benefit whatsoever** on the driver. Thus, when the driver accepts money for gasoline or the like, the guest statute does **not** apply. Similarly, when a passenger is a prospective customer of the driver and is being transported for mutual business interests, the courts have generally held that there has been "indirect" benefit; thus, the passenger is not to be deemed a guest and may accordingly collect from her host for injuries caused by simple negligence.

e. **Trend Away from Such Statutes. [§ 365]**

In recent years, most jurisdictions have repealed their guest statutes. In some other states, the courts have ruled them unconstitutional as a denial of equal protection.

F. BREACH OF DUTY. [§ 366]

Usually, the most important part of a negligence analysis is determining whether the defendant in fact **breached** the applicable standard of care.

This is simply a matter of applying the facts given in the question and discussing **(from both sides)** whether the defendant fell below the applicable standard of care. Typically, then, the focus is whether the defendant acted as a reasonably prudent person would act under the same or similar circumstances. Though a question for the trier of fact, you need to be able to marshal the arguments from the perspective of the plaintiff and the defendant. In other words, explain what the parties will argue to the jury and then analyze.

1. **Clarity Caveat. [§ 367]**

    This element of breach of duty is often referred to by judges, lawyers and professors as "negligence," although breach of duty is actually only one element of the negligence cause of action (that is, duty, cause in fact, proximate cause, and damages remain as separate and additional elements).

2. **Exam Hint. [§ 368]**

    > An analysis of breach often appears to students as rather easy. Be careful, however, to avoid speaking in generalities and be certain to apply the applicable legal rules (as broad and ill-defined as they may be). Identify and state specifically what you are claiming to be the defendant's unreasonable conduct (and there may be several possible bases of unreasonable conduct.)

3. **Unreasonable Risks. [§ 369]**

    All risk is not actionable. Defendant is only liable for the creation of **unreasonable** risks. The key then is to analyze "reasonableness." Do not analyze the reasonableness of Defendant's conduct too generally.

    a. **Balancing Test—The Calculus of Risk. [§ 370]**

        Judge Learned Hand in *United States v. Carroll Towing Co.*, 159 F.2d 169 (2d Cir. 1947), fashioned an equation designed to analyze the reasonableness of conduct. Under this test, a defendant will be found to have breached the obligation to use reasonable care if the burden he faced in preventing the injury is less that the probability that the accident would occur multiplied by the magnitude of the likely harm the injury would inflict. This formula was presented by Judge Hand as an algebraic equation: $B < P(L)$ = unreasonable conduct. In the equation, B represents burden, P represents probability, and L represents the magnitude of loss. It is a broad principle that conduct is deemed to be unreasonable (i.e., that the defendant has breached) if the probability and gravity of injury to third persons exceed the burden of adequate precautions and the social utility of the defendant's conduct.

(1) Probability. [§ 371]

The first factor requires consideration of how likely it is that the harm-causing event will come about. In *Carroll Towing*, this was the likelihood that a ship would break loose from its moorings.

(2) Magnitude. [§ 372]

The question of magnitude of the loss focuses on what would be the likely harm if the harm-causing event comes about. Thus, in *Carroll Towing*, magnitude of the loss was the likely harm suffered when a ship gets loose in a crowded harbor. Note that it is the likely harm, not the actual harm suffered, that is the appropriate focus.

(3) Burden. [§ 373]

The product of liability and magnitude must be balanced against the burden of avoiding the injury to determine whether the defendant failed to act reasonably. In determining burden, consider what action the defendant might reasonably have been expected to take because usually a person's conduct will not be considered unreasonable unless one or more appropriate alternatives were available. Evaluate the pros/cons of these alternative measures. Also, consider the value society places on the activity in which the defendant was engaged.

(4) Factors Debatable. [§ 374]

These factors will be highly arguable with the plaintiff and the defendant having very different views of probability, magnitude, and burden.

(5) Economic Analysis. [§ 375]

Some commentators strongly advocate that this calculus of risk is an economic formula. Most, however, recognize that it is just a broad framework for thoughtful analysis encompassing intangibles (e.g., liberty interests) as well as concrete monetary concerns.

4. Custom. [§ 376]

Generally, a reasonable person conforms his conduct to the **customs or standards of the community** of which he is a member. Thus, evidence of the custom of a community, business, or industry is admissible, though not conclusive. Custom evidence is relevant to the determination of the reasonableness of the defendant's conduct. Ultimately, custom fits into the calculus of risk. The existence of a custom tends to indicate that the burden of avoidance is not too great and that there is some recognized probability of harm.

a.   **Non-Conformity to Custom. [§ 377]**

Showing **non-conformity** to a custom is highly relevant to show negligence. What a community does often establishes a **minimum** level of conduct deemed reasonable. However, a failure to follow customary methods may be irrelevant without preliminary proof that (a) what was actually done was not only different **but more dangerous** than what was usually done and (b) that the custom was adopted by others to avoid the kind of harm suffered by plaintiff.

> **(1) Example. [§ 378]** Patsy is injured moving some crates by hand. She sues her employer, Discs, Inc. Patsy seeks to introduce evidence that all similar companies use dollies to move the crates. This evidence is relevant, and may thus be considered by the trier of fact in Patsy's attempt to prove the unreasonableness of Discs' conduct, **provided she can show that the reason other companies use dollies is to ensure the safety of workers.**

b.   **Conformity to Custom. [§ 379]**

Compliance with custom is evidence of the defendant's lack of negligence, though the fact that the defendant acted as most others act is not necessarily compelling. This is particularly true when the defendant asserts conformity with a **business or industry custom** as evidence of the lack of unreasonableness, since the custom may well be based on cost and efficiency factors rather than on safety notions. Accordingly, there is a principle of "**customary negligence**," under which the trier of fact finds that the custom itself is unreasonable.

> **(1) Example. [§ 380]** Paxton sues for cargo lost at sea during a storm while being carried aboard a ship owned by Dim Co. Paxton contends that Dim was unreasonable by failing to equip the ship with a radio so that it could have learned about the impending storm. Dim may still be found to be unreasonable even if most (or even all) other ships do not equip themselves with radios, as the trier of fact could find the entire practice of not using radios unreasonable in light of the probability, magnitude and burden. (See, *The T.J. Hooper*, 60 F.2d 737 (2d Cir. 1932)).

5.   **Proof of Breach by Circumstantial Evidence. [§ 381]**

While the facts surrounding a tort action are normally clear by the time the case reaches the appellate courts (since these courts are generally bound by the findings of fact by the trial court), in real life practice proving exactly what happened is often quite difficult. Rarely is there direct evidence (e.g., an eyewitness), so circumstantial evidence is needed. Circumstantial evidence is proof from which one may draw reasonable inferences (e.g., fresh dog paw prints in snow are circumstantial evidence that a dog has recently walked by).

a. **"Slip and Fall" Cases. [§ 382]**

In order to recover in slip and fall cases, Plaintiff must show that Defendant knew or should have known about the condition that caused Plaintiff to fall. Thus, circumstantial evidence is needed to show that the condition existed long enough for the defendant to have been unreasonable in its failure to discover it (e.g., the banana peel on which the plaintiff slipped was flattened, black and gritty).

> **(1) Example. [§ 383]** Plyx slips in the produce aisle while shopping at Dumbo Market. He suffers a broken leg as a result of the fall and sues Dumbo Market for negligence. Plyx shows that he fell on a piece of lettuce that was on the floor of the produce aisle. If this is all the evidence of Dumbo Market's fault that Plyx provides at trial, Dumbo Market's motion for a directed verdict will be granted. There is not enough evidence from which a reasonable jury could infer that Dumbo Market was at fault for not discovering and remedying the dangerous condition. If Plyx shows that the lettuce on which he fell was smashed and dirty, the case will proceed to the jury for them to decide whether to infer unreasonable conduct by Dumbo Market.

b. **Res Ipsa Loquitur. [§ 384]**

When the plaintiff has little or no evidence showing exactly what the defendant did unreasonably, she will often attempt to prove breach by utilization of a special form of circumstantial evidence—the doctrine of **res ipsa loquitur** ("the thing speaks for itself").

(1) Rationale. [§ 385]

The gist of the doctrine of res ipsa loquitur is that the unique facts surrounding the accident in question are such that a reasonable person would logically conclude that the negligence of the defendant was the cause of the plaintiff's injury. The plaintiff is thus attempting to show that the injury was probably due to negligence and that the negligence was probably that of the defendant.

(2) Exam Hint. [§ 386]

Consider res ipsa loquitur whenever the plaintiff is having trouble showing exactly how her injury came about.

(3) Elements of Res Ipsa Loquitur. [§ 387]

The classic formulation of the doctrine identified three elements: (a) the event must be one which **would not normally happen unless someone were negligent**; (b) the event was caused by an instrumentality in the **control of the defendant;** and (c) the **event was not caused by any voluntary contributing action of the plaintiff.**

c. The Harm-Causing Event Would Not Happen in the Absence of Negligence. [§ 388]

(1) Unusual Acts. [§ 389]

Certain acts, by their unusual nature, indicate that **someone** must have been negligent. For example, if a flour barrel falls out of a second story window of a flour mill, logic and common experience would indicate that someone was negligent. Note that the exact nature of the negligence need not be proven or even logically inferable— it does not matter whether the negligent act was pushing the barrel out, leaving the barrel too close to the window so that vibrations would cause it to fall, improperly maintaining the mill floor or the barrel, or any other specific cause. All that is required is that the **likely causes point to negligence.**

(2) Unusual Act Not Required. [§ 390]

Although res ipsa loquitur is easiest to prove when the act itself is highly unusual, such an unusual act is not necessarily required. Thus, if moments after Daisy parks her car, the car rolls down the street and injures Petunia, Petunia can prove Daisy's negligence under res ipsa loquitur since cars do not normally roll down a hill in the absence of negligence.

(3) Negligence Need Not Be Only Possibility. [§ 391]

The plaintiff is not required to prove that negligence is the only explanation. The plaintiff need only show that negligence is the **most likely** explanation. Thus, in the Daisy-Petunia example immediately above, the finding of breach under res ipsa loquitur would not be precluded by

Daisy pointing out that it is possible that the car rolled down the hill because of an earthquake or because some unknown person released the emergency brake and threw the transmission into neutral.

d. Defendant Was the Responsible Party. [§ 392]

Plaintiff must prove that the negligence was probably that of the defendant.

(1) Exclusive control. [§ 393]

Proof of exclusive control is not actually required as long as Plaintiff can show that Defendant had control at the time of the alleged negligence and, thus, was probably the responsible party.

(2) Vicarious Liability Sufficient. [§ 394]

It is not necessary that the defendant was **personally** responsible for the act of negligence so long as he could be properly held to be vicariously liable for the acts of all those who might have been directly responsible (e.g., the negligence was of one of the plaintiff's employees). Vicarious liability is discussed in §§ 895–933.

(3) Application to Groups. [§ 395]

The "of the defendant" requirement causes major problems when the evidence supports a reasonable inference that **one or more, but not all** of a group of persons was negligent and no one person is responsible for the entire group. Notwithstanding some narrow exceptions that will be noted immediately below, the general rule requires a plaintiff to show by a preponderance of the evidence exactly which person is responsible for her injuries. Failure to do so will lead to a **non-suit or a directed verdict**; the case will fail due to the plaintiff's lack of proof.

(a) The Case of *Ybarra v. Spangard.* [§ 396]

In the well-publicized case of *Ybarra v. Spangard*, 154 P.2d 687 (Cal. 1944), the plaintiff suffered a traumatic injury while he was unconscious during a medical operation. The attending doctors and nurses and an orderly were all sued. No defendant was present at all times during which the injury might have happened, and at no time were all defendants present. The case was allowed to get past a motion for non-suit, despite the lack of evidence leading to a rational inference that any particular defendant was negligent.

(i) Limitations of *Ybarra*. [§ 397]

Even in jurisdictions following the rationale of *Ybarra* (and some have expressly refused to do so), the plaintiff will normally lose if all he can prove is that some one of a small group of people was negligent (e.g., plaintiff proves he was run down by a hot pink three-wheel car, and the three defendants each own one of the only three such vehicles in existence). In *Ybarra*, the court noted that there was a pre-existing relationship between the plaintiff and all the defendants, that the unique facts of the surgical setting (the plaintiff was unconscious and necessarily under the care of various independent contractors), and that the medical profession's "conspiracy of silence" all made it unjust for Ybarra to lose his claim as a matter of law. None of these characteristics are present in the hot pink car example.

e. No Voluntary Contributing Action by the Plaintiff. [§ 398]

Traditionally, the plaintiff must introduce evidence removing any inference of his or her own fault.

> **(1) Example. [§ 399]** Pru is injured when a bottle of soda purchased from Disco exploded in her face. While soda bottles do not ordinarily explode in the absence of negligence, Pru must introduce evidence that she was not careless in handling the bottle after purchasing it.

(2) Effect of Comparative Fault. [§ 400]

Proof of the lack of fault by the plaintiff is no longer necessarily crucial in those jurisdictions that have adopted comparative fault. (See § 464). The plaintiff's unreasonable conduct in these jurisdictions will lead to a reduced recovery, but will not preclude the use of res ipsa loquitur.

f. **Procedural Effect of Res Ipsa Loquitur. [§ 401]**

(1) **Rule of Superior Access. [§ 402]**

On the theory that res ipsa loquitur is justified by notions of fairness and the defendant's superior access to information, some of the older cases held that once the doctrine is applied, the burden of proof as to breach shifted to the defendant. In such a jurisdiction, a directed verdict must be entered in favor of the plaintiff unless the defendant introduces evidence disproving his fault which is at least equal to the natural inferences created by the circumstances of the injury. A few jurisdictions continue to require the plaintiff to prove the defendant has superior access to information before res ipsa loquitur will be permitted.

(2) **Rule of Circumstantial Evidence. [§ 403]**

Most courts, on the other hand, have held that res ipsa loquitur is **simply a form of circumstantial evidence**. As such, once the doctrine is shown to be applicable, the plaintiff has established his prima facie case of negligence but there is no presumption of negligence. Put another way, the judge may not take the case away from the jury by finding that there is no cause of action as a matter of law, but the jury is not **required** to find for the plaintiff even if the defendant fails to introduce evidence on the matter. The key benefit of res ipsa loquitur, then, is that the case gets to the jury.

g. **Res Ipsa Loquitur Inapplicable to Intentional Torts. [§ 404]**

Accidents, by their nature, are largely unintentional. Where the defendant has acted intentionally or recklessly, res ipsa loquitur is inapplicable. Of course, in such cases, normal rules of circumstantial evidence may aid the plaintiff in a manner closely analogous to res ipsa loquitur.

---

(1) Example. [§ 405] Paul sues Dumas for trespass to land after Dumas drove a tractor onto Paul's land. If Paul can prove that the only way that the tractor could have been driven was if Dumas had followed a procedure of specific tasks in a specified order, the logical inference that Dumas knew what he was doing (since intent to do the act which results in the trespass is all that is required) ought to allow Paul to get his case before the jury. This is not res ipsa loquitur.

---

h. Final Res Ipsa Loquitur Pointer. [§ 406]

Res ipsa loquitur is a doctrine of circumstantial evidence which assists the plaintiff with his proof of **breach** in a negligence case. It does not supplant full and independent analysis of the other negligence elements (e.g., proximate cause, damages), nor does the doctrine have any application outside the negligence context. Further, you should not use res ipsa loquitur unless you cannot identify what constitutes the defendant's specific alleged unreasonable conduct. Only when the situation "smells" of negligence but you cannot identify what exactly the defendant did wrong do you want to employ the doctrine.

> **(1) Res Ipsa Loquitur Example. [§ 407]** Pava was walking down a street when he suddenly lost consciousness. The facts show that as he passed Dell's flour warehouse, he was hit on the head by a falling barrel of flour. Pava sues Dell. Without res ipsa loquitur, Pava's case would be dismissed because he could not prove what Dell did wrong. Relying on res ipsa loquitur, however, Pava can try to persuade a jury that barrels do not usually fall out of windows absent negligence, and that Dell was probably the responsible party. If the jury is so persuaded, the jury may infer that Dell was unreasonable. Dell, of course, is free to put on evidence of Dell's due care. (See *Byrne v. Boadle*, 159 Eng. Rep. 299 (1863)).

G. CAUSE IN FACT (OR ACTUAL CAUSE). [§ 408]

After the plaintiff has proven that the defendant owed a duty and failed to comply with the applicable standard of care, the next issue is whether more likely than not the defendant's conduct was a **cause in fact** (or **actual cause**) of the plaintiff's harm. This is generally a question of fact to be resolved by the trier of fact.

1. The "But For" Test. [§ 409]

The **"but for" test** requires proof that the plaintiff's injury would not have occurred **but for** the defendant's negligent conduct. This requires precise identification of the aspect of the defendant's conduct that was negligent and a determination of whether the plaintiff's injury would have occurred even without this negligent conduct.

> **a. Example. [§ 410]** Dave collided with a car driven by Chip in which Pedro was a passenger. Dave's only negligence was a failure to signal for a left turn. If Chip was not looking and would not have seen Dave's signal had he made one, Dave's negligence is not the cause in fact of Pedro's injury, and Pedro would recover nothing from Dave. Note that this is so even though Dave owes a duty to Pedro and breached it by his unreasonable conduct.

2. Multiple Causes and the "Substantial Factor" Test. [§ 411]

The traditional **but for** test breaks down when concurrent causes create a single injury, but either would have been sufficient to cause the identical harm alone.

> **a. Example. [§ 412]** Dizzy and Daffy, unknown to each other, are both negligently driving their motorcycles when they pass Pinky, a horseback rider. Pinky's horse is frightened and throws her to the ground. Neither motorcyclist was the "but for" cause of Pinky's injury if the horse would have been frightened by either defendant alone.

b. Resolution of Problem. [§ 413]

Obviously, it would be absurd to relieve both Dizzy and Daffy of liability in the above example simply because Pinky would have been injured to the same degree by either one. In such cases, the courts will disregard the "but for" test and find that they have both caused the injury so long as each was a **substantial factor** in causing the injury.

3. May Be More Than One Cause. [§ 414]

Plaintiff need not necessarily establish Defendant's negligence as the sole or even primary cause of Plaintiff's injury so long as that negligence is an integral part of the chain of events leading to the injury. Thus, two defendants who acted independently are both causes-in-fact of an injury if their negligent acts combine to cause a single injury.

> **a. Example. [§ 415]** Romulus negligently allows a flammable chemical to collect in an alley behind Spock's store. Klingon negligently throws a match into the pool formed by the chemical and Spock's store is burned to the ground. Since the fire could not have happened without Romulus's negligence, he clearly was a cause in fact of Spock's injuries even though his act was not sufficient, by itself, to cause the fire. Similarly, Klingon's act was a cause in fact of the damages because the fire would not otherwise have occurred. Each was a "substantial factor" of the harm.

4. Problems of Proof. [§ 416]

a. Multiple Negligently Inflicted Injuries. [§ 417]

If the plaintiff suffers a broken arm due to Defendant-1's negligence and a broken leg due to Defendant-2's negligence, each defendant is responsible only for the injuries she caused. However, situations involving "divisible harm" are rare. More likely, the situation involves multiple, though independent tortfeasors, who combine to cause indivisible harm to Plaintiff. While the plaintiff can prove his total injury, the overlap creates difficulty in proving how much injury each accident separately caused. Upon proving duty, breach, and that each defendant was a "substantial factor" of Plaintiff's injury, the defendants are jointly and severally liable for the harm suffered by Plaintiff. (See §§ 965–975.)

b. **Alternative Liability Theory—Uncertainty as to Which Negligent Defendant Caused Single Injury. [§ 418]**

In *Summers v. Tice*, 199 P.2d 1 (Cal. 1948), two hunters negligently fired their shotguns in the plaintiff's direction and a shotgun pellet lodged in his eye. It was impossible to prove from which gun the errant pellet came, and it was equally likely that it came from either gun. Both hunters were given the burden of disproving cause-in-fact and held jointly liable when they could not meet the burden. The rationale was that it was fairer to place the burden of proof as to the issue of causation on the defendants, **both of whom were negligent**, than on the innocent, injured plaintiff.

(1) **Application of *Summers*. [§ 419]**

For the alternative liability theory to be employed, each defendant must have acted unreasonably and each must have been sued by the plaintiff. Thus, absent the ability of the plaintiff to establish breach on the part of each defendant, there is no "*Summers*" issue regarding causation. Further, the greater the number of defendants, the less likely it is that a court will follow *Summers*.

(2) ***Ybarra* Distinguished. [§ 420]**

Note that **Ybarra v. Spangard** (discussed in § 395) is not merely a logical extension of the rule of *Summers v. Tice*. **In *Summers*, all of the defendants were proven to have acted negligently, and the only issue was cause-in-fact;** in *Ybarra*, the plaintiff could not prove that **any** of the defendants had acted negligently.

(3) **Market Share Liability. [§ 421]**

In *Sindell v. Abbott Laboratories*, 607 P.2d 924 (Cal. 1980), the California Supreme Court adopted a modified version of the alternative liability theory to be used in situations where the plaintiff sues a number of negligent defendants who manufactured a generic harmful product and where the plaintiff, through no fault of her own, is unable to identify which company manufactured the product that caused Plaintiff's injury. The court held that once a plaintiff brings enough defendants into court so that "a substantial percent of the market" is represented, the burden of proof shifts to the defendants to show that they are not the manufacturer of the harm-causing product used by the plaintiff. If the defendants cannot sustain this burden, each defendant is liable to the plaintiff for her injuries based on each defendant's **market share**. Several jurisdictions have adopted some variation of this approach. Many jurisdictions that have adopted some form of market share liability use a national market to determine the amount of each defendant's liability and, in most, defendants are only severally liable (meaning they pay only the percentage of the plaintiff's injury represented by their market share). In a somewhat controversial decision, the high court of New York determined that the DES manufacturing defendants will be liable based on their share of the national market even if they prove they did not provide the DES to the plaintiff's mother. See *Hymowitz v. Eli Lilly and Company*, 539 N.E.2d 1069 (N.Y.1989).

c. Medical Uncertainty: Loss of a Chance. [§ 422]

The "but for" test has been rejected in some jurisdictions where the defendant's malpractice reduces a plaintiff's chance of recovery and where the plaintiff never had a probable chance of survival. For example, due to Dr. Doom's negligence, Ply's cancer was undetected. Had it been detected, Ply would have had a 40% chance of survival. By the time the condition is actually discovered, the cancer is incurable. Under traditional notions of cause-in-fact, Ply could not recover from Dr. Doom, because Ply could not show that "but for" the doctor's malpractice, Ply probably would have survived. To avoid this result, some jurisdictions have characterized Ply's injury as "the loss of a chance of survival." As such, Ply could recover some damages for the negligence that deprived her of a 40% chance of survival.

H. PROXIMATE (OR LEGAL) CAUSE. [§ 423]

A defendant who owed a duty, breached it, and was the cause in fact of harm to the plaintiff will not be held liable for negligence unless she was a **proximate cause** (sometimes called the **legal cause**) of the plaintiff's harm. All courts agree that, at some point, it would be unfair to hold a defendant liable for all of the consequences caused by her negligent conduct. **Proximate cause is concerned with policy considerations limiting the scope of liability.** Most of the limitation of liability is based upon the concept of foreseeability—that is, generally, courts find that the defendant is the proximate cause of foreseeable risks or consequences, but not of harm which is deemed wholly unforeseeable.

1. **Relation to Duty Issue. [§ 424]**

   There is a very close relationship between the issue of duty and the issue of proximate cause. Indeed, both concepts are designed to answer the single public policy question: "Is the defendant obligated to protect the plaintiff from the injury which did in fact occur?" Traditionally, however, the issues have been treated separately so that the duty issue is primarily concerned with defining the **relationship** between the plaintiff and the defendant, while the proximate cause issue is concerned with whether the defendant is responsible for the **consequences** flowing from his conduct, given the relationship. Another key difference is that duty is regarded as a question of law for the judge while proximate cause is seen as a question of fact for the trier of fact.

2. **Identifying Proximate Cause Issues. [§ 425]**

   As indicated above, courts are concerned with proximate cause issues in an effort to place some limits on the potentially unlimited circle of liability. This danger is primarily present when: (a) the harm is extremely widespread; (b) the magnitude of the injury is grossly out of proportion to the defendant's negligent conduct; (c) there was a very unusual or unexpected (thus unforeseeable) result; or (d) there were multiple parties or factors which contributed to the ultimate resulting injury or harm.

3. **Often Not a Key Issue. [§ 426]**

   Just as duty is usually readily established in a negligence case, proximate cause is usually easily shown. Typically there are no intervening forces and the risk created by the defendant's conduct mirrors what happened to the plaintiff. The discussion that follows analyzes those rather unusual situations which raise a potential proximate cause issue.

4. **Direct versus Indirect Causes. [§ 427]**

   There are different approaches taken to proximate cause. The traditional approach (and one that many torts professors greatly criticize) divides proximate cause problems into cases involving **direct causes and indirect causes.** If you did not discuss proximate cause this way in class, however, you should not use this terminology in briefs, in class, or on exams!

   a. **Concepts Defined. [§ 428]**

      Direct causation cases involve situations where nothing intervened between the defendant's negligence and the harm suffered by the plaintiff. **Indirect causation** is found when any occurrence—whether the act of another person, the conduct of an animal, or an act of nature—happens after the negligent act in question and constitutes a necessary link in the chain leading from that act to the injuries suffered by the plaintiff.

b.   "Set Stage." [§ 429]

The circumstances already in existence, including the forces already in motion at the time of the defendant's negligence, are **never** intervening causes; the defendant is said to have acted on a set stage. Thus, the unusual susceptibilities of the plaintiff (the Eggshell Skull Rule) never break the chain of proximate cause. Intervening forces arise after the defendant's negligent act.

c.   Direct Causes. [§ 430]

(1)   Traditional View. [§ 431]

The traditional view was that all direct causes are proximate causes, no matter how unforeseeable. (Note, however, that the plaintiff still must be a foreseeable plaintiff in jurisdictions following the Cardozo view in *Palsgraf*).

> **(a) Example. [§ 432]** In the famous case of *In re Polemis*, an agent of the defendant negligently dropped a wooden plank in the hold of a ship. The plank caused a spark which ignited fumes in the hold, and the resulting fire substantially damaged the ship. The court held that even though a fire which destroyed the entire ship was not foreseeable, the defendant was liable since the act of dropping a board into the hold of the ship was negligent (because it created a risk of **some** harm to the ship) and there were no intervening causes. The plaintiff's harm was directly traceable to the defendant's breach of duty.

(2)   Modern Trend. [§ 433]

(a)   Personal Injury: Eggshell Skull Rule. [§ 434]

Insofar as personal injuries are concerned, the courts continue to hold that all direct causes are proximate. Thus, if Dorvel negligently kicks Parmel in the knee, Dorvel is the proximate cause of all of Parmel's physical injuries. This is true even if the blow would only have bruised a normal person but Parmel was permanently crippled due to a pre-existing injury which Dorvel could not have foreseen.

(b) Injury to Property: Foreseeability Is Key. [§ 435]

Expressly or impliedly rejecting *In re Polemis*, many courts have held that the defendant is not the proximate cause of injuries which were beyond the scope of foreseeable risk. A defendant is not the proximate cause of harm that is **highly extraordinary.**

d. Indirect Causation Cases: Foreseeability Is the Key. [§ 436]

Indirect causation cases are those in which someone or some force came into active operation after the defendant's negligence and before the harm to the plaintiff.

(1) Basic Rule. [§ 437]

If the defendant could **reasonably foresee** the intervening act or force, then the intervening act or force is **not superseding** and the defendant is said to be the proximate cause. If, on the other hand, the intervening act or force is **not** reasonably foreseeable, generally speaking, it is considered superseding and the defendant is not the proximate cause of plaintiff's harm.

(2) The Foreseeable Results Theory. [§ 438]

Even if a particular intervening act or force is found to be unforeseeable, the defendant nevertheless may be found to be the proximate cause of an injury if the **ultimate result was foreseeable.**

> **(a) Example. [§ 439]** Dasco maintains a weakened power pole which would fall if subjected to moderate force. Pam is injured by the falling pole after it was struck by Fletcher, a negligent hang glider. Even though it was not foreseeable that the pole would be struck by a hang glider, the **result was foreseeable** and thus Dasco was the proximate cause of Pam's injury.

(3) Result Must Be Within the Risk. [§ 440]

The defendant's conduct is not the proximate cause of the plaintiff's injuries unless the possibility of the harm actually resulting was one of the risks that make the conduct negligent. While normally this is not a problem, there are a few cases where the result is clearly not within the risk.

> **(a) Example. [§ 441]** Doris is driving at an excessive speed and runs into a fallen tree, thus injuring Pat. If Doris could have avoided the tree had she been driving at a slower, reasonable speed, the resulting injury to Pat is clearly within the risk. However, suppose the tree fell on top of the car as Doris drove by; while speeding is still a cause-in-fact of the accident (if only in the sense that the car would have been somewhere else when the tree fell had Doris been driving at a slower speed), the risk of having a tree fall on her car as she drove by a specific spot was not what made her conduct negligent.

(4) Limitations of Risk Analysis. [§ 442]

If one **generalizes** enough about the risks that made the conduct negligent, almost every case can be brought within the general description. If one **particularizes** the specific facts of any accident, the specific accident is almost never foreseeable. Thus, risk analysis merely frames the issue rather than providing answers in most non-routine proximate cause problems. The parties, of course, will characterize the risk differently often to serve their own ends.

> **(a) Example. [§ 443]** Dallas negligently maintains a road and Pirate's car becomes stuck in a mud hole. In attempting to extricate the car, Pirate's peg leg becomes entangled in the rope, breaking his good leg. Obviously, the precise nature of this unusual accident was unforeseeable. On the other hand, it is foreseeable that people will suffer personal injury in extricating cars stuck in mud holes.

(5) Repetitive Cases. [§ 444]

Although application of the proximate cause principles can be difficult in any given case, there are some repetitive situations which have produced some fairly well-settled rules which can be used or argued by analogy.

(a) Intentional or Criminal Intervening Conduct of Third Parties. [§ 445]

Although it is sometimes said that the subsequent intentional torts or criminal acts of a third party which cause an injury are superseding causes, freeing a merely negligent defendant from liability, this is not necessarily true. While such conduct is not normally foreseeable, the possibility of such conduct may in fact be specifically foreseeable in a given situation or may be one of the risks that made the defendant's conduct negligent in the first place.

> **(i) Example. [§ 446]** Dozier, a security guard, negligently fails to lock the doors of a building which is then burglarized. Dozier is liable for the resulting loss even though the burglary can be classified as an intervening illegal act of a third person. The very risk created by Dozier's negligence is that a burglary would occur.

(b) Rescuers. [§ 447]

As noted in § 200, the defendant is liable for injuries to a person who reasonably attempts to rescue one imperiled by her negligence. The rule has been applied beyond injury to the rescuer himself and covers cases where the rescuer aggravates the injuries to the original victim or even ends up injuring third parties. Because of a policy to encourage rescue attempts, liability has been imposed despite the freakishness of the particular facts or unforeseeable intervening events.

> **(i) Example. [§ 448]** Fisher negligently left his truck on a highway at night without setting out flares. A car containing Gunter crashed into the truck and caught fire. Lynch managed to extricate Gunter from the burning car. Gunter, however, was deranged by the accident and shot Lynch with a pistol he had hidden under the car's floor mat which Lynch was using to pillow Gunter's head. Fisher was held liable for Lynch's injury. *Lynch v. Fisher*, 34 So.2d 513 (La. App. 1948).

(c) Injuries Received in Subsequent Treatment of Original Injury. [§ 449]

If the defendant is responsible for an injury, he will usually be liable for **aggravation** of the injury caused by its subsequent treatment. Under this rule, the defendant is liable for injuries sustained in an **ambulance accident** on plaintiff's trip to the hospital, **medical malpractice of plaintiff's doctor in treating the injury, and aggravation of the injury in the course of rehabilitation** (as when plaintiff's weakened leg gives way as he is walking to strengthen it). When the aggravating conduct becomes too extreme (and thus highly unforeseeable), the original tortfeasor will not be liable for the additional harm. So while usually the initial tortfeasor will be liable (along with the negligent physician) for injuries aggravated by subsequent medical malpractice, if the surgeon is so intoxicated that she removes the wrong organ, this is so extraordinarily negligent that the initial tortfeasor will not be liable for this additional harm. Obviously, the line here is a fuzzy one.

(6) Suicide. [§ 450]

At one time, the plaintiff's suicide was always labeled superseding event for which the original defendant was not responsible, even if the plaintiff's suicidal state was caused by the defendant's tortious conduct. In negligence cases, the old rule may be giving way when the plaintiff's conduct resulted from an **uncontrollable impulse** resulting from a disordered mental state caused by his original accident (as opposed to a conscious choice simply following a period of depression). The defendant's liability is more arguable where his tortious conduct was **intentional,** particularly if he intended the severe mental distress which led to the suicide.

(7) Factors Breaking Chain of Proximate Cause. [§ 451]

Notwithstanding normal foreseeability analysis, two factors are routinely held to break the chain of proximate cause.

(a) Termination of Risk: Higher Ethical Duty. [§ 452]

A person's legal responsibility sometimes ends under proximate cause when a second actor who is expected to use great care intervenes but fails to exercise the expected care.

> **(i) Example. [§ 453]** Reduction negligently left a dynamite cap at a construction site and the cap is found by Charlie, a small child. Charlie's parents see Charlie playing with the cap and know what it is, but they allow him to keep it. Jack, Charlie's playmate, is injured when the cap explodes. The conduct of Charlie's parents is an independent intervening event, insulating Reduction from liability. Reduction's potential liability ended when the parents failed to protect Charlie from the **known danger.** *Pittsburg Reduction Co. v. Horton*, 113 S.W. 647 (Ark. 1908). Modern analysis would look to see if the parents' negligence was so gross, and therefore so unforeseeable, that the conduct would be characterized as superseding conduct, thereby insulating Reduction from liability for its clearly unreasonable conduct.

(b) Significant Lapse of Time. [§ 454]

A very long lapse between the time of the defendant's act and the time the plaintiff is harmed has prompted some courts to ignore the "foreseeable results" theory.

5. Modern Approach to Proximate Cause. [§ 455]

While most of the above-stated rules continue to apply, the modern focus in proximate cause tends to divide the analysis into three categories: extent of harm, type of harm, and manner of harm.

a. Extent of Harm. [§ 456]

As discussed in § 421 above, the defendant takes the victim as he finds her and is liable for all consequences no matter how extraordinary. This is so even where Defendant precipitates a pre-existing condition in Plaintiff.

> **(1) Example. [§ 457]** Darren collides with Pebbles, breaking her leg. Pebbles, due to years of alcohol abuse, is predisposed to delirium tremens and dies of delirium tremens after a couple of days in the hospital. Defendant is the proximate cause of the death if his negligence precipitated the attack of delirium tremens. *McCahill v. New York Transportation Co.*, 94 N.E. 616 (N.Y. 1911).

b. Type of Harm—the Risk Rule. [§ 458]

Courts no longer employ the "directly traceable" test of *Polemis*. The modern focus is on the foreseeability of the harm suffered by Plaintiff under a "risk rule" analysis. The issue is whether the harm actually suffered by Plaintiff is within the risk created by Defendant's negligence. One needs to consider what it is that made Defendant's conduct unreasonable.

> **(1) Example. [§ 459]** Dawn owns a vicious dog, Cuddles, that she unreasonably allows to escape from the yard one night. Cuddles runs into the street, causing a gasoline truck to swerve to avoid a collision. The truck driver loses control and the gas leaks, causing an explosion that destroys Pookah's house. Pookah sues Dawn. Dawn can make a persuasive argument that the risk created by negligently letting Cuddles out of the yard did not include the burning of a house.

c. Manner of Harm. [§ 460]

Arguably, the manner the harm came about should be irrelevant provided that the injury suffered was within the risk created by Defendant's negligence. In fact, most intervening conduct (acts of nature, acts of third parties, etc.) occurring between Defendant's negligent act and Plaintiff's injury does not relieve Defendant from liability. However, occasionally the intervening force is so unforeseeable that it is deemed superseding, thereby relieving the negligent actor of liability. It is typically highly debatable whether certain intervening conduct is superseding. Often the more culpable the intervening force, the less foreseeable it is.

> **(1) Example. [§ 461]** DorkCo negligently fails to secure a work site. Rex, an epileptic who negligently failed to take his medication, suffers a seizure and enters the work site, injuring Pat. In Pat's action against DorkCo, the intervening negligent conduct of Rex will likely not be deemed superseding. Thus, DorkCo (along with Rex) will be liable to Pat for her injuries. If, however, Rex was Pat's archenemy who drove onto the work site intending to harm Pat, Rex's conduct would likely be deemed superseding, insulating DorkCo from liability. See *Derdiarian v. Felix Contracting Corp.*, 414 N.E.2d 666 (N.Y.1980).

PROXIMATE CAUSE

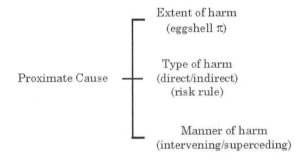

I. COMPENSABLE DAMAGES. [§ 462]

Negligence requires that there be **actual** damage. The issue of damages is discussed in a later part of this summary. (See §§ 949–964.)

J. NEGLIGENCE DEFENSES. [§ 463]

After considering the prima facie case, remember to discuss any affirmative defenses that the defendant may raise. "Defenses" are not the counter-arguments raised by Defendant to Plaintiff's prima facie case (e.g., Defendant's contention that she used reasonable care). Rather, here we are focusing on those issues that arise after Plaintiff has established a prima facie case for negligence (i.e., Plaintiff has proven duty, breach, cause in fact, proximate cause and damages). These defenses must be proven by Defendant by a preponderance of the evidence; the burden of proof is on the defendant.

CHAPTER II

1. Contributory Negligence. [§ 464]

Contributory negligence is conduct by the plaintiff which falls below the standard of care to which she should adhere for her own safety and which is a cause in fact of her harm. **Virtually all the concepts considered above in the prima facie negligence case apply equally when examining the plaintiff's conduct.** Contributory negligence is a complete bar to plaintiff's recovery. Thus, if Defendant was 99% at fault and a jury found Plaintiff to be 1% at fault, Plaintiff would recover **nothing due to her contributory negligence.** Almost all states have abandoned contributory negligence for comparative fault.

a. Reasonable Person Standard. [§ 465]

In most cases, the plaintiff's conduct must be examined under the reasonable person test (i.e., did the plaintiff's conduct fall below the standard of a reasonable person under like circumstances?). This is an objective test and requires a consideration of the same factors discussed in determining whether a defendant's act or omission was negligent.

(1) Dual Standards. [§ 466]

Some courts will analyze a less demanding standard to the plaintiff whose contributory negligence is in issue than to a negligent defendant.

(a) Mental Characteristics of Adult. [§ 467]

While the mental disabilities of an adult **defendant** are generally ignored (See § 292), some states will consider such defects in determining whether an adult **plaintiff** was contributorily negligent, at least when the defendant had a clear duty to protect the plaintiff from his own folly.

> **(i) Example. [§ 468]** Mochen was institutionalized due to a mental deficiency. Employees of the defendant hospital failed to supervise Mochen's activities and he was injured in attempting an unreasonably dangerous escape. The court held that the issue of contributory negligence must be determined by considering Mochen's mental defects. *Mochen v. State of New York*, 352 N.Y.S.2d 290 (N.Y.A.D. 1974). Recall that if Mochen had been the defendant his mental disabilities would have been irrelevant.

(b) Children Engaged in Adult Activities. [§ 469]

This same rationale may apply to a child involved in an adult activity, who, as a defendant, is held to the adult standard of care, but who, as a plaintiff, may be held to a child standard even though engaged in an adult activity.

b. Effect of Statute on Contributory Negligence. [§ 470]

The relevance of the plaintiff's violation of a statute, including the availability of excuse, is generally governed by the same rules that were discussed under the heading "standards of care" (See § 284.) with regard to the defendant's negligence. Accordingly, where there is an applicable statute, a plaintiff may be "contributorily negligent per se."

c. Where Defendant's Negligence Is in Violation of a Criminal Statute. [§ 471]

Normally, the only effect of a violation of a criminal statute is to establish that the defendant's conduct is negligent. Thus, most of the time, contributory negligence will still be a defense. However, in a few cases where the statute violated by the defendant is a **paternalistic measure designed to protect people like the plaintiff from their own folly,** contributory negligence may not be a defense. Thus, if Dingo has violated a statute making it unlawful to sell fireworks to children, the action of a child-buyer who is injured when the fireworks explode is unaffected by the child's contributory negligence.

d. Cause in Fact. [§ 472]

For the plaintiff's contributory negligence to constitute a bar to recovery, it must be a cause-in-fact (using either the "but for" or "substantial factor" test) of her injuries.

> **(1) Example. [§ 473]** Darryl negligently parked his car in the middle of a road. One evening, Parker collided with Darryl's car and sued for his injuries. Darryl contends that Parker was contributorily negligent for failing to have his headlights on as required by statute. Though Parker's failure to have the headlights illuminated is probably negligence per se, Parker is not contributorily negligent unless Darryl can prove that it is more likely than not that Parker would have avoided the collision had he had his headlights lit. *See Martin v. Herzog,* 126 N.E. 814 (N.Y. 1920).

(e) Willful and Wanton Misconduct. [§ 474]

Just as the plaintiff's contributory negligence is no defense to an intentional tort, **it is no defense if the defendant's conduct is willful and wanton or reckless.** While the difference between negligence and recklessness is often more one of degree than kind, obviously the issue is whether the defendant's conduct is extremely careless.

(f) Last Clear Chance. [§ 475]

Contributory negligence is not a defense if the defendant had the **last clear chance** to avoid the accident, a rebuttal to the defendant's defense of contributory negligence. Theoretically, the rule may be based on the assumption that the defendant's conduct is more blameworthy than the plaintiff's conduct if the defendant has the last clear chance to avoid the accident. In fact, however, the rule seeks to determine only who was negligent last.

f. Effect of Contributory Negligence. [§ 476]

At common law, **any** negligence of the plaintiff which contributed to his injuries (i.e., was a cause in fact and proximate cause), no matter how slightly, served as a **complete defense** to the plaintiff's action. Contributory negligence is all or nothing; plaintiff gets full damages or no damages.

g. Modern Rule: Comparative Negligence. [§ 477]

Today, virtually all states have replaced the absolute bar of contributory negligence with a **partial defense** of **comparative negligence.** Such jurisdictions compare the fault of the plaintiff and defendant and simply reduce the plaintiff's recovery by the proportion that her own negligence bears to the total negligence.

(1) "Pure" Comparative Negligence. [§ 478]

Under the **"pure"** form of comparative negligence, in effect in states which have adopted comparative negligence by case law, a plaintiff is **always** entitled to recover something from a negligent defendant, no matter how serious his own negligence. Thus, if Pat is 90 percent at fault and Dan is 10 percent negligent, Pat can recover for 10 percent of her injuries.

(2) Modified Comparative Negligence. [§ 479]

Most comparative negligence statutes, however, limit recovery to cases where the plaintiff's negligence is **not as great as** or **not greater than** the defendant's negligence. Thus, if Pat is 49 percent negligent and Dan is 51 percent negligent, Pat recovers 51 percent of her damages; but if

Pat is 51 percent negligent and Dan is 49 percent negligent, Pat recovers nothing.

(a) Special Problems. [§ 480]

(i) Special Verdicts. [§ 481]

A significant number of comparative negligence statutes provide for special verdicts, with the jury reporting how much, in percentages, each party has been negligent. The court then applies the statutory formula to apportion the total damages, as found by the jury, on the basis of the percentage of each party's negligence.

(ii) Multiple Party Cases. [§ 482]

Comparative negligence is especially complex in cases involving multiple plaintiffs and/or multiple defendants and/or counterclaims. Some statutes have special provisions for apportioning damages in relation to the degree of fault of each defendant, replacing common law rules on indemnity and contribution.

(3) Effect of Comparative Negligence on Specific Common Law Rules of Negligence. [§ 483]

Many of the common law rules of negligence, including the doctrine of assumption of risk (§ 484) and most of the special contributory negligence rules discussed earlier, are subject to reevaluation in light of the adoption of comparative negligence. The most important changes to these doctrines identified so far are discussed below.

(a) Assumption of Risk. [§ 484]

To the extent that assumption of risk is a synonym for a particular kind of contributory negligence, it is usually covered by the rules of comparative negligence (i.e., the plaintiff should still recover a portion of his damages, at least if his fault is less than the defendant's). There are, however, cases where assumption of risk means that the defendant owed no duty to the plaintiff, in which case the plaintiff can recover nothing even under a comparative negligence statute.

(b) Wanton Misconduct. [§ 485]

The common law rule that contributory negligence is not a defense to wanton or reckless conduct was clearly designed to mitigate the harshness of the absolute bar of contributory negligence and is no longer needed in comparative negligence jurisdictions. Thus, an unreasonable plaintiff could have her recovery reduced to some degree even though the defendant behaved recklessly. Typically, comparative fault is not applied in the context of intentional wrongdoing, however.

(c) Last Clear Chance. [§ 486]

Last clear chance should not logically survive enactment of a comparative negligence law (since the rule was really intended to lessen the harshness of the rule of contributory negligence) and most states have so held.

2. Assumption of Risk. [§ 487]

Assumption of the risk should be kept in mind as a defense separate and apart from comparative fault/comparative negligence. This area is complicated because there are different forms of assumption of the risk: express assumption of the risk; implied assumption of the risk; and primary assumption of the risk.

a. Express Assumption of the Risk. [§ 488]

Express assumption of the risk is really a contractual waiver whereby the plaintiff by oral or written words relieves the defendant of the defendant's obligation to act non-negligently toward the plaintiff. Most jurisdictions recognize this defense provided that the language is clear and provided that the waiver is not void as against public policy.

> **(1) Example. [§ 489]** Before permitting a person to ski at its lodge, Ski-town requires patrons to sign a written waiver agreeing to relieve Ski-town of liability even if due to its negligence. If Polly, who signed the waiver, is injured because Ski-town negligently failed to mark an area as out of bounds, Polly, in most jurisdictions would lose her negligence claim due to express assumption of the risk.

(2) Invalid Waivers. [§ 490]

A defendant may not assert express assumption of the risk for conduct that is more culpable than negligent. Thus, a plaintiff may still recover for her damages upon proof that the defendant was reckless or intentional. Further, if the activity is a necessity, such as medical treatment, forcing the plaintiff to sign a waiver will be deemed as void as against public policy. See *Tunkl v. Regents of University of Cal.*, 32 Cal.Rptr. 33, 383 P.2d 441 (Cal.1963), in which the California Supreme Court struck down a waiver that sought to relieve a hospital from liability for malpractice as a condition of treatment.

b. Implied assumption of the risk. [§ 491]

Implied assumption of the risk is an affirmative defense based on the plaintiff's conduct. The defendant must prove that the plaintiff 1) knew the risk, 2) understood the risk, and 3) voluntarily elected to expose herself to the risk.

---

(1) Example. [§ 492] Polly gets into Drew's car, noticing that Drew reeks of alcohol and spotting several bottles on the floor near Drew. While driving, Drew loses control of the car and hits a tree, injuring Polly. In Polly's negligence action against Drew, Drew may successfully assert that Polly assumed the risk because Polly knew that Drew was intoxicated, understood the dangers of riding with an intoxicated driver, and voluntarily got into the car with Drew. If, however, Polly was so intoxicated herself that she did not notice Drew's condition, then there would be no assumption of the risk.

---

(2) Unreasonable Assumption of Risk. [§ 493]

If the plaintiff's decision to subject himself to the risk is unreasonable, both contributory negligence and assumption of risk will be defenses. This would be the case in the above example.

(3) Reasonable Assumption of Risk. [§ 494]

Assumption of risk is most confusing when the plaintiff's decision to undergo the risk is **reasonable.**

(4) Full Duty of Care. [§ 495]

Generally, if the defendant owes the plaintiff an obligation to make a dangerous condition safe, the plaintiff's action is unaffected if his assumption of risk is reasonable.

> **(a) Example. [§ 496]** Poe attempts to cross a street at a pedestrian crosswalk. He notices that many cars are speeding and some are ignoring pedestrians in the crosswalk. After some delay, Poe attempts to cross the street. Since drivers of the cars owe Poe a full duty of care, Poe's conduct does not bar his recovery unless it was unreasonable.

c. Primary and Secondary Assumption of the Risk. [§ 497]

Some jurisdictions distinguish between primary and secondary assumption of the risk. Secondary assumption of the risk is the true affirmative defense discussed above where the defendant has the burden of showing that the plaintiff knew, understood, and voluntarily encountered a specific risk. Primary assumption of the risk, on the other hand, signifies that the defendant does not owe the plaintiff a duty to protect against the defendant's negligent conduct in light of the nature of the activity.

> **(1) Example. [§ 498]** Paula and Dex were on opposing sides in a "friendly" game of touch football, when Dex negligently smashed Paula's finger. Under primary assumption of the risk, Dex owed Paula no duty to avoid negligently inflicting this harm because such negligently caused injury is an inherent risk of a football game. See *Knight v. Jewett*, 834 P.2d 696 (Cal.1992).

DEFENSES TO NEGLIGENCE

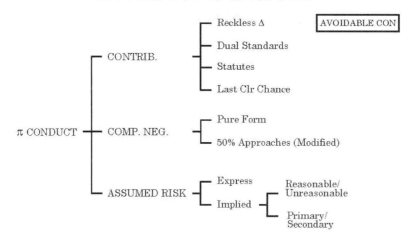

REVIEW PROBLEMS—NEGLIGENCE

Problem 1. Dale, age twelve, takes his parents' car without their permission. Due to his negligent driving he collides into Penny. The impact is not too great and it causes only minor denting to Penny's car. However, because Penny is predisposed to schizophrenia, the collision causes Penny to become schizophrenic. She is expected to be institutionalized for the remainder of her life. What is Dale's liability?

> **Answer:** Because Dale is engaging in an "adult" or inherently dangerous activity, in most jurisdictions he will be held to the adult standard of care of a "reasonably prudent [adult] person." The facts state that he has failed to use reasonable care, so breach is not a problem. Cause in fact is also not a big hurdle for Penny because if it were not for Dale's negligent driving, Penny would not (then) have become schizophrenic. Under proximate cause, Dale is clearly liable for the dents to Penny's car as they are harms clearly within the risk of Dale's negligent conduct. Further, because of the "egg-shell plaintiff" rule under which the defendant accepts the plaintiff in the plaintiff's pre-injury condition, Dale is also the proximate cause of Penny's schizophrenia. He takes her as one predisposed to the illness. It is likely, however, that he would not have to pay all of Penny's damages since it is likely that a jury would find that Penny would have become schizophrenic at some future point had this collision never have occurred. Note also that, absent a statute, Dale's parents are not vicariously liable for the harm that Dale caused.

Problem 2. Darla owns a tract of undeveloped land. Parton asks Darla if Parton can eat his lunch on the property and Darla consents. While on the property, Parton falls into a hole that had been covered by brush that was not known to Darla. Does Darla owe a duty to Parton?

> **Answer:** At common law, Parton would be characterized as a licensee because he was on the land with the owner's consent, but was not conferring an economic benefit. Accordingly, no duty would be owed to warn of dangers that were not known to the landowner Darla. Under a strong minority approach, there would be a duty owed here, as a duty of reasonable care is owed to all land entrants. The focus would then be on whether Darla breached this duty in this instance.

Problem 3. Dr. Dox is a nationally board-certified surgeon. During surgery on Pablo, Dr. Dox severed an artery. Pablo's expert, a board-certified surgeon practicing in a distant state, testified that surgeons would not proceed in the manner selected by Dr. Dox, and that if Dr. Dox had chosen the customary method, Pablo's artery would not have been severed. Dr. Dox contends that she believed her approach was better than the customary approach, though it involved a risk of severing an artery. Dr. Dox puts on no other testimony. What is the result of Pablo's negligence action against Dr. Dox?

> **Answer:** Because Pablo is bringing a medical malpractice action, the custom of the profession sets the standard of care. In most jurisdictions Dr. Dox will be held to a national standard of care, because she is board certified. In these jurisdictions, Pablo's expert's testimony is highly relevant, establishing both the standard of care (the custom) and breach (failure to meet the custom). While Dr. Dox would try to assert that she was complying with an approach followed by a "respectable minority school," her simple assertion that she believed her approach was better will not be adequate. Thus, she is liable for malpractice.

Problem 4. Early one Tuesday morning at 5:30 a.m. while riding in the City Center, twelve-year-old Dale collided into Penny while Dale was riding to school to attend an early basketball practice. Dale was unable to stop his bicycle because he failed to check to see that the brakes were in working order. A local city ordinance provides that "no vehicles (automobiles, motorcycles, bicycles, etc.) shall be permitted in the City Center on Tuesday mornings from 5 am–6 am." The ordinance was passed to facilitate weekly street cleaning and trash pickup in the usually busy City Center. Penny, a pedestrian, suffered a broken leg due to the force of the collision. Analyze Penny's action against Dale.

> **Answer:** Penny will bring a negligence action against Dale. There is no real duty issue since Dale was acting affirmatively—misfeasance. Accordingly, he would owe a general duty to foreseeable plaintiffs and Penny would be such a foreseeable plaintiff.
>
> A larger issue is to determine what is the appropriate standard of care to which Dale will be held. Penny will likely try to persuade a court to use the statute as the standard of care. Under the "negligence per se" doctrine, if the statute is adopted as the standard of care, Dale's breach of duty is found by his violation of the statute (unless excused).
>
> Should the statute be adopted as the standard of care? For the statute to be adopted, the plaintiff has to be in the protected class and the statute has to have been enacted to protect against the harm suffered. Though some debate would be possible, it is unlikely that a judge would use the statute since it was designed to facilitate street cleaning/trash pickup, and not to protect against collisions. Also, the statute is designed to help the street cleaners, not people like Penny.
>
> Assuming the statute is not used, the case proceeds under another standard of care. Here the new standard of care will probably be that used for children, and Dale will be compared to other children

of the "same age, experience and intelligence." It is unlikely that he is engaged in an adult activity.

If a child of the same, age, experience and intelligence would have checked the brakes, then cause-in-fact is no hurdle for Penny. "But for" Dale's negligence, she would not have been harmed. Proximate cause is no hurdle either since there are no intervening forces nor is the actual harm suffered beyond the risk created by Dale's negligence. Finally, Penny has suffered damages.

Multiple Choice Questions 1–2 are based on the following fact situation.

Driver, whose driver's license has expired, stops in a bar on his way home from work and drinks heavily.

When Driver leaves the bar at 11:00 p.m., he forgets to turn on his lights. A block from his home, Driver stops for a red light and his car is struck by a car belonging to Careless. Careless had negligently parked his car without setting the handbrake. Both cars are damaged.

1. If Driver sues Careless in a contributory negligence jurisdiction, Driver will probably

    (A) lose because his license had expired.

    (B) lose because he was drunk and he did not turn on his lights.

    (C) lose because Careless' negligence was not foreseeable.

    (D) win because his violations of the law were not actual causes of his injury.

2. If Careless sues Driver, Careless will probably

    (A) lose if, but only if, the law requires him to set the hand brake.

    (B) lose because he was negligent and Driver was not.

    (C) win because public policy favors recovery against drunk drivers.

    (D) win because Driver would not have been at the place of the collision had he not stopped at the bar.

Multiple Choice Questions 3–7 are based on the following fact situation.

Blue Flame Gas Co. had furnished natural gas to the prior tenant of a building. The current tenant had requested removal of the gas service and Blue Flame took out the service and capped the pipe immediately outside the building. The gas was still under pressure in the capped pipe.

George, age 35, was driving his auto with Joan, age 44, as a passenger. The two of them had had several drinks in the last few hours. George lost control of his vehicle and crossed over to the wrong side of the street and went up and over the curb, striking the pipe as he crashed into the building. This resulted in the gas becoming ignited, causing the car to burst into flames and the building to burn down.

The present tenant's business was interrupted for three months.

The gas pipe was 12 feet from the street, 3 feet behind the sidewalk, and 20 inches above the ground.

3. In a suit by the tenant against George for damages for negligence, George's drinking would be

    (A) a rebuttable presumption of negligence.

    (B) negligence per se.

    (C) evidence of negligence.

    (D) sufficient to make out a prima facie case of negligence.

4. In a suit by Joan against George for damages, if there is no guest statute, George's best argument is that

    (A) whatever the degree of George's negligence, it is imputed to Joan under the theory of joint venture.

    (B) if George is at fault, it is imputed to Joan as a passenger in the car.

    (C) since loss of control implies a mechanical defect, George was not a cause of Joan's injuries.

    (D) Joan's action is barred by assumption of risk.

5. In a suit by the tenant against George for damages, the extra damage caused by the presence of the gas in the gas pipe

    (A) prevents George from being the actual cause of the damage.

    (B) is an intervening cause relieving George of liability.

    (C) is a condition of the premises that is not highly unforeseeable so that it is not a superseding cause.

    (D) is not a foreseeable hazard of negligent driving, and therefore George is not liable.

6. In a suit by the tenant against Blue Flame for negligence, which of the following is the most likely holding with respect to the relevance of George and his automobile?

    (A) Blue Flame is not liable because it is not an actual cause.

    (B) Blue Flame is not liable because its negligence, if any, is passive while that of George is active.

    (C) George is a trespasser and strictly liable so that Blue Flame is not a joint tortfeasor.

    (D) There is a jury question as to whether George is a foreseeable intervening cause.

7. In a suit by the owner of the building against George, the most likely holding on damages is that George is

    (A) liable only for so much of the damage to the building as would have occurred had there been no fire.

    (B) liable for one-half of the damages.

    (C) not liable at all because the owner was out of possession.

    (D) liable for the entire amount if he is liable at all.

Multiple Choice Questions 8–9 are based on the following fact situation.

Childs, a ten-year-old boy, was selling homemade potholders door-to-door. He came to the home of Owner and knocked on the front door. Getting no answer, he went around to the back and climbed the eight-foot brick fence.

Childs discovered a trampoline in the backyard, climbed upon it, and started jumping. The trampoline was in a state of bad repair. It belonged to a third party but had been picked up by Owner and taken to Owner's home to "rethread" with fresh elastic ropes. The old ropes suddenly snapped, and Childs was thrown to the ground, breaking his arm.

Leaving the yard, Childs failed, because of tears in his eyes, to see a water sprinkler head which Owner had installed in the grass at the intersection of Owner's property and the sidewalk. He stumbled over the sprinkler head, fell, and broke his leg.

8. In a suit by Childs against Owner for damages, the most likely holding would be that

    (A) Childs was an invitee because the trampoline constituted an attractive nuisance.

    (B) Childs was a licensee because the presence of young children on the land was readily foreseeable.

    (C) Owner owned no duty to Childs because he was not attracted onto the land by the trampoline.

    (D) Owner owed no duty to take reasonable precautions to protect young children against the hazards of the trampoline.

9. In a suit by Childs against Owner for damages, the best argument on either side regarding the hazard of the sprinkler head is that

    (A) it is an absolute nuisance because of its location.

    (B) Owner is liable for damages stemming from it under the theory of res ipsa loquitur.

    (C) Owner owes a duty of due care to all persons under the theory of attractive nuisance.

(D) Owner's duty to Childs is that which is owed to a user of the sidewalk or a technical trespasser.

Multiple Choice Questions 10–12 are based on the following fact situation.

The Glen Gables National Bank recently replaced its old burglar alarm with an advanced and super-sensitive device that has a direct connection to the Glen Gables Police Department. Because of the sensitivity of the new burglar alarm, it can be easily triggered by static electricity such as that commonly generated by dusting cloths and feather mops. For this reason the entire janitorial staff of the bank was explicitly instructed to keep clear of the alarm, or, if it were necessary to remove dust or dirt from or near the point where it is located, to have the bank's security officer temporarily disconnect it during the cleaning operation.

Despite these instructions, Minnie Maid, a janitor employed by the bank, dusted the alarm, thereby setting it off. Officer Tracy of the Glen Gables Police Department was immediately dispatched in a City of Glen Gables police car to answer the alarm. While on his way to the bank, and traveling above the speed limit, Officer Tracy collided with a car driven by Joy Ryder. Ryder suffered serious personal injuries and extensive property damage to her car.

The collision occurred at an uncontrolled intersection and, under the applicable traffic law, Ryder had the so-called "right of way." However, another provision of the same traffic law requires drivers of motor vehicles to yield to police vehicles emitting warning flashes and/or sounding sirens. Officer Tracy was both sounding his siren and emitting warning flashes at the time of the collision, but Ryder was unable to see the warning flashes because her view was blocked by a building, and she did not hear the siren because of the volume of her recently installed stereo tape player.

Just prior to the collision, Officer Tracy had remarked to a companion officer in the car, and with reference to the Ryder vehicle, "I hope that driver yields."

10. In a suit by Ryder against Tracy, the most likely holding in a negligence suit is that Ryder is

(A) contributorily negligent as a matter of law for failing to yield the right of way.

(B) barred by assumption of risk for turning her stereo too loud.

(C) excused from the requirement to give up the right of way if she could not in fact see the light or hear the siren.

(D) not contributorily negligent since Tracy had also violated the vehicle code.

11. In a suit by Ryder against Glen Gables National Bank for negligence, which of the following is the most likely holding if Ryder is deemed not to have been negligent?

    (A) The bank is not liable because the risks of dusting off an alarm do not include an automobile collision.

    (B) The bank is not liable because it was not a cause in fact of the accident.

    (C) The bank is not liable because it is hardly foreseeable that a person would be injured in an automobile collision in the precise way this one occurred as a result of using such an alarm mechanism.

    (D) The bank is liable because a jury could reasonably find that its negligence caused the collision.

12. In a suit by Ryder against the City of Glen Gables, the city is most likely to be held to be

    (A) not liable because of sovereign immunity.

    (B) not liable because if Tracy was negligent, he necessarily exceeded his authority.

    (C) liable because contributory negligence would be no defense because vicarious liability is strict.

    (D) liable because the negligence of Tracy is imputed to the city.

Multiple Choice Questions 13–15 are based on the following fact situation.

Contrary to an ordinance which makes the sale of liquor to a minor a misdemeanor, Ann sells a bottle of liquor to Bob, a sixteen-year-old who came into Ann's bar. Cal, another customer of Ann, teased Bob about his baby face, and when Cal turns his back on Bob, Bob hits Cal over the head with the still full liquor bottle, doing him severe damage.

13. In a suit by Cal against Bob for damages, the most appropriate theory is that Bob is liable for

    (A) negligence in becoming intoxicated and taking the risk of getting out of control.

    (B) assault in threatening Cal.

    (C) battery in striking Cal.

    (D) negligence in violation of the ordinance.

14. In a suit by Cal against Ann, the most likely holding is that

    (A) Ann is vicariously liable for the acts of Bob, regardless of negligence, because of the statute.

(B) Ann was negligent in selling liquor to Bob, and that constitutes a breach of duty to all who are injured as a result of Bob's actions in using the product.

(C) there is insufficient evidence of proximate causation of the head injuries.

(D) Cal is barred from recovery because he started the fight.

15. Assume that Cal can prove that Bob would not have hit him but for intoxication resulting from liquor served to him by Ann. If Cal sues Ann

(A) there can be no liability unless the ordinance provided for civil suits for damages.

(B) Cal will lose because he is not within the class of people sought to be protected by the statute.

(C) Ann cannot be liable under the ordinance because it is irrelevant to her fault.

(D) Ann is liable to Cal because she was negligent.

ANSWERS TO THE MULTIPLE CHOICE QUESTIONS

Answer to Question 1.

(D) is correct.

A is clearly wrong because Driver's alleged contributory negligence of failing to have a license is neither a cause-in-fact nor proximate cause of the collision. B is also clearly wrong for similar reasons; Driver's drinking and failure to turn on his lights did not contribute to the accident. C is wrong because A and B are both wrong and there is no other basis for finding Driver contributorily negligent. D is correct because Driver will not be found to be contributorily negligent because his unreasonable conduct was unrelated to the harm he suffered.

Answer to Question 2.

(B) is correct.

A is wrong since Careless may be negligent even if his conduct violates no statute. C is an insufficient basis for allowing recovery since, even if Driver was drunk, his drunkenness was not a cause of the accident. D is wrong since Driver's stopping at the bar, while a cause in fact of the accident, is not a proximate cause of the accident. Based on the facts, B is the best choice.

Answer to Question 3.

(C) is correct.

Of the options given, C is the best. The drinking alone is not proof of negligence nor does it create a presumption of negligence. It may serve as evidence of intoxication, which is not established here, but an intoxicated person is not necessarily negligent in a given situation. Tenant would still have to prove all elements of her prima facie case. Thus, A, B, and D are incorrect.

Answer to Question 4.

(D) is correct.

A is wrong because there is no imputation of negligence from host to guest and, since Joan had no right to equal control of the vehicle, there was no joint venture. B is similarly wrong on the law. C is wrong because loss of control does not necessarily imply mechanical defect. Since Joan knew that George had been drinking, assumption of risk is a plausible holding. Thus, D is correct.

Answer to Question 5.

(C) is correct.

The gas is not a subsequently arising cause, but a condition of the premises which a negligent party takes as she finds, even if not foreseeable. Thus, B and D are wrong. A is wrong because there is no question that George is a "substantial factor" in damage.

Answer to Question 6.

(D) is correct.

There is a causal nexus between Blue Flame and the harm because Blue Flame was a substantial factor. A is wrong accordingly. The relevant issue is whether George's intervening conduct is so unforeseeable that it should be superseding. This is for the jury to decide on these facts. B and C are wrong statements of law.

Answer to Question 7.

(D) is correct.

As a rule of damages and causation, George can be individually liable for the entire damage. He is jointly and severally liable with Blue Flame. At best, he could seek contribution from Blue Flame. Thus, A, B, and C are wrong.

Answer to Question 8.

(D) is correct.

Owner has no duty to a child trespasser because the attractive nuisance doctrine would not apply here because Owner had no reason to suspect that children would enter her back yard. Thus, A is incorrect. C is incorrect as the prevailing rule is now that the trespassing child need not be attracted by the dangerous condition. B is incorrect on the facts.

Answer to Question 9.

(D) is correct.

Even if the attractive nuisance applied to the trampoline injury, it does not apply to the sprinkler injury. Thus, C is wrong. Options A and B are not supported by the facts.

Answer to Question 10.

(A) is correct.

Ryder's violation of the statute would constitute contributory negligence per se. Thus, D is wrong. Ryder would not be excused from hearing the siren under these conditions, so C is wrong. B is wrong because there is no basis for assumption of risk on these facts.

Answer to Question 11.

(D) is correct.

While the result in D is not necessarily required, it is for a jury to decide the foreseeable risks created by the Bank employee's negligence. The Bank employee's negligence was certainly a substantial factor in Ryder's harm. Thus, B is wrong. Choice A and C suggest the lack of proximate causation. They are wrong because the precise manner that the harm comes about need not be foreseen as long as the general type of harm suffered is foreseeable. Based on the facts here, a jury could reasonably find that a collision was reasonably foreseeable.

Answer to Question 12.

(D) is correct.

A is not the best choice because sovereign immunity no longer applies to actions which are non-governmental in character (such as driving a car), so A is wrong. While the tortious acts of an employee may be imputed to the employer, liability is not strict simply because it is vicarious. Thus C is wrong. Option B is wrong on its facts.

Answer to Question 13.

(C) is correct.

Battery is not only the most obvious recovery, but the only one clearly correct on the facts. Option A is wrong because the facts indicate that Bob had not yet begun to drink. Option B is factually wrong because Cal could not have had any apprehension of harm since his back was turned to Bob. Option D is wrong as the statute regulates **sellers,** not **buyers.**

Answer to Question 14.

(C) is correct.

A is wrong because the sole relevance of the statute is to help determine whether Ann's conduct was negligent. Option B is wrong because the resulting harm was not within the risk which made Ann's conduct negligent; what makes selling liquor to a minor dangerous is the risk that the minor is likely to become intoxicated, not that he will use the bottle as a weapon when he is sober. Option D is incorrect because Cal's teasing does not make him the aggressor or otherwise justify Bob's act.

Answer to Question 15.

(D) is correct.

The statute appears to set a relevant standard of care, and Cal's proof helps establish that the result was within the risk. Options A, B, and C are wrong as a matter of law.

CHAPTER III

STRICT LIABILITY

A. IN GENERAL. [§ 499]

Under certain limited situations, a plaintiff may recover for injuries sustained as a result of some act or omission of the defendant, **even if the defendant used utmost care.** In these rare situations the plaintiff need not prove fault on the part of the defendant; no evidence of negligence or intent is needed. However, the plaintiff will have to prove more than just the fact that she was injured by the defendant. This doctrine is known as **strict liability.** Though occasionally referred to as "absolute liability," that term is misleading since there are defenses that may be asserted by Defendant to enable Defendant to avoid liability. Strict liability is appropriate in very few situations where the following are involved: wild animals; abnormally dangerous activities; defective products (this last category is discussed in the next section).

1. Social Policy. [§ 500]

In those situations which fall within the recognized areas of strict liability, liability is imposed as a matter of **social policy.** The theory that if defendants engage in certain dangerous activities, they must pay their own way, including for harm caused to others. Put another way, the issue is who should bear the loss if there is no real blame on either side. There is much debate among scholars and courts about the propriety of liability without fault.

B. STRICT LIABILITY AT COMMON LAW. [§ 501]

1. Animals. [§ 502]

a. Wild Animals. [§ 503]

The possessor of naturally **wild animals** (i.e., lions, tigers, bears, etc.) is strictly liable for injuries to another, since he is held to know that they are likely to inflict serious harm. This is true even if they are "tame."

> **(1) Example. [§ 504]** Pumpkin is bitten by Dell's pet tiger Whiskers. Dell is strictly liable even if Whiskers is tame and had never bitten anyone before.

b. Domestic Animals. [§ 505]

A defendant is **not** strictly liable for injuries caused by a naturally **domestic animal** (i.e., dog, cat, or other creature usually regarded as harmless) unless there is proof that she **knew or should have known of the dangerous propensities** of the animal.

(1) What Constitutes Notice. [§ 506]

The defendant is under no duty to discover the traits of his animal, but he is expected to possess common knowledge and can't ignore characteristics that would put a reasonable person on notice. Note that the fact that one's dog has once bitten someone is sufficient to establish that it may do it again, but this is **not** notice that it will collide with someone and knock him down.

(2) Special "Dog Bite" Statutes. [§ 507]

Some states provide by statute that in the case of dogs, the owner will be liable for a bite to anyone who was neither trespassing nor guilty of provocation, even though the dog has no vicious propensities. Statutes generally refer only to **dog bites**, not scratches or other injuries, nor do they cover cats or other animals.

2. Abnormally Dangerous Activities. [§ 508]

Along with developments in liability for defective products, this has been the area of greatest importance for modern strict liability. There have been great developments over the last century attempting to define when a defendant is strictly liable to a person the defendant has injured by engaging in a certain activity.

a. *Rylands v. Fletcher.* [§ 509]

Two attempts to create a coherent theory of liability without fault were made in the case of *Rylands v. Fletcher*. Justice Blackburn in one opinion suggested that a person would be strictly liable when he has brought onto his land something that is likely to do harm if it escapes. Lord Cairns altered the rule (perhaps unwittingly) on appeal by holding that one who introduces something onto the land which is a "non-natural" use of the land is strictly liable for harm caused. These approaches are different. Under Blackburn's view, strict liability was applied because Rylands brought on to his land large quantities of water for a mill which escaped, flooding the plaintiff's mines. Under the Cairns approach, Rylands was strictly liable because he was using his land for milling in an area that is a mining area. Both approaches can be asserted as a basis for strict liability, although, as discussed below, U.S. courts have a more modern approach to strict liability that builds off the *Rylands* principles.

b. Modern Law—The Restatement. [§ 510]

According to the **Restatement (Second)** sections 519 and 520, one who engages in an **abnormally dangerous activity** is strictly liable for resulting injuries (the original **Restatement** used the term "ultrahazardous activity").

c. What Is an Abnormally Dangerous Activity? [§ 511]

According to the Restatement, in determining whether an activity is abnormally dangerous, the following factors will be weighed by a **judge:** (a) the **probability of harm** to the person, land, or chattels of others; (b) the **likely gravity** of the potential harm; (c) the actor's **inability to eliminate the risk** by the exercise of reasonable care; (d) the extent to which the activity is **not a matter of common usage;** (e) the **inappropriateness of the activity** to the place where it is carried on; and (f) the extent to which its **value to the community is outweighed by its dangerous attributes.**

> **(1) Examples. [§ 512]** Common examples of abnormally dangerous activities include **blasting, excavations,** operation of **oil wells,** and **mining operations. (NOTE:** One must take special care to analyze the surroundings of the activity, however, damage incurred by blasting in the city involves strict liability, while blasting on a deserted island might not.)

d. Criticism of the Restatement Approach. [§ 513]

Some courts have refused to engage in the balancing suggested by the Restatement, contending that such balancing injects too much negligence into the analysis. These jurisdictions look at the activity (e.g., blasting) and decide whether it should be deemed abnormally dangerous in all instances. Indeed, the Third Restatement of Torts has moved away from the balancing approach, advocating that strict liability should apply where the defendant engages in an activity that "creates a foreseeable and highly significant risk of physical harm even when the reasonable care is exercised by all actors" and "the activity is not a matter of common usage."

e. Exam Hint. [§ 514]

> Whether a certain activity is abnormally dangerous is often a highly debatable issue. Use the Restatement factors and argue each factor from both sides. If unclear, harken back to the policies underlying liability without fault for an abnormally dangerous activity. Remember that fault is required for tort liability in most instances. Strict liability will not apply to common activities, such as air travel.

3. Dangerous Products. [§ 515]

Strict liability has had perhaps its most significant impact on the liability of the supplier of chattels. These problems are discussed in § 533, the **Products Liability section of this summary.**

4. Cause in Fact. [§ 516]

The plaintiff must show by a preponderance of the evidence that the defendant's participation in the abnormally dangerous activity was, at least, a substantial factor in the plaintiff's injury. The cause-in-fact rules discussed in the Negligence chapter (§§ 395–409) apply to strict liability as well.

5. Proximate Cause—Result Within the Risk. [§ 517]

Because of the basic unfairness of holding a person liable even though he was not at fault, courts have tended to be a bit more lenient in relieving the defendant of liability due to a lack of **proximate cause** in strict liability cases than they have been in negligence actions. Indeed, the Restatement Second § 519 includes a built in "risk rule" providing that one is strictly liable only "for the kind of harm, the risk of which makes the activity abnormally dangerous." Thus, strict liability will be applied only if the resulting injuries suffered were within the risk that made the activity abnormally dangerous in the first place. Unforeseeable intervening conduct by third parties could be superseding thereby relieving a defendant from liability.

> **a. Example. [§ 518]** Demo's blasting results in the death of some of Paula's minks. While Demo is clearly strictly liable if an explosion hurls stones and crushes some of the animals, Demo is **not** strictly liable if the noise of the blast so frightens the adult minks that they kill their young. In other words, the risk that make blasting dangerous does not include the risk that an animal will devour its young.

6. Defenses and Privileges. [§ 519]

a. Contributory Negligence No Defense. [§ 520]

Traditionally, contributory negligence is not a defense to cases of strict liability. Thus, the plaintiff's unreasonable conduct by itself is irrelevant.

> **(1) Example. [§ 521]** Paco's cow is killed when Darth's tiger escapes and breaks into Paco's barn. In most states, Paco's negligence in maintaining the barn is irrelevant in his action based on strict liability.

b. Assumption of Risk Is a Defense. [§ 522]

On the other hand, assumption of risk is a defense to an action based in strict liability. Thus, if the plaintiff **voluntarily** undertakes to expose herself to a **known risk,** she will normally be barred by **assumption of risk.**

> **(1) Example. [§ 523]** Peggy sees that Donner's blasting is hurling large rocks. Peggy's act of approaching the area where the rocks are falling while aware that the rocks are being hurled will normally be a defense if she is struck and injured.

c. Effect of Comparative Negligence. [§ 524]

The modern trend imports the rationale of comparative negligence into the strict liability context. Accordingly, courts have held that the plaintiff's unreasonable conduct (even where it does not constitute assumption of the risk) is a partial defense in such cases.

d. Privilege. [§ 525]

Occasionally, certain acts which normally result in strict liability will be privileged in certain circumstances. Thus, a "controlled burn" set to help prevent a catastrophic forest fire or the maintenance of a public zoo will generally be privileged so that a person injured as a result of such activities can recover only if the defendant was negligent.

COMMON LAW STRICT LIABILITY
(overview)

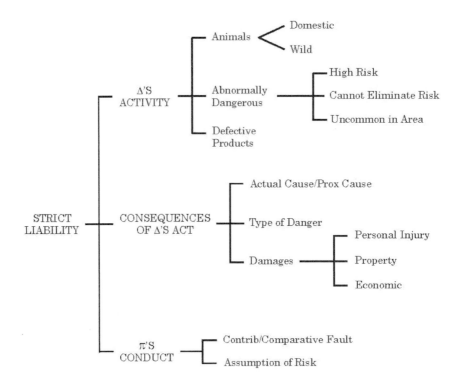

C. SPECIAL STATUTORY FORMS OF STRICT LIABILITY. [§ 526]

1. Worker's Compensation. [§ 527]

Today, every American jurisdiction has adopted a **worker's compensation act** which makes the employer strictly liable for an injury to her employee occurring while the employee was acting **within the scope of employment.** The theory behind such actions is that injuries to workers, like the breakage of equipment, is inherent in business and thus must be considered a cost of business to be borne by the employer (who in turn can pass it on to the consumer).

a. Scope of Act. [§ 528]

Most worker's compensation acts exclude from their coverage farm workers, domestic workers, railroad workers, and those who work for businesses with few employees; those persons are left to their common law remedies.

b. **Compulsory Insurance. [§ 529]**

Worker's compensation statutes require the employer to purchase insurance, and the insurance rates are regulated so that the burden is equalized over the entire industry. A failure to obtain insurance subjects the employer to criminal action and permits the employee to sue at law (in which case the employer still may not raise contributory negligence, assumption of risk, or other traditional defenses).

c. **Measure of Damages. [§ 530]**

Generally, the injured employee receives full compensation for medical expenses plus a percentage of her average weekly wages for the period she is unable to work. The amount of recovery for **disfigurement or permanent disability** (e.g., the loss of an arm or eye) is fixed by statute or determined by a worker's compensation board. The amount and type of damages is typically quite limited.

d. **Relation to Common Law Remedies. [§ 531]**

If the employee is within the protection of the act, **worker's compensation is the sole remedy available for injuries** caused by his employer and fellow employees. Any common law action which he might have against other parties, however, is unaffected.

e. **No Formal Defenses. [§ 532]**

Neither contributory negligence, assumption of risk, nor the fellow servant rule (which held that an employer was not responsible for injuries caused by the injured party's co-worker) **is a defense.**

2. **No-Fault Automobile Insurance. [§ 533]**

The **no-fault automobile insurance** systems adopted in many states can best be thought of as a form of strict liability that attaches to the car. Under such a plan, the insurer of a car which is involved in a traffic accident is strictly liable for injuries occurring to any person who is **not an occupant of another vehicle** (e.g., the car's driver, the passengers, pedestrians).

> **a.** **Example. [§ 534]** Aldo insures his car with Wepay Insurance Company. While Aldo is driving his car with Betty as a passenger, the car goes out of control striking Chang, a pedestrian, and a car belonging to Luigi. Wepay is liable for the injuries to Aldo, Betty, and Chang, but Luigi can recover only from his (Luigi's) insurance company; this is true whether Aldo was reckless, negligent, or totally blameless (although he will be denied recovery if his conduct was **intentional**).

b. **Compulsory Insurance. [§ 535]**

A failure to obtain insurance may subject the offender to criminal penalties, cause her to be personally liable for all injuries that would normally have been covered by insurance, and/or cause her driver's license and/or automobile registration to be revoked.

c. **Amount of Loss. [§ 536]**

No-fault insurance acts provide for compensation only for out-of-pocket expenses, not for pain and suffering.

d. **Foreclosure of Tort Action. [§ 537]**

In systems which provide for compensation for large losses of the injured party, an action against another driver is generally barred unless there is very serious injury.

CHAPTER IV

PRODUCTS LIABILITY

A. IN GENERAL. [§ 538]

"Products liability" is the broad term applied to situations where someone has suffered harm caused by a product. Do not confuse this term with the cause of action of "strict product liability," which is one of the several theories on which a products liability action may be based.

B. SEVERAL THEORIES. [§ 539]

The biggest problem that most students have with products liability questions is the fact there are **several distinct theories that are potentially relevant,** each of which has its own special elements and defenses. Whenever the facts reveal that someone has suffered personal injury or property damage one must consider the following theories which may be available: (a) liability based upon **negligence;** (b) **strict products liability**; (c) liability based upon a **representation** made regarding the quality or nature of the product; and (d) liability based upon breach of **warranty** (express and implied). All of these theories could be raised in a products liability exam question and all would need to be discussed (unless the call of the question limits the scope of the question). As a practical matter, negligence and strict products liability are the topics on which most torts classes focus most heavily because they are the most important causes of action.

C. BASIC STRATEGY. [§ 540]

1. Exam Hint. [§ 541]

> **KEEP THEORIES SEPARATE.** While some of the cases themselves fail to differentiate clearly between the various theories and often use the vocabulary of one form of the action when they are actually discussing another, it is critical to keep the theories separate analytically. Do not try to discuss several theories together or you will probably get hopelessly confused (or at least the reader will be). **Each theory should be fully analyzed before turning to the next.** Sometimes the call of the question in a products liability exam question will limit the focus of the question, telling you, for example, to analyze a problem only under a strict products liability theory. The call of the exam question is particularly important in the products context.

2. Ask Five Questions. [§ 542]

For each theory, you must consider five basic questions:

a. Gravamen. [§ 543]

What is the **gravamen** of the action (i.e., what is the action really about)? What are the elements of this cause of action?

b. Defendants. [§ 544]

What **kinds of persons are potentially liable** under this particular theory?

c. Plaintiffs. [§ 545]

What **kinds of persons can recover** under this theory?

d. Damages. [§ 546]

What damages does the injured plaintiff seek?

e. Defenses. [§ 547]

What **defenses** may be raised to an action based on this theory?

PRODUCTS LIABILITY
(overview)

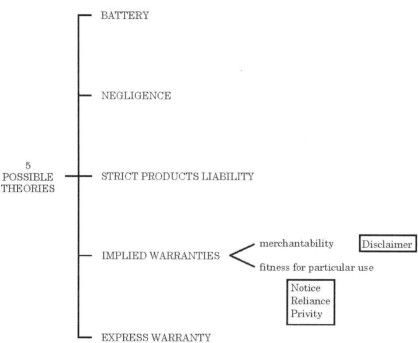

D. NEGLIGENCE. [§ 548]

Negligence should always be considered as a separate basis of recovery for harm caused by a defective product. **Everything discussed in the general negligence analysis applies equally to a case involving a product**. In other words, one must analyze the problems of duty, standards of care, breach of duty, cause in fact, proximate cause, damages, and negligence defenses (contributory negligence/comparative fault and assumption of risk). At this point, only some specifics particularly applicable to negligence liability for defective products are noted.

1. **Gravamen: Breach of Duty of Due Care. [§ 549]**

Under the **negligence** theory of products liability, the manufacturer, wholesaler, or retailer is liable to the plaintiff if that defendant **breached the duty of due care through unreasonable conduct. The focus is on the defendant's conduct.** The **conduct** of each defendant must be analyzed separately to determine if that defendant failed to use reasonable care. A purely objective test is employed.

2. **Duty: Privity of Contract Not Required. [§ 550]**

Everyone involved in the **chain of commercial distribution** owes an obligation of due care to **anyone foreseeably endangered** by the defective product. Privity, under which liability extended only to a party to the contract, has been universally rejected as a requirement in a negligence action.

> a.   **Example. [§ 551]** Parker bought a car from Cartown that had been manufactured by Detroit Co. Due to negligence by Detroit Co., Parker was injured when his brakes failed. Parker, as a foreseeable plaintiff, may sue Detroit Co. even though he has contractual privity only with the retailer, Cartown. Note that it is unlikely Parker would be able to show any negligence by Cartown. *MacPherson v. Buick Motor Co.*, 111 N.E. 1050 (N.Y. 1916).

3. **Standards of Care. [§ 552]**

Usually, the standard of care to be applied requires the defendant to act as a reasonably prudent manufacturer, retailer, etc. would have acted under the same or similar circumstances.

4. **Breach Analysis. [§ 553]**

Again, the typical breach analysis will involve the use of the Hand formula balancing the burden against the probability times the magnitude. (See § 359.)

5. Negligence Relating to Individual Unit. [§ 554]

Of course, each **individual unit** of a given product line must be manufactured and handled with due care. Thus, there can be negligence as to an individual unit because of its failure to work or operate properly for any number of reasons, as when a jar is cracked due to the defendant's unreasonableness or a screw is improperly tightened.

6. Negligence in Design. [§ 555]

Negligence in design is an issue when each unit of a particular product line has the same dangerous characteristics. The focus is on the defendant's conduct in designing the product as it was marketed. Ultimately the analysis of burden involves the feasibility of a safer design and the cost of safer products, balanced against the severity and likelihood of harm. **As in any negligence analysis, one must propound a hypothetical alternative course of conduct which is safe**. If no known technology will produce a safer product, there is no negligence in product design unless the product is so dangerous that a jury determines that no reasonable defendant would have sold it at all.

7. Cost of Safer Design. [§ 556]

Since negligence requires the weighing of risk with the cost of safety, if a safer product requires unreasonably higher costs, there is no negligence in product design even if a safer product is technologically feasible. For example, it is not unreasonable to fail to make a small economy car as crashworthy as a large, expensive sedan.

8. Custom. [§ 557]

In the determination of reasonableness, the defendant's compliance with or deviation from custom is highly relevant (though not determinative).

9. Duty to Warn. [§ 558]

Even if the dangers of the product are not such that a prudent person should redesign it or withdraw it from the market (i.e., there is no negligence in the design, manufacture, or handling of the product), there may be an **obligation to warn** consumers about dangers of which they are likely to be unaware. As a negligence cause of action, the test is whether a reasonably prudent manufacturer should have known about a significant danger and should have warned about it. **Hint:** Once it is found that a reasonably prudent manufacturer should have known about a significant danger, it is likely that the manufacturer is negligent for failing to warn because of the tiny burden a warning would entail.

> **a.   Example. [§ 559]** Drugco manufactures the only known drug which is effective in controlling a serious disease. If the use of the drug is sometimes accompanied by harmful or unanticipated side effects, Drugco has an obligation to warn of these side effects even if it need not (or **should not**) take the drug off the market provided that it should have been aware of these risks and provided that a reasonable manufacturer would have warned about them.

b.   Warning May Be Insufficient. [§ 560]

Many courts have held that a warning is insufficient if the degree of danger is high and the difficulty in making it safe is slight. (**NOTE**: Whether the obligation is to make safe or to warn is crucial because if the defendant's only duty is to warn, the plaintiff will have a very tough cause in fact hurdle, requiring proof that the plaintiff would not have used the product had there been an adequate warning.)

10. Duty to Inspect. [§ 561]

a.   Manufacturer's Duty to Inspect. [§ 562]

The **manufacturer's** duty of due care includes the duty to make reasonable inspections and tests; **in most cases, this duty cannot be delegated to the wholesaler or retailer**.

b.   Wholesaler's Duty to Inspect. [§ 563]

It is generally said that the **wholesaler** has no duty to inspect (her only duty is to warn of known dangers), but a court might well impose such a duty when there is some clear indication that a reasonable inspection would reveal a danger and where a reasonable wholesaler would have thus inspected.

c.   Retailer's Duty to Inspect. [§ 564]

The **retailer's** obligation of reasonableness rarely involves an obligation to inspect products. There is no obligation to inspect unless the retailer first has reason to know that the product is likely to be defective (e.g., if the product comes from a manufacturer of dubious reputation, she has had previous experience with defects in the same or similar products, the shipping containers show signs of abuse, etc.).

11. Proof of Breach and Res Ipsa Loquitur. [§ 565]

Breach in products liability cases can be proven by direct evidence, or by circumstantial evidence, including res ipsa loquitur.

a.   **Res Ipsa Loquitur as Circumstantial Evidence. [§ 566]**

While there are cases where the facts raise a fair inference of the manufacturer's negligence (e.g., a decayed human toe is found in a sealed tin of pipe tobacco), there are other cases where the manufacturer can argue that the inference is impermissible because such defects cannot be eliminated by ordinary care (e.g., a piece of broken clam shell in a barrel of clams). There is endless room for argument in particular cases as to whether a reasonable inference of negligence can be drawn from a particular defect. **Hint:** In products cases in which something disgusting is found in a product, think res ipsa loquitur as the basis to prove breach in a negligence action. (**NOTE:** Res ipsa loquitur is a negligence-related concept; it has no role in the strict products liability analysis discussed below.)

b.   **Uncertainty as to Who Was Negligent. [§ 567]**

Sometimes a plaintiff has trouble identifying which of several possible defendants was negligent. There are cases where the plaintiff's proof shows that **either** the manufacturer, wholesaler, or retailer was negligent, but not which one. This generally would prevent the plaintiff from asserting res ipsa loquitur. However, the plaintiff will be able to assert res ipsa loquitur if she is able to show that under the facts the problem more likely than not resulted from the conduct of a specific defendant. (For example, Perez finds a mouse in a bottle of Squirt soda. It is sufficient for him to show more likely than not the mouse must have gotten into the bottle at the bottling plant.)

12. **Causation. [§ 568]**

As in any negligence cause of action, the plaintiff must prove that the defendant's negligence was a cause-in-fact and proximate cause of her injuries. Thus, even if the plaintiff proves that her auto's faulty suspension makes it unreasonably likely to overturn and that her car in fact overturned, she still must prove that the defective suspension was a cause-in-fact of the particular accident (i.e., the faulty suspension was a substantial factor in the overturning of the car) and that there were no unforeseeable intervening acts.

a.   **Cause-in-Fact and Warning. [§ 569]**

When there is a warning issue, cause-in-fact can be a **huge** hurdle for the plaintiff who must show by a preponderance that if there had been a warning (or if there had been an adequate warning), she would have heeded it and, thus, would not have been harmed by the product.

> **(1) Example. [§ 570]** Peter sues Drugco when he suffers an allergic reaction to its product. Even if Peter can show that Drugco should have known about the allergic reaction and that a reasonable manufacturer would have warned about the risks in light of this knowledge, Peter must also establish that, had there been an adequate warning, more likely than not he would have heeded it.

b. Proximate Cause. [§ 571]

The plaintiff must show that the harm suffered by the plaintiff was foreseeable and that there were no superseding causes (as where a retailer discovers a manufacturer's negligence yet sells the product anyway).

13. Possible Defendants. [§ 572]

a. Manufacturers. [§ 573]

The manufacturer is, of course, liable for all injuries caused by **negligence in design.** If the injury is caused by a defect in the **particular unit,** however, the manufacturer is liable only if the plaintiff can show that the unsafe condition existed **at the time it left the manufacturer's control** and the condition was due to the manufacturer's unreasonable conduct.

b. Wholesalers and Retailers. [§ 574]

As a general rule, wholesalers and retailers are liable only for their own negligence in handling the product. They are liable for injuries caused by negligence of their predecessors in the chain of distribution only in rare situations where it would have been reasonable for them to inspect the product.

14. Possible Plaintiffs. [§ 575]

As mentioned above, all courts now follow the rule that **privity of contract is not required** for a plaintiff to recover in negligence. Anyone who was foreseeably endangered by the defendant's conduct may sue.

15. Defenses. [§ 576]

The rules regarding the negligence defenses of contributory negligence, comparative fault and assumption of risk discussed in the **Negligence** chapter of this outline fully apply to products liability cases based on negligence.

E. STRICT PRODUCTS LIABILITY. [§ 577]

Under the theory of **strict products liability**, now recognized in virtually every American jurisdiction, a plaintiff may recover from any commercial supplier who places an article on the market which is in a **defective condition. Liability attaches although the supplier has exercised all possible care in the preparation and sale of the article in question.** There are numerous justifications articulated to support liability without fault in the area of defective products, including: the manufacturer is best able to spread the costs of these product-associated injuries as a cost of doing business through insurance; safer products will result from imposing strict liability on the manufacturer; consumers necessarily rely on the expertise of manufacturers; and the manufacturer is in a better position to remedy any product defects. These justifications have been challenged, however, with opponents claiming strict products liability imposes excessive liability.

1. Strict Products Liability Checklist. [§ 578]

The following approach to strict products liability may prove helpful:

a.   Is this a proper plaintiff (i.e., user, consumer, bystander, etc.)?

b.   Is this a proper defendant (i.e., manufacturer, retailer, in the business, etc.)?

c.   Was the product defective when it left defendant?

d.   Was the product unforeseeably altered or misused?

e.   What kind of defect is involved?

f.   If a design defect, does the product fall within comment (k)?

g.   Based on the kind of defect, was the product at issue defective?

h.   Was the defect a cause-in-fact and proximate cause of Pplaintiff's injuries?

i.   Are there any strict products liability defenses?

2. Gravamen: Marketing a Defective Product. [§ 579]

The gist of an action based on strict products liability is that the defendant sold a product which contained a **defect** and the plaintiff was injured thereby (Restatement Second § 402A). The "defect" may be a manufacturing error, a design problem, or a failure to warn the user of the product's hazards (or an inadequate warning).

3. What Constitutes a Defect. [§ 580]

Under Restatement § 402A, the determination of whether a product is defective is primarily a question of **consumer expectation**. The focus is upon what an ordinary consumer would expect.

4. Manufacturing Defect. [§ 581]

Where a product is produced in a manner that is other than that intended by the manufacturer, this is a manufacturing defect. Manufacturing defects are generally easy to identify, the classic case being a mouse in a bottle of soda. Thus, there are no special analytical problems with regard to determining when an individual unit of a product line is defective under the ordinary consumer expectation test of Restatement § 402A—the main problems are typically those of proof. The plaintiff must prove that the defect existed at the time it left the defendant.

5. Unreasonably Dangerous. [§ 582]

The language of Restatement § 402A requires that a product be both "defective" and "unreasonably dangerous." The latter phrase means that a product must be dangerous beyond that which an ordinary consumer would expect. Thus, there is no liability merely because butter contains cholesterol, liquor intoxicates, or knives cut. Led by the influential California Supreme Court, most jurisdictions have rejected the "unreasonably dangerous" language because it "rings of negligence" and because it appears to increase the burden of proof on plaintiffs in strict products liability cases.

6. Design Defects. [§ 583]

A more challenging form of defect is a **design defect**. Here the defendant's entire product line is being challenged. If the manufacturer was unreasonable in choosing the design, there may be liability in negligence. However, even where the defendant manufacturer has not acted unreasonably, there are cases where a design is "defective" under the theory of strict products liability. The proper focus is on the product, not on the defendant's conduct. While modern developments in the area of strict products liability for design defects have arguably blurred the distinction between strict liability and negligence, there remain critical differences between the theories.

a. Unknown Product Characteristics. [§ 584]

The easiest case for arguing a distinction between strict products liability and negligence is where the product has dangerous characteristics of which the manufacturer could not reasonably have known at the time of distribution. In an action based on strict products liability, it is usually irrelevant whether the seller knew, should have known, or even could have known of the defect. **Knowledge of the defect is imputed to the defendant in strict products liability** in many jurisdictions. Some courts have resolved the issue by holding that a product is defective if a manufacturer would have been negligent for failure to withdraw or redesign the product or warn consumers of the dangers of the product, assuming it knew of the defect.

b.   Restatement § 402A Comment (k): Unavoidably Unsafe Products. [§ 585]

Some products are so beneficial and unique that, notwithstanding certain risks, they are not subject to being deemed defective in design. Assuming adequate warnings are given, these highly useful products are outside the scope of design defectiveness where there are no alternative designs. The most obvious products that fit into this category are prescription drugs and vaccines, though other products fall within comment (k) protection.

(1)   Prescription Drugs. [§ 586]

Some jurisdictions have determined that all prescription drugs fall into comment (k) protection. *Brown v. Superior Court*, 751 P.2d 470 (Cal. 1988). In these jurisdictions, the only possible strict products liability claim would be for the lack of an adequate warning or for a manufacturing defect. Other jurisdictions require a showing of great value of the drug and no safer alternatives before a prescription drug is entitled to comment (k) protection.

(2)   Exam Hint. [§ 587]

Be careful about being too quick to conclude that a certain product falls within comment (k). If there are possibly safer alternatives and/or the product is not of enormous societal value, comment (k) protection is unlikely. If there is room for debate, be certain to analyze the defectiveness of the product fully after discussing the possible application of comment (k).

c.   Tests for Design Defectiveness. [§ 588]

Most jurisdictions have two tests for the determination of whether a product is defective in design: the ordinary consumer expectation test of Restatement § 402A and the risk/utility balancing test.

(1) Ordinary Consumer Expectation Test. [§ 589]

This test focuses on what an ordinary consumer would expect when using a product in its intended or foreseeable manner. Many times, due to the complicated nature of the design of many products, an ordinary consumer has no real expectation about design. Also, under the ordinary consumer expectation test, products with obvious shortcomings are not defective because they are no more dangerous than the ordinary consumer would expect. For example, goggles lacking side protection may be deemed to be non-defective because the ordinary consumer could not expect such side protection when it is obviously missing from the product.

(2) Risk/Utility Balancing Test. [§ 590]

Most jurisdictions permit a plaintiff to try to establish a design defect by showing that the risk of the product as designed outweighs its utility. Under this approach a jury weighs the following factors: gravity of the danger posed by the challenged design, the likelihood that such danger would occur, the mechanical feasibility of a safer alternative design, the financial cost of an improved design, and the adverse consequences to the product and to the consumer that would result from an alternative design. (See, *Barker v. Lull Engineering Company, Inc.*, 573 P.2d 443 (Cal.1978).)

(a) Burden of Proof. [§ 591]

A few jurisdictions shift the burden of proof to the defendant to prove that the utility of the product as designed outweighs its risks.

(b) Example. [§ 592] Detroit Co manufactures a new economy car called The Stallion. To promote fuel efficiency, Detroit Co. designed the car with the gas tank placed further to the rear than other cars. Pru was injured when her Stallion exploded after being rear-ended by another driver. Even if Detroit Co. did not know of this risk of explosion, in some jurisdictions, Detroit Co. will be strictly liable if the risks posed by the design outweigh its utility with a jury considering the likelihood of harm, its potential gravity, and the cost and feasibility of alternative designs. The value of the current design-fuel efficiency-will be considered too.

---

d. Difference from Negligence. [§ 593]

The risk/utility balancing test has been criticized as injecting negligence into a strict liability forum. The risk/utility balancing, however, is done with knowledge of the defect imputed to the defendant. Further, under strict products liability more defendants may be liable than in negligence. Strict products liability differs from negligence because in strict products liability the plaintiff can recover against any commercial defendant who placed the product (or passed on the product) in the marketing chain. No proof of fault need be shown.

e. State of the Art. [§ 594]

Few issues are more challenging than the question of what evidence is admissible to show that a product is or is not defective in design. It is not relevant that the defendant did not know of the problem with the product or even that it was reasonable in not knowing, as this is just negligence. It is, however, relevant that, at the time the product was marketed, there were no safer designs available (i.e., that the product was "state of the art"). Conversely, the plaintiff may introduce evidence of alternatives that were **knowable** (i.e., alternatives that could have been known) at the time the product was marketed.

f. Third Restatement of Torts. [§ 595]

The Third Restatement of Torts, which only becomes law if a jurisdiction elects to adopt it, has made risk/utility balancing for a design defect closer to a negligence analysis by stating that knowledge of the defect should not be imputed to the defendant, that the burden of proof should stay on the plaintiff, and that almost always a product will be non-defective absent a reasonable alternative design. Some courts have rejected the Third Restatement approach while others have found it persuasive.

7. Warning Defects. [§ 596]

The final type of defect is a warning defect under which a product is defective in design due to a lack of a warning or due to an inadequate warning.

a. Test for Warning Defect. [§ 597]

In a majority of jurisdictions, the test for a warning defect is whether the manufacturer should have known about the danger and should have warned about it. In this context, then, the test for defectiveness in strict product liability parallels that of negligence, **except** that under strict product liability theory those in the marketing chain (the retailer, for example) will be liable even without any fault on its part. A minority position, represented by the much-publicized (but rarely followed) *Beshada v. Johns-Manville Products Corp.*, 447 A.2d 539 (N.J. 1982), imposes strict liability for failure to warn even where the manufacturer should not have known (or even could have known) of the danger. Some jurisdictions permit liability when the defendant **could have** known of the risk.

b. Cause-in-Fact Hurdle. [§ 598]

Cause-in-fact poses a challenge for plaintiffs claiming a product defect due to an inadequate warning as the plaintiff must show that she would not have used the product had the warning been adequate.

> **c.   Example. [§ 599]** Drek Co. failed to warn that its over-the-counter appetite suppressant creates a risk of stroke in people with high blood pressure, a danger of which Drek Co. was aware. Penn, who had undiagnosed high blood pressure, suffered a stroke from using the product. Penn would have to show he probably would not have used the product had it included a warning of stroke in people with high blood pressure.

d. Inadequate Warning. [§ 600]

Just as a product may be defective because it lacks a warning, a product may be defective because the warning provided is inadequate. A jury deciding whether a warning was adequate considers the placement, language, color, and design of the warning.

8. Misuse and Alteration. [§ 601]

A product is not defective when it has been used in an unforeseeable manner or has been unforeseeably altered. Though some courts speak of "misuse and alteration" as a defense, it really goes to whether a product is defective in the first place.

> **a.   Example. [§ 602]** Pablo stands on a chair manufactured by Dunce Co. in order to reach a vase on a high shelf. The chair collapses under Pablo's weight and he is seriously injured. He sues Dunce Co. in strict products liability claiming that the chair was defective. Dunce Co. claims that it is not liable because of Pablo's misuse—a chair it to be sat upon, not to be stood on. While Dunce Co. is correct that the intended use of a chair is to be sat upon, there will be no misuse because Pablo's conduct was foreseeable.

9. **Proof of Defect. [§ 603]**

The plaintiff must establish that a defect existed at the time the product left the defendant's control. This is easy when a new car goes out of control as the purchaser is driving it off the showroom floor. It is much harder when time has elapsed and several owners have been in the picture.

10. **Applications Beyond Products. [§ 604]**

   a. **Services. [§ 605]**

   Strict products liability does not extend to persons who are solely engaged in furnishing services. A few cases have permitted strict products liability where there was a hybrid of products and services. For example, in a New Jersey case, *Newark v. Gimbel's, Inc.*, 258 A.2d 697 (N.J. 1969), strict liability was extended when a merchant supplied **both** products and services (a hairdresser applied a hair dye to the plaintiff's hair and the plaintiff was badly burned). The court's approach is controversial and has not gained wide acceptance.

   b. **Sales of Buildings. [§ 606]**

   There is also a trend toward extending strict liability to building contractors for defective construction of buildings, at least when the buildings are mass-produced (as in the case of tract houses).

11. **Possible Defendants. [§ 607]**

Strict products liability is limited to those engaged in the **commercial distribution** of products (e.g., manufacturers, wholesalers, retailers, etc.). Many jurisdictions have imposed liability beyond **sellers** and have subjected **lessors, bailors,** and other **non-seller commercial suppliers** to strict liability for defective products. The defendant must be in the business of dealing in that product and must have placed the defective product into the marketing chain. An occasional seller is not a proper defendant.

   a. **Manufacturers. [§ 608]**

   The **manufacturer** is liable only for design defects and defects in individual products which existed when they left its control.

   b. **Wholesalers and Retailers. [§ 609]**

   A **wholesaler** or **retailer** is strictly liable for a defective product so long as the defect (whether a design defect or an individual defect) **existed when it left his control**. Unlike the situation in products liability actions based on negligence, a wholesaler's or retailer's liability is **not** dependent upon its own negligence or failure to inspect, and it is totally irrelevant whether or not it could have found the defect after a reasonable inspection. Thus, in actions based on strict liability in tort, the **retailer** is the easiest defendant from whom to obtain recovery.

12. Possible Plaintiffs. [§ 610]

Strict products liability clearly extends to **any user or consumer** of the defective product. While the **Restatement** takes no position as to whether **bystanders** can recover under this theory (e.g., a defective car goes out of control and hits a person on the sidewalk), the majority view now extends liability to all persons foreseeably endangered by the defective product, including bystanders.

a. Strict Liability Inflicted Emotional Distress. [§ 611]

Many jurisdictions will permit recovery of bystanders who are emotionally harmed according to the jurisdiction's test for bystander recovery for negligently inflicted emotional distress. Thus, if the jurisdiction is a "zone-of-danger" jurisdiction (See § 250), a plaintiff who fears for her own safety while witnessing a close relative suffer serious harm due to a product defect will be permitted to recover for her emotional distress.

13. Defenses. [§ 612]

Contributory negligence traditionally was not a defense to an action based on strict products liability. **Assumption of risk,** however, was a defense when the plaintiff knew of the defect and understood the danger posed by it (even if his exposure to it was not unreasonable). Most jurisdictions that have adopted comparative fault now permit a jury to reduce a plaintiff's recovery when that plaintiff has engaged in unreasonable conduct. (See *Daly v. General Motors Corp.*, 575 P.2d 1162 (Cal. 1978))

> **a. Example. [§ 613]** Penny is drying her hair with a blow dryer manufactured by DenCo. Due to a defect, the blow dryer begins to smoke and then combust. Because she was daydreaming, Penny did not notice the smoke or sparks even though a reasonable person would have. Traditionally, Penny would get full recovery because she did not actually perceive the danger. Most jurisdictions now would permit the jury to reduce Penny's recovery due to her unreasonable conduct.

STRICT PRODUCTS LIABILITY (SPL)

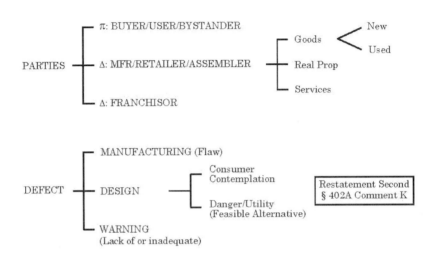

F. LIABILITY BASED UPON STATEMENTS CONCERNING THE NATURE OR QUALITY OF THE PRODUCT. [§ 614]

First, one need **not** consider liability based upon statements concerning the nature or quality of a product unless the facts indicate that a representation has in fact been made. However, when a problem reveals that there has been a **representation of quality** by a seller, both Restatement Second § 402B and warranty issues should be considered.

1. **Misrepresentation Under Restatement § 402B. [§ 615]**

   a. **Gravamen: Misrepresentation of Material Fact. [§ 616]**

      In an action based upon Restatement § 402B, the plaintiff must prove that there was a **misrepresentation of material fact** regarding the **nature or quality** of the product which caused an injury.

   b. **Misrepresentation. [§ 617]**

      The misrepresentation need not be malicious, intentional, or even negligent so long as the product does not, in fact, live up to the defendant's statements concerning the quality of the product. Liability under § 402B is, accordingly, strict.

c.   Misrepresentation Must Be Material. [§ 618]

Not every variation between the representation and the true facts is actionable—the misrepresentation must be **material.** In this context, the false statement must be of a type upon which a reasonable person would rely.

d.   Misrepresentation Must Cause Injury. [§ 619]

Even if the defendant has misrepresented a material fact, the untrue fact must be causally related to the plaintiff's injury or there is no liability under Restatement § 402B.

e.   Representation as to Quality. [§ 620]

The representations of quality about a product must be fairly specific or they cannot be the basis of liability.

f.   "Puffing." [§ 621]

A statement is **not** a representation of fact if it only relates to the **general value** of the product or is obviously merely the **seller's opinion or commendation** of the goods. Mere "puffing" (e.g., "this is the finest widget made in America today") is insufficient since common experience tells the buyer that such statements are entirely self-serving and likely to be overstatements.

g.   Puffing or Representation of Quality? [§ 622]

Whether a statement is mere puffing or an express representation depends upon the specificity of the statement and whether it was reasonable for the plaintiff to rely thereon. Representations which specifically relate to **safety**, however, will rarely be considered puffing, since a contrary rule might encourage a seller to misrepresent his goods concerning this most important fact.

h.   Special Reliance or Relationship. [§ 623]

Statements of opinion **can** be actionable, however, if the seller **purports to be an expert or holds a special position of trust or confidence.**

i.   Communication of the Statement. [§ 624]

(1) Public Communication. [§ 625]

Restatement § 402B provides that one is liable if she makes a misrepresentation **to the public.** Many writers believe there is no essential reason why Restatement § 402B should not be applicable if the representation is made to the plaintiff only, and the authors of the Restatement express no opinion as to whether such a private misrepresentation should be actionable.

(2) Manner of Communication. [§ 626]

The **manner** by which the statement may be communicated is irrelevant. A product label, newspaper, television, radio advertisement, or a descriptive brochure may constitute an actionable misstatement.

j. Possible Defendants: Commercial Sellers. [§ 627]

Restatement § 402B applies only if the defendant is **in the business of selling chattels of that kind.**

> **(1) Example. [§ 628]** Disco, the owner of a record shop, places an advertisement in a local paper offering to sell his sports car stating that the car "can make hairpin turns at 30 miles per hour." Pacman sees the ad and buys the car. Pacman is injured when he crashes in an attempt to turn a corner at 30 miles per hour. Even if Disco's statement was not puffing, Disco would not be liable under Restatement 402B because he is not a commercial seller of automobiles.

k. Possible Plaintiffs: Those Who Relied on Misrepresentation. [§ 629]

Under Restatement § 402B, a commercial seller is liable for injury to **anyone who relied** on the misrepresentation.

(1) Privity of Contract Not Required. [§ 630]

If a manufacturer makes a representation of quality in his advertising or labeling and the purchaser reads and relies upon it and is subsequently injured, the purchaser can sue the manufacturer although he did not deal directly with him (i.e., the plaintiff purchased the product from a retailer). Similarly, if Zeno buys a hammer from Del and then lends the hammer to Pal, Zeno's neighbor, Pal may recover from Del if he was aware of Del's misrepresentation, relied on it, and was injured thereby.

(2) When injured Party Has Not Read or Heard Misrepresentation. [§ 631]

In theory, there is no liability for a misrepresentation if the injured party has never heard it, because the injury was obviously not caused by reliance. There is a respectable argument that there should be liability based upon such representations even if they were not read, for assertions of quality are self-imposed standards paid for by the purchaser whether or not he knows of it.

(3) Reliance in Use Sufficient. [§ 632]

The representation need not be part of what induced the purchaser to buy the goods. Reliance is required only in connection with the **use** of the product.

> **(a) Example. [§ 633]** Pretty buys a bottle of hand lotion manufactured by Drugco even though she had never seen or heard of the product before finding it on her supermarket shelf. Inside the package is a brochure that says, "Also good for minor cuts and abrasions." Pretty subsequently used the lotion on a cut, which was infected thereby. Pretty may recover even if she had never contemplated using this or any other lotion on cuts prior to reading Drugco's leaflet after her purchase.

l. Defenses. [§ 634]

Once it is determined that a representation of material fact has been made, the defendant is **strictly liable** if the product fails to perform as promised and the plaintiff is injured thereby.

(1) Contributory Negligence and Assumption of Risk. [§ 635]

As in other cases of strict liability, the traditional rule is that **assumption of risk is a defense** to actions based on misrepresentation of a material fact while ordinary **contributory negligence is not a defense.**

(2) Impossibility No Defense. [§ 636]

The defendant may be liable **even if it is impossible** for her to make good the representation. Thus, if a seller states that her glass is "shatterproof," she cannot defend an action based on an injury caused by the shattering of her glass on the ground that there is no known technology for making a glass that will not shatter.

2. Breach of Express Warranty Under UCC § 2–313. [§ 637]

Liability under the Uniform Commercial Code (UCC) is very similar to liability under Restatement § 402B. The major differences are set out below.

a. Gravamen: Breach of Express Warranty. [§ 638]

Instead of using language of misrepresentation, the UCC refers to **breach of express warranty.** Nevertheless, the "affirmation of fact or promise ... which ... becomes part of the basis of the bargain" (the basis of an express warranty under UCC § 2–313) is the functional equivalent of a "misrepresentation of a material fact," and the rules relating to puffing are the same. **Under the UCC, however, there is no requirement of a public** representation.

b. Possible Defendants. [§ 639]

(1) Any Seller May Be Liable. [§ 640]

UCC § 2–313 is **not** limited to representations by commercial sellers. Thus, for example, an accountant who sells her used adding machine to a neighbor can be liable for breach of express warranty under the UCC.

c. Possible Plaintiffs. [§ 641]

Privity is not required for an action based upon an express warranty. Privity is required for implied warranties, however.

d. Defenses. [§ 642]

Assumption of risk and misuse of the product are defenses to an action under UCC § 2–313, but contributory negligence is not. In addition, the following concepts also limit the plaintiff's ability to recover from the defendant:

(1) Failure to Give Notice. [§ 643]

UCC § 2–607 requires the buyer to **notify the seller** of any breach of warranty "within a reasonable time" after discovery of breach. The provision may be a trap for the unwary injured plaintiff, and a number of theories have developed to excuse the requirement in personal injury cases. While this rule is founded on strong public policy—not only is it fair to the defendant by enabling him to assemble his evidence before it disappears, but it gives him an opportunity to protect others potentially injured by identical or similar products—many courts have excused failure to give notice when there was no privity of contract between the plaintiff and the defendant in all cases of **personal injury or in cases when the plaintiff is an uninformed layperson.**

(2) Disclaimer. [§ 644]

An attempted **disclaimer** of an express warranty is inoperative except to the extent that the purported disclaimer limits the warranty by clarifying its meaning.

> **(a) Example. [§ 645]** If one part of a contract warrants that a knife is "rustproof," a later statement that "the seller disclaims all warranties" is of no effect. On the other hand, if one part of the contract warrants that the knife is "rustproof" and a later statement says "this knife will not rust so long as it is not subjected to prolonged exposure to intense heat and humidity," the latter provision validly defines and limits the scope of the warranty.

G. IMPLIED WARRANTY. [§ 646]

In the beginning of the twentieth century, anger over the marketing of unwholesome food caused many courts to look for a theory that would give appropriate relief to an injured plaintiff even if he could not prove negligence. The theory developed is called **breach of implied warranty.**

1. Implied Warranty in Contract. [§ 647]

While the doctrine of implied warranty **in contract** is seldom used to provide recovery to tort victims suffering personal injury in view of the generally more favorable cause of action based on strict products liability, UCC §§ 2–314 through UCC 2–318 provide a possible theory of recovery. As is the case with express warranty, once the plaintiff proves a breach of implied warranty, the defendant is liable for injuries caused thereby without having to prove fault.

a. Gravamen: Breach of One of Two Warranties Accompanying a Sale of Goods. [§ 648]

b. Implied Warranty of Merchantability. [§ 649]

There is an implied warranty in the sale of goods that they are "of fair average quality within the description" and "fit for the ordinary purposes for which such goods are used" [UCC § 2–314]; this is known as the **warranty of merchantability.** The concept obviously goes beyond products which are dangerous.

c. Implied Warranty of Fitness for a Particular Purpose. [§ 650]

As opposed to fitness for "ordinary" purposes, there is a **warranty of fitness for a particular purpose if the buyer relies on the seller's skill and judgment to furnish goods for that special purpose** [UCC § 2–315]. This warranty arises if the seller recommends a particular product after having been apprised by the buyer of his particular needs.

d. Requirement of a Sale of Goods. [§ 651]

Both warranties require that there be a sale of a product—there are no implied warranties in contracts for **services.** Courts have, however, extended the warranties by analogy to **bailments** and **leases** when policy considerations justify such a result.

e. Possible Defendants. [§ 652]

(1) Who Gives Implied Warranties. [§ 653]

(a) Warranty of Merchantability. [§ 654]

The warranty of **merchantability** requires that the defendant be a merchant in goods of that kind; it does not arise in the case of casual, isolated sales.

(b) Warranty of Fitness for Particular Use. [§ 655]

The warranty of **fitness for a particular purpose,** however, does not require that the seller be a merchant, but the warranty will seldom arise in the case of a sale by someone other than a merchant, as the buyer would not be likely to rely on the seller's skill and judgment unless the seller was a merchant in goods of that kind.

f. Liability to Remote Parties. [§ 656]

The seller's liability to **remote parties** depends upon which version of UCC § 2–318 is in effect in the jurisdiction.

g. Possible Plaintiffs. [§ 657]

Under the UCC, the injured party need not have relied on the warranty. Instead, the UCC attempts to define **classes of protected persons** in three alternative versions of UCC § 2–318.

(1) Alternative A. [§ 658]

Under UCC § 2–318, Alternative A, the seller is liable for **personal injuries** to **his buyer, members of his buyer's household,** and **guests in his buyer's home.** This is the Alternative adopted in most jurisdictions.

(2) Alternative B. [§ 659]

Alternative B to UCC § 2–318 is broader than Alternative A as it provides that a warranty extends to **any natural person who could be expected to use, consume, or**

be affected by the goods, and who suffers personal injury by the breach.

(3) Alternative C. [§ 660]

Alternative C extends liability to the same persons as does Alternative B except that it is **not limited to injuries to the person** (i.e., it covers damages to the plaintiff's property) and is not confined to natural persons (i.e., a corporation may also sue). Note that liability for non-personal injury may be disclaimed, however.

> **(a) Example. [§ 661]** Charlemagne purchases a power mower which is impliedly warranted not to throw out debris, but during use the mower throws a rock, injuring Pippin, Charlemagne's son. Under any version of UCC § 2–318, Pippin is a person protected by the warranty and may recover for breach of express warranty. Had Pippin been a passerby on a public street, he would not have been able to recover under Alternative A, although he might have an action under Alternative B or C. If the only damage suffered by Pippin had been the breakage of his glasses, he could collect only under Alternative C.

h. Defenses. [§ 662]

In addition to the defenses of assumption of risk, misuse, and failure to follow directions, the UCC continues to limit liability for implied warranty in two significant respects.

(1) Failure to Give Notice. [§ 663]

As noted in the discussion of express warranty, UCC § 2–607 requires the buyer to notify the seller of any breach of warranty "within a reasonable time" after discovery of breach.

(2) Disclaimer. [§ 664]

Implied warranties can be disclaimed unless (a) there is a statutory duty (e.g., if a statute requires certain components of used cars to be in working order); (b) the disclaimer is not sufficiently "conspicuous" [UCC § 2–316(2)]; or (c) the disclaimer is held to be unconscionable [UCC § 2–302]. Some courts have held **all** disclaimers unconscionable in consumer cases or in cases of persons injured by mass-produced goods, or have held that disclaimers are binding only on the purchaser (and not third parties). It is also possible to argue that a particular disclaimer is ambiguous or inapplicable. Finally, the Magnuson-Moss Act prohibits disclaimer of implied warranties when goods cost $15 or more and are covered by a written warranty. Strict products liability theory avoids the problem of disclaimer entirely.

i. Exclusivity of Warranty Cause of Action. [§ 665]

Where a plaintiff suffers personal injury or property damage due to a product defect, that plaintiff may bring an action in strict products liability, negligence, or in warranty. As noted above, the warranty action, as a contract-based action, is subject to different defenses than the tort-based strict product liability action. The warranty action is limited to contract damages and is subject to the contract statute of limitations. Where a plaintiff is suing for injuries brought about by the product malfunctioning and injuring itself (as opposed to injuring persons or **other** property), most jurisdictions restrict the plaintiff to an action based in the law of warranty.

> **(1) Example. [§ 666]** Pava's truck fails to start due to a defective engine part manufactured by Darn Co. Pava seeks to recover for the engine repairs and for business lost to Pava when she was unable to make deliveries due to the broken truck. In most jurisdictions, Pava could only bring an action in warranty for these losses. Note that if the defect caused the engine to explode, starting a fire that burned down Pava's house, she would be entitled to bring an action in strict products liability or negligence as well.

REVIEW PROBLEMS—PRODUCTS LIABILITY

HairCo. manufactures a commercial hair dryer, known as the Vulcan V, that uses a heating component made by Warm, Inc. Vidal, the proprietor of a trendy hair salon, purchased a Vulcan V from Dryer Supplier, a retailer in commercial hair care dryers. While under the Vulcan V dryer at Vidal's shop, Teresa suffered severe burns due to a malfunction in the hair dryer's heating component.

Question 1. If Teresa wishes to bring an action based on strict products liability which defendants may be sued successfully?

Answer: For purposes of strict products liability, a proper defendant is anyone who is in the business of dealing with the product in issue who places the defective product in the stream of commerce. Clearly the manufacturer of the defective component part, Warm, Inc., is a proper defendant, as is the assembler, HairCo. Further, courts have concluded that the retailer (here, Dryer Supplier) is also an appropriate defendant. Whether Vidal is strictly liable is a more difficult issue though most courts would not find him to be a proper defendant for purposes of strict products liability. Most courts distinguish between goods and services, finding only the former a basis for strict liability.

Question 2. What is it Teresa will have to show in order to recover in her action in strict products liability?

> **Answer:** Teresa will have to prove that the product was defective, cause in fact, proximate cause, and damages. To determine the proper test to find defectiveness, Teresa would have to first determine whether the defect was one of manufacture or design. If the Vulcan V hair dryer malfunctioned due to a manufacturing defect (because the heating component was aberrational on this one hair dryer), the plaintiff can prove a defect by showing that the product was more dangerous than an ordinary consumer would expect. If all of the heating components had the potential to malfunction, it is likely that there is a design defect. To prove a design defect (in most jurisdictions), Teresa would have to be able to show either that the product failed to meet ordinary consumer expectations or that the risk of the product as designed outweighs its utility (so called risk/utility balancing).

Question 3. If Teresa seeks to recover in negligence, who is most likely the proper defendant?

> **Answer:** In order to recover in negligence, Teresa must show unreasonable conduct on the part of the defendant. The most likely defendant to have been negligent is the manufacturer of the component part, Warm, Inc. Teresa would have to show Warm, Inc. was unreasonable in the manner it designed or tested the heating unit. HairCo. is only liable if it should have discovered the problem, which is unlikely as long as Warm, Inc. is a generally reputable company. Similarly, it is unlikely that fault can be shown as to Dryer Supplier. Vidal can be liable only if he or one of his employees should have discovered the problem heating component through the exercise of reasonable care.

Multiple Choice Questions 1–4 are based on the following fact situation.

Owner contracts with Plumbing for the installation of a water heater. Plumbing agrees to provide a suitable heater. It buys a heater manufactured by Hot Trane from Peers, a wholesaler.

This line of heaters has two safety devices: (1) a thermostat and (2) a lead plug which blows out in the event of excessive heat to allow steam to escape to prevent the tank from exploding. This line of thermostats was designed to operate correctly when a certain screw is turned one turn counterclockwise; however, on this particular heater, the thermostat does not operate in the normal fashion unless the screw is removed completely.

Plumbing's installer made the one turn as is usually sufficient. However, in checking out the adequacy of the lead plug, he jammed it in such fashion that it did not operate correctly.

Shortly after installation, the tank exploded, doing considerable damage to Owner's house. It also caused severe damage to Walker, who was walking by Owner's house at the time of the explosion.

1. In a suit for damages by Owner against Plumbing, which of the following is the most likely holding?

    (A) The only basis for liability is in negligence because a water heater is part of the realty.

    (B) There is no tort action because this is a case of misfeasance in the performance of a contract.

    (C) Plumbing is strictly liable because the heater was defective.

    (D) Plumbing is not liable because the heater was defective when Plumbing bought it.

2. In a suit by Owner against Peers based on negligence the most likely holding is that Peers is

    (A) liable for failing to discover the defective thermostat.

    (B) not liable because it had no duty to inspect.

    (C) not liable because it is not a retail dealer.

    (D) not liable because there was no privity of contract.

3. In a suit by Owner against Hot Trane based on strict products liability, Hot Trane proves that the thermostat was manufactured by Thermo. The most likely result of this fact is that

    (A) Hot Trane is still liable for distributing a defective product.

    (B) Hot Trane is not liable because it is not an actual cause of the damage.

    (C) Hot Trane is subject to liability only in negligence because it was not the manufacturer of the defective part.

    (D) Thermo is the only proper defendant because Hot Trane might reasonably rely on being supplied a safe part.

4. In a negligence suit by Walker against Owner, the most likely holding is that Owner is

    (A) liable because he was negligent in the selection of the installing company.

    (B) liable because he is vicariously liable for the negligence of his employee.

    (C) not liable because Walker is a bystander.

    (D) not liable because the negligence was that of an independent contractor.

ANSWERS TO THE MULTIPLE CHOICE QUESTIONS

Answer to Question 1.

(C) is correct.

This is a products liability situation even though the tank is installed on realty and pursuant to a contract. Thus, A and B are incorrect. D is also wrong. Plumbing is liable because the tank is in defective condition.

Answer to Question 2.

(B) is correct.

Under modern products liability theory, wholesalers can be accountable without privity; thus C and D are incorrect. Wholesalers generally are not unreasonable in failing to inspect, however, and therefore a failure to inspect is not negligent. Thus, A is incorrect and B is the right choice.

Answer to Question 3.

(A) is correct.

A manufacturer is strictly liable for injuries caused by a defective product even if the defect is in a part supplied to the manufacturer. Thermo may be liable, but that does not immunize the manufacturer. Hot Trane is strictly liable for placing the defective product on the market. Thus, C is wrong. B is wrong because Hot Trane's act of selling the product was a substantial factor of Owner's injury. D is also incorrect because it focuses on the reasonableness of Hot Trane, which is irrelevant to strict product liability.

Answer to Question 4.

(D) is correct.

The negligence was not that of **employee** since Owner had no right to control the installer's actions. Thus, installer is an independent contractor and this situation does not seem to fall within the exceptions regarding non-vicarious liability of owner hiring independent contractor. Thus, B is wrong. No facts support a finding of fault on Owner's part so A is not the best choice. C is wrong because Walker's bystander status is irrelevant.

CHAPTER V

DEFAMATION AND PRIVACY

A. DEFAMATION. [§ 667]

1. Introductory Points. [§ 668]

Defamation is one of the oldest torts. It is designed to protect against reputational harm. Students often find the law of defamation challenging because it raises difficult constitutional issues as well as some complex common law tort principles. By tracing the progression of the law, one can best grasp the interrelationship of the constitutional and common law principles.

2. Defamation Checklist. [§ 669]

To approach a defamation question, it is well to begin by considering the common law pleading requirement, followed by absolute privileges and qualified privileges (including constitutional issues). A useful checklist follows:

1) Is the statement defamatory?

2) Is it of and concerning the plaintiff?

3) Is it defamatory on its face or are other facts necessary to make it defamatory?

4) Was it published?

5) Is it libel or slander?

6) If libel, is it libel per se or libel per quod?

7) If slander or libel per quod, can the plaintiff prove special damages or does the defamatory statement fall into one of the special categories?

8) Is there an absolute privilege?

9) Is there a qualified privilege, including a constitutional privilege?

10) If there may be a constitutional privilege, consider:

   a) the status of the plaintiff

b) the classification of the subject matter, and

c) the type of damages sought

11) Is the statement false?

These requirements will be discussed below.

3. Common Law Principles—The Prima Facie Case. [§ 670]

Whether a statement constitutes libel or slander (See § 763 below), the plaintiff must prove (a) that the defendant made a **defamatory statement** (b) **of or concerning the plaintiff** (c) which was **published to a third party** and (d) that the plaintiff suffered **special damages** or the defamation fell within a **special category of defamation not requiring proof of special damages.** Also consider what showing, if any, is required regarding the falsity of the alleged defamation and regarding defendant's fault. Fault, falsity, and damages have been greatly affected by the constitutional developments discussed in detail below.

a. Defamatory Statement. [§ 671]

Traditionally, a statement was considered defamatory if it exposed the plaintiff to **public hatred, contempt, scorn, shame or ridicule.** While the traditional view is still followed in most jurisdictions, the **Restatement Second** provides that a statement is defamatory if it tends to deter others from associating with the plaintiff or if it **lowers the esteem in which she is held by third parties.**

(1) Difference Between the Tests. [§ 672]

Most statements that would be defamatory under one test would also be defamatory under the other; this is certainly true if the statement relates to the plaintiff's honesty, integrity, or morality. On the other hand, suppose that Doug erroneously reports that Paco is dead. It is quite possible that this will subject Paco to substantial ridicule, although it is unlikely that his reputation would be adversely affected. Conversely, assume Donna publishes an article stating that Prudence is penniless. While this may fail to be defamatory under the common law definition (as it would not tend to hold one up to ridicule, scorn, etc.), it may be defamatory under the Restatement provision.

(2) Insults and Obvious Jokes are Not Defamatory. [§ 673]

As a general rule, insults, no matter how abusive, are not defamatory. If Dale accuses Parth of having canine ancestry, it is unlikely that others will shun or think less of Parth. Nor would the hearer believe such a statement. Similarly, **obvious** jokes, such as a comedian's quip that "Parth is to the political right of Attila the Hun," are not actionable for the same reasons.

(a) Alternative Theory. [§ 674]

Note that extreme insults or jokes in bad taste **may** constitute extreme and outrageous conduct giving rise to an action for intentional infliction of emotional distress (§§ 87–99). However, simple parody will not.

(3) Defamatory in Whose Eyes? [§ 675]

It is not necessary that the statement cause the plaintiff to be hated, held in contempt, or ridiculed by everyone (or that his reputation in the community in general be adversely affected). On the other hand, it is not enough that some person or aberrant group shuns or thinks less of the plaintiff. In essence, a **statement is defamatory if any substantial and morally respectable group might react in a negative manner toward the plaintiff due to the statement.** Some courts express this point differently, noting that the statement must be defamatory to a "**right-thinking group.**" This latter approach has been criticized as being too vague and narrow, however.

(4) Alternative Theory. [§ 676]

When an injurious statement is not defamatory because the plaintiff cannot prove that she was subjected to hatred, contempt, or ridicule (or that her reputation was harmed), an action based upon **false light** privacy (See §§ 803–809) might be available. As will be discussed later in § 803, that tort focuses upon the injury to the plaintiff's sensibilities rather than on the reaction of third parties to the statement.

(5) Possible Innocent Meaning. [§ 677]

At early common law, a statement was not defamatory if it had **any** possible innocent meaning. Today, courts consider the logical inferences of a statement to determine whether it is defamatory. Matters of phrasing, punctuation, etc. may affect whether a defamatory meaning is possible. While the statement "Parton was seen with a new date" is probably not defamatory, the statement could be defamatory if written as follows:

"Parton" was seen with a new "date." The use of quotations around the word "date" might potentially be construed as implying that Parton was in the company of a prostitute.

(6) Judge and Jury's Role. [§ 678]

A judge must decide whether the statement in issue is capable of a defamatory interpretation. If it is, the jury then decides if the statement was defamatory in the context at issue.

b. Of or Concerning the Plaintiff. [§ 679]

In order to recover for defamation, the plaintiff must prove that the defamatory statement referred to him (or was "of or concerning the plaintiff").

(1) Explicit Reference Not Required. [§ 680]

It is not necessary that the plaintiff be explicitly named or identified in the statement or that the defendant even intend that her statement refer to the plaintiff. It is sufficient that there be persons who have sufficient external knowledge (referred to as **"colloquium"**) which leads them to believe that the statement referred to the plaintiff and their understanding was reasonable.

---

(2) Example. [§ 681] Acme Law School's weekly paper, **Res Ipsa**, publishes an article accusing "a female torts professor at this school" of robbing a bank. If Professor Patty is the only female torts professor at Acme Law School, she could establish colloquium by asserting that fact in her complaint.

---

(3) Plaintiff Must Be a Living Person. [§ 682]

The defamatory statement must be of or concerning a **living natural person.**

(a) No Right in Decedent's Estate. [§ 683]

The estate of a deceased person has no right to bring an action based on the defamation of the decedent, whether the defamation occurred before or after death. Similarly, even a pending defamation suit does not survive the death of the person defamed. This is because the legally protected interest in the tort of defamation is reputational harm.

(b) Business May Sue for Disparagement. [§ 684]

While it is often said that business entities cannot be defamed, they may maintain a similar action under the tort of **disparagement.** That tort is discussed in §§ 822–840.

(4) Group Defamation. [§ 685]

A troublesome "of and concerning" problem is the situation of group defamation. For example, if defendant, the conductor of the local symphony, refers to her audience as "boisterous baboons, uneducated, uncouth, and unwashed," can any member of the audience say that the statement was of or concerning him?

(a) Basic Test. [§ 686]

The basic test of whether a plaintiff was defamed when the statement, by its terms, referred only to a group to which the plaintiff belongs is whether the average, reasonable person would ultimately conclude that this particular person was defamed (i.e., the reasonable person would shun or think less of this plaintiff).

(b) Key Factors. [§ 687]

The key factors in resolving the issue are (a) to how many members of the group did the statement purport to refer (i.e., did Defendant say "All members of the audience. . . ." "Most members of the audience. . . ." "Some members of the audience. . . ." or "One member of the audience. . . .")?; (b) how large was the group (i.e., did the audience consist of 15,000 people, 100 people, 20 people, or 5 people)?; and (c) can the plaintiff show special facts which indicate that the statement **particularly** referred to him?

(c) Guidelines. [§ 688]

If the group is very large (e.g., "all lawyers"), no individual member is defamed, even if the statement purports to be all-inclusive; this category includes, according to one case, a defamation of a group of 162 labor leaders. If the group is very small, even an imputation that the description only applies to some may be actionable (e.g., each of nine models was defamed by the statement "Some Neiman models are call girls").

(d) Specific Circumstances Also Relevant. [§ 689]

Aside from these factors and guidelines discussed above, the specific circumstances surrounding the statement in question are also relevant in determining if it was of or concerning the plaintiff. Thus, if Dawn looks directly at Parker, the only landlord in the room at a meeting of a tenants' union, and says "All landlords are greedy, heartless bloodsuckers," Parker may have been defamed.

c. Publication. [§ 690]

Since the essence of defamation is to protect the plaintiff from the adverse reactions of third parties, the defamatory statement is actionable only if it was **published** (i.e., conveyed) to a third person.

> **NOTE:** In this context the word "published" is a term of art which extends far beyond the common use of the term. If Dan orally conveys to his friend, Francis, a defamatory comment about Page, this is sufficient "publication."

(1) Publication Requires Understanding. [§ 691]

A defamatory statement is not published to a third party unless it is understood. Thus, if Dezi calls Percy names in Spanish and no one who heard the statements other than Percy understands Spanish, there has been no publication sufficient to make out a prima facie case in defamation.

(2) Belief of Statement Need Not Be Proven. [§ 692]

The plaintiff is not required to prove that anyone who heard the statement believed it to be true. This rule is justified because such belief is virtually impossible to prove. However, if the statement is so outrageous that no one could believe it as true, it will not be defamatory.

(3) Publication Must Be at Least Negligent. [§ 693]

The defendant must be **at least** negligent with regard to publication if the plaintiff is to succeed in his action for defamation. Normally, this is not hard to prove as, in most cases, the defendant typically has intentionally communicated the statement to one or more third parties. However, assume that Dalton defames Porter and the sole third person who overhears the statement is only in a position to do so because he was burglarizing the closed office next door. Under these circumstances, there is no cause of action in defamation since Dalton was not even negligent with regard to publication.

(4) Special Situations. [§ 694]

(a) Republication Rule. [§ 695]

The republication rule provides that one who republishes defamation is subject to liability just as if she had published it originally. Every restatement of the defamatory matter constitutes another publication and the "restater" may be liable accordingly for defamation. This is true even if the republisher attributes the source of the defamation to the original publisher. Thus, every individual copy of a defamatory book or newspaper could be seen as a basis for a separate cause of action. Most states, however, have adopted a rule that the entire edition of a printed work is to be treated as a single publication (the "single publication" rule). A new edition or a new printing would still be seen as a new publication, however.

> **(i) Example. [§ 696]** Dale tells Shirley that Pru embezzled funds from Pru's employer. Shirley later tells Laverne, her housemate, "Dale told me today that Pru embezzled funds from her employer." Pru could recover against Dale and Shirley for defamation. (Even though Shirley's statement is literally true because she attributes the statement to Dale, Shirley is liable as a republisher.)

(b) Publication by the Plaintiff. [§ 697]

Normally, the plaintiff cannot recover for defamation if all third parties to whom the statement was communicated were informed of the defamatory statement by the plaintiff himself. There are, of course, exceptional cases such as those when the defendant sends the plaintiff a defamatory letter **knowing** that she is blind or illiterate or that other persons are likely to read her mail (as a secretary might read letters mailed to a business executive).

d. Damages—Existence of Special Damages or Exception. [§ 698]

A source of great confusion is the extent to which a plaintiff must establish damages as an element of her prima facie case. As a general rule, the existence of **some** special damages (See

§ 702) **or** a recognized exception to the requirement must be shown for the plaintiff to state an action for defamation unless the communication is libelous on its face.

e. **Libel or Slander. [§ 699]**

The damage pleading requirements vary depending on whether the defamation is characterized as **"libel" or "slander."** Thus, it is useful to distinguish between the two forms of defamation for proper labeling.

(1) Definitions. [§ 700]

In the simplest terms, **slander** is the name given to oral defamation while **libel** refers to defamation in a permanent form (typically a writing, but a cartoon, statue, or similar representation may also constitute a libelous statement).

(2) Special Problems of Electronic Media Broadcasts. [§ 701]

Jurisdictions disagree about whether defamatory statements conveyed on radio and television broadcasts constitute libel or slander.

(a) Resolution by Definition. [§ 702]

A few cases, focusing on the written-oral distinction, have held that defamatory broadcasts made from a film or tape are libel, while those broadcast live are slander. Alternatively, it has been held that a broadcast read from a prepared script is libel while an extemporaneous defamation is slander.

(b) Resolution by Rationale. [§ 703]

Other states, supported by most of the commentators and the **Restatement Second** have entirely rejected the distinctions discussed above as being ridiculously artificial. Instead, they have gone back to the underlying rationale justifying the distinction—it is easier to recover for libel because such statements, due to their permanence and the respect given to the written word, are far more likely to injure the plaintiff than transitory oral statements. Since under this view, media broadcasts reach thousands and even millions of persons and are often treated with great reverence (many persons presume them to be undeniably true), they must be treated as libel because of their tremendous capacity to injure the plaintiff.

(c) Resolution by Policy. [§ 704]

Other jurisdictions, on public policy grounds, have held that treating mass media broadcasts as libel, which eases the plaintiff's burden, unduly interferes with free speech, and have declared that all defamation transmitted by radio or television is slander.

(3) Presumption of General Damages: Libel and the Common Law. [§ 705]

At common law, once the plaintiff established his prima facie case for libel, no proof of damages was required. **General damages,** such as injury to feelings and reputation, were compensable without any direct proof of such harm, because it was presumed that the libel would cause reputational harm to the plaintiff. Libel, because it was written and, thus permanent in form, was viewed as more harmful than slander and presumed to cause reputational harm.

(4) Damages and Slander. [§ 706]

At common law, slander was generally viewed as less hurtful than defamation and, accordingly, in most situations reputational harm was not presumed for slander as it was for libel. Instead, in an action for slander, in order to recover any damages at all, the plaintiff had to plead and prove **special damages. Thus, "special damages" is a term of art used to describe a prima facie element of a defamation action, not a measure of recovery.** To help avoid this confusion, the **Restatement Second** uses the term "special harm."

(a) Special Damages Defined. [§ 707]

"**Special damages**" is pecuniary injury directly resulting from a third party's reaction to a defamatory statement.

(b) Pecuniary Injury. [§ 708]

Loss of customers, employment, or a contract are the normal type of special damages which **can** make out a prima facie case for libel or slander. However, more personal types of economic injury (e.g., disinheritance, loss of an advantageous marriage, or loss of a free vacation) also qualify, although loss of friends does **not** constitute special damage since it is not pecuniary in nature. On the other hand, assuming that the plaintiff does get to present her case to the jury by proving special damages, her recovery is not limited to these special damages; the jury may then provide damages for reputational harm as well as it sees fit.

(c) Response of Third Party. [§ 709]

While it is irrelevant whether the third party actually believes the statement, there is no special damage unless the injury flows directly from a third party's reaction to the statement.

(d) Slander Per Se. [§ 710]

At common law, certain types of defamatory statements (even slanderous statements) were actionable **without proof of special damages** because they could be presumed to injure the plaintiff significantly. Given the difficulty in proving special damages, there is a great incentive for the plaintiff to try to fit into one of the exceptions. In the case of slander (oral defamation), the transitory nature of the communication makes harm so unlikely that damages will be presumed (and thus special damages need not be proven) only if the statement was **slander per se.** The basic categories of what constitutes slander per se are:

(i) Trade or Profession. [§ 711]

A defamatory statement which adversely relates to the plaintiff's particular trade or profession is slander per se because direct financial injury can be logically presumed. This requires a careful consideration of **this particular plaintiff's** occupation. Thus, it would be slander per se to say that a lawyer is illiterate, a security guard is dishonest, or a soldier is a coward. Note, however, that since honesty is not crucial to being a soldier, nor bravery crucial to being a lawyer, nor literacy crucial to being a security guard, such imputations are not slander per se.

(i-a) Aspersion of Plaintiff's Goods Distinguished. [§ 712]

Technically, aspersions of a plaintiff's goods or products are actionable, if at all, in a suit for disparagement (discussed in §§ 822–830) not defamation. However, such statements often bear directly on the plaintiff's character as well, at least when there is an implication that the managers of the business know of the defect. (If a butcher shop sells rotten meat, what does that say about the butcher?)

(ii) Crime. [§ 713]

It is slander per se to accuse the plaintiff of having committed a serious crime (i.e., one involving moral turpitude such as embezzlement, rape, or murder). An accusation that the defendant jaywalked would not suffice.

(iii) Present Loathsome Disease. [§ 714]

Some diseases are so loathsome that an implication that the plaintiff is **presently** so afflicted seriously affects the willingness of others to deal with him and thus constitutes slander per se. This category covers venereal diseases and other sexually transmitted diseases.

(iv) Woman's Lack of Chastity. [§ 715]

Under traditional theory, an accusation that a **woman** is unchaste is slander per se. There is authority to the effect that a woman is unchaste if she has indulged in obscenity of language, indecency of conduct, or undue familiarity with men. This medieval notion has generally given way to holding that an unmarried woman is chaste if she is still a virgin and a married woman (or widow or divorcee) is chaste so long as she has not engaged in extra-marital intercourse. This entire category of slander per se has been attacked as being unrealistic, outmoded and unimportant in our modern society and/or as being unconstitutionally discriminatory, and some courts have abandoned it. Others have interpreted it as applying to sexual impropriety in general regardless of gender.

(v) Other Possible Categories. [§ 716]

A few courts have held other types of slander to be slander per se (e.g., accusations of homosexuality, impotence, or of being a communist), but none have gained widespread acceptance.

f. Dispute as to Libel. [§ 717]

Since the more permanent nature of a libel makes harm to the plaintiff far more likely than in the case of slander, all jurisdictions dispense with the requirement of proving special damages more readily in libel cases. Exactly when special damages must be proven in the case of libel depends on the jurisdiction.

(1) Restatement View. [§ 718]

The **Restatement, Second** and a substantial number of jurisdictions follow the rule that **all** libel is actionable without proof of special damages.

(2) Other View. [§ 719]

Some states distinguish between **libel on its face** and **libel per quod.**

(a) Libel on Its Face. [§ 720]

A statement is **libel on its face** if no external knowledge (inducement) or innuendo is necessary to understand the defamatory nature of the statement (e.g., "P is a drunk" or "P is thief"). As to this type of libel, the traditional view is the same as the **Restatement view—it is actionable without proof of special damages.**

(b) Libel Per Quod. [§ 721]

A statement is **libel per quod** if the defamatory nature does not appear from the defendant's statement alone. For example, there is nothing libelous per se in writing "P (an actress) has found an artistic and intellectual equal in her new co-star, Clyde"; however, if it can be established by external facts ("inducement") that Clyde is an orangutan, the defamatory nature of the statement is obvious. In traditional jurisdictions, **libel per quod is actionable without proof of special damages only** if the defamatory sting of the statement falls within one of the **slander per se categories.** (In this case, note that the statement about Plaintiff's intellect would not allow suit without proof of special damages, but the statement about her acting ability relates to one of the slander per se categories—competency in her profession.)

g. **Issue of Truth or Falsity: Common Law. [§ 722]**

To be actionable, a defamatory statement must be untrue. At common law, however, falsity was **presumed** upon proof that the statement was defamatory; thus the defendant had the burden of proving truth in the nature of a defense, rather than the plaintiff having to prove falsity as a part of her prima facie case.

(1) **Impact of the First Amendment. [§ 723]**

Relatively recent decisions by the United States Supreme Court have changed the common law rule in most contexts, thereby requiring the plaintiff to prove falsity as part of her prima facie case. (See §§ 763–783 below.)

h. **Fault: Common Law. [§ 724]**

At common law, defamation was basically a strict liability tort—the defendant's good faith, reasonable belief that the statement was true was not a defense nor was it relevant that the statement was interpreted by third parties in an unintended manner or that the defendant did not intend his statement to refer to the plaintiff. (However, there was a fault element with regard to publication and fault is relevant to the qualified privileges.)

---

(1) Example. [§ 725] A photographer for The Daily takes a picture of a man and the woman accompanying him. The man tells the photographer that the woman is his wife. The Daily prints the photo with the caption, "Husband and wife enjoying the warm evening air." The man is actually married to Penny. Under common law defamation rules, Penny recovers against The Daily even though they had no reason to suspect that the caption was defamatory.

---

(2) **First Amendment. [§ 726]**

As will be discussed in some detail below, it is with regard to fault that the most dramatic change has occurred over the last few decades. The United States Supreme Court, starting with *New York Times v. Sullivan* in 1964, has drastically changed the "fault" aspect of the tort of defamation in most contexts.

4. Common Law Defenses. [§ 727]

a. Truth. [§ 728]

Truth is an absolute defense to all actions for libel or slander. At common law recall that the defendant had the burden of proving truth, however.

(1) Substantial Truth. [§ 729]

To prove truth, the defendant does not have to prove the literal truth; proof that the defamatory impact was **substantially true** will prevent the defendant's liability.

> **(2) Example. [§ 730]** Poindexter sues the Daily because it reported that Poindexter had been convicted of "sexual assault" when Poindexter had in fact been convicted of rape. Daily would not be liable because it could prove the statement to be substantially true. The difference between the actual truth and the statement as published is not enough to be material and thus the defendant will prevail.

(3) Must Relate to Defamatory Sting. [§ 731]

To be a defense, the truth must relate to the "defamatory sting" of the statement—partial or technical truth is not enough.

> **(a) Example. [§ 732]** Doug says "Prissy worked in a house of prostitution." Since the clear implication is that Prissy had been a prostitute, it is an insufficient defense to prove that she had worked in such an establishment as a cloakroom attendant.

> **(b) Example. [§ 733]** Dokie says "I think that Pome is a thief" or "I've heard that Pome is a thief." The defamatory implication is clear and the mere couching of the statement in language of opinion or as a report of what others have said is not enough to establish truth as a defense.

(4) Alternative Theories. [§ 734]

Whenever technical truth of an allegedly defamatory statement is in issue, "false light" and/or "true" privacy, discussed in §§ 811–817, are possible alternatives theories of liability. If the statement is clearly substantially true, then privacy, not defamation, is the appropriate route.

b. Absolute Privileges. [§ 735]

Absolute privileges are, as the name implies, complete and full privileges—**they cannot be defeated by the defendant's bad motives, negligence, or even deliberate falsehood.** Normally, absolute privileges are a function of the special status of the defendant and the context of the statement in relation to that status. They are afforded to certain persons because, due to those persons' special position, it has been determined that they should not worry about potential liability when expressing themselves.

(1) Statements in the Course of Judicial Proceedings. [§ 736]

(a) Persons to Whom Applicable. [§ 737]

An absolute privilege is available to **all participants** in judicial proceedings—the judge, grand and petit jurors, attorneys, and witnesses. Thus, pertinent statements made in judicial contexts are not subject to an action for defamation.

(b) Statements Must Be Pertinent. [§ 738]

The statement must be "relevant" to the purpose of the proceeding, although not in the sense of evidence law; all that is necessary is that the statement be **arguably pertinent** to the subject under inquiry. The statements must have a reasonable relationship to the judicial proceedings and have occurred in the course of the proceedings. The point is that the defendant cannot use the judicial proceeding as an open forum to defame her enemies if the statement has absolutely no relationship to the proceeding.

(c) Proceedings to Which Applicable. [§ 739]

The privilege extends to conventional hearings and trials, grand jury proceedings, and quasi-judicial administrative proceedings.

(d) Attorney's Statements. [§ 740]

An attorney is absolutely privileged to make statements about a potential or existing case provided his statements are made in furtherance of the litigation and serve the interests of justice. This line is blurry, however, and an attorney speaking about a potential case at a press conference may be found to lack the required nexus to the furtherance of litigation required for the absolute privilege to attach.

> **(i) Example. [§ 741]** During the cross-examination of Plyn, the attorney, Dell, asks Plyn, "Are you still a member of the Nazi party?" Dell knows Plyn has never been affiliated in any way with Nazis, but wants to harm Plyn's credibility before the jury. Plyn loses a defamation action because Dell's statement is absolutely privileged.

(2) Statements in the Course of Legislative Proceedings. [§ 742]

The legislative privilege is established for federal legislators by the United States Constitution and, generally, by state constitutions for state legislators.

(a) Legislators. [§ 743]

Unlike the judicial proceeding privilege, the legislative privilege has no limitations insofar as the legislator himself is concerned (i.e., **there is no requirement that the statement of a legislator be relevant to the matter before the legislature**). Total leeway is afforded the legislator provided the statement is made in the course of legislative proceedings. The law is less certain about comments not directly part of legislative proceedings, such as work-related telephone calls.

(b) Witnesses Before Legislative Hearing. [§ 744]

Witnesses in legislative hearings have a narrower privilege, analogous to that of witnesses in judicial proceedings. Their statements are privileged only if they are plausibly related to the subject matter of the hearing.

(3) Public Statements by Other Government Officials. [§ 745]

An absolute privilege is generally granted to **high** officials relating to the scope of their office. While the privilege of subordinate officials is narrower and generally applies only to statements of the type required by their duties, a qualified privilege of the type discussed in §§ 735–753 will be available for most statements not falling within the absolute privilege.

(4) Communication Between Spouses. [§ 746]

In many states, communications between a husband and wife are absolutely privileged.

---

(5) Note: May Not Be Repeated Elsewhere. [§ 747] While a statement made in one of the contexts mentioned above is absolutely privileged, **repeating the statement outside of that setting is not.** For example, if an attorney tells the press that a prosecution witness is "a liar and known dope addict," the statement is **not** privileged even though the identical courtroom accusation is. (In such cases, the **qualified** privilege to report transactions at public proceedings (See § 755), may apply, however.)

---

c. Qualified Privileges. [§ 748]

Aside from the special relationships subject to absolute privilege, there are other important interests which could be seriously injured by the common law's strict liability approach to defamation. Thus, a number of **qualified (or conditional) privileges** exist which may be raised as defenses. These qualified privileges are based on the social utility of protecting statements made in response to moral, legal, or social duty and are conditioned on publication being in a reasonable manner and for a proper purpose. In other words, the qualified privileges may be lost by excessive publication or improper motive.

(1) Meaning of "Qualified." [§ 749]

The privileges discussed below are qualified by three conditions (i.e., they do not act as defenses unless **all three** conditions are met).

(a) Good Faith. [§ 750]

The defendant must **honestly and subjectively** believe that the statement is true and is necessary to protect the interest in question (i.e., she is not motivated solely by spite or ill will).

(b) Reasonableness. [§ 751]

Generally, the defendant's belief must also be **objectively reasonable.** Some states eliminate this consideration entirely while others will allow this element to be defeated only by a showing of gross negligence or recklessness.

(c) Limited Disclosure. [§ 752]

Publication must be limited in scope so that only facts relevant to the interest to be protected are disclosed and only those who could be expected to act on the information are notified.

(2) Interests Protected. [§ 753]

(a) Statements in Defendant's Own Interest. [§ 754]

A defendant is not liable for defamatory statements made in order to protect his own interests. Thus, statements meant to discredit an accuser of the defendant or to otherwise exculpate the defendant are covered by this qualified privilege.

> **(i) Example. [§ 755]** Pippin accuses Dolly of stealing their employer's goods. Dolly responds by saying, "You're the thief, not me." This statement is covered by a qualified privilege.

(b) Statements in Interest of Third Party. [§ 756]

A person has a similar qualified privilege to make statements in the interest of a third party, at least if there is some **pre-existing relationship** between the defendant and the third party or the defendant is asked about a matter by the third party (as opposed to the defendant being an officious intermeddler).

> **(i) Example. [§ 757]** Dr. Darla, Irene's family physician, is privileged to warn Irene of Dr. Darla's suspicion that Dr. Pax, a specialist who Irene has considered seeking for treatment, may be incompetent.

(c) Statements in Common Interest. [§ 758]

Another privilege is recognized for statements made in the interest of both the defendant and a third party (e.g., financial data filtered through a mutual credit organization).

(d) Statements in the Public Interest. [§ 759]

The privilege for statements made in the public interest includes statements relating to public officers and employees, persons in licensed professions, merchants, and others capable of injuring the public as a whole.

(i) Scope of Privilege. [§ 760]

This privilege is broad in one respect and narrow in another. While the nature of the facts which may be revealed is broader than in most other cases, the publication must be limited to those in a position to protect the public from the person defamed.

> **(ii) Example. [§ 761]** Darla, a police officer, believes that Pogo, a fellow officer, is consorting with suspected criminals. Darla is privileged to convey this suspicion, but only to appropriate police authorities (e.g., Pogo or Darla's supervisor or an internal affairs division of the department). A disclosure of her beliefs to the press for public distribution would normally be held to violate the privilege.

(e) Reports of Public Proceedings. [§ 762]

A defendant has a qualified privilege to report what happened at a meeting open to the public (e.g., a trial, legislative proceeding, or administrative fact-finding hearing).

(i) Must Be Accurate Report. [§ 763]

The report must be an accurate recounting of what happened. Unreasonable characterization, summary, or editorializing will defeat the privilege.

(f) Fair Comment: Literary and Artistic Criticism. [§ 764]

The privilege of "fair comment" covers comments about literary and artistic works. (The same privilege also applied at common law to comments about public officials, public figures, and matters of public concern, but the former law as to those issues has been made obsolete by the constitutional developments discussed in § 757 and following).

(i) Only Protects Opinions. [§ 765]

This "fair comment" privilege protects only the opinions and conclusions of the defendant and does not extend to misstatements of fact. Moreover, the privilege will be lost if the critic falsely states her actual opinion (an issue virtually impossible to prove) or if her **sole** purpose was to harm the plaintiff.

(ii) "Fairness" of Comment. [§ 766]

While there is some debate about this, the **Restatement** takes the position that the comment does **not** have to be "fair" in an objective, reasonable-person sense in order to qualify for the privilege so long as it is held in good faith.

(g) Opinion. [§ 767]

It is often stated that a statement of opinion is incapable of being defamatory, and this is generally true. A **pure** statement of opinion cannot be proven to be defamatory because it cannot be shown to be true or false. Thus, if Paula seeks to sue Deena because Deena wrote: "Paula is a lousy dresser," no defamation action will lie.

(i) Opinion Based on Fact. [§ 768]

Opinion that appears to be based on fact, however, will be actionable. This is true even though the defendant couched her statement with words of opinion (e.g., "My opinion is . . . ").

> **(ii) Example. [§ 769]** If Don's restaurant review stated that the food at Paulie's Place was "disappointing," there would be no basis for a defamation action because this is a statement of pure opinion. However, if the review stated: "I think that Paulie's Place serves week-old tomatoes," an action could lie because the statement can be interpreted as based on fact.

5. Constitutional Defenses and Limitations. [§ 770]

As alluded to above, the United States Supreme Court has ruled that several elements of the common law of defamation unduly interfere with the First Amendment guarantees of freedom of speech and freedom of the press. Accordingly, since 1964, defamation law has undergone dramatic changes and will continue to do so. These constitutional decisions have affected burdens of proof, fault, damages, and falsity.

a.   Study Approach. [§ 771] It is important to understand the specific holding of each of the constitutional cases and to highlight what issues are yet unresolved. In essence, the Court has been struggling with the proper balance between the plaintiff's right to be compensated for reputational harm and the need to protect the freedom of press and speech.

b.   Fault. [§ 772]

At common law, defamation was a strict liability tort. This has been changed in most contexts, however, by the Supreme Court's creation of qualified privileges that require plaintiffs to prove varying degrees of fault based upon the status of the plaintiff and upon the kind of damages the plaintiff is seeking.

c.   Status of the Plaintiff. [§ 773]

It is critical now to determine the status of the plaintiff in order to assess the proof she must have to recover for defamatory statements. Ask yourself whether the plaintiff is a public official, a public figure (and, if so, what kind), or a private person.

d.   Public Officials. [§ 774]

Because of the importance of open debate concerning those in charge of public affairs, the rights of public officials to sue in libel or slander must be limited or free speech will be unduly chilled (See *New York Times Co. v. Sullivan*, 376 U.S. 254, 84 S.Ct. 710 (1964)).

(1)   Who Is a Public Official? [§ 775]

The term **public official** includes not only elected politicians and appointees to high office, but also **candidates** for such office and **public employees** who have substantial responsibility for governmental affairs (e.g., those who have significant **decision-making** powers, not just ministerial functions).

(2)   Scope of Privilege. [§ 776]

The privilege with regard to a public official relates to **any act which bears on her qualification for office,** not just to her public acts or the carrying out of her official duties. Indeed, for some public figures it is hard to conceive of statements not related to their position (e.g., statements about the President of the United States).

(3) Defeat of Privilege: "Actual Malice." [§ 777]

The privilege relating to public officials is not absolute, however. It is **qualified** in that it is defeated if the plaintiff proves "actual malice." **Actual malice (or constitutional malice) is a constitutional term of art meaning knowledge of falsity or reckless disregard of the truth or falsity of the statement. Thus, it is wholly distinct from common law malice which means spite or ill will.**

(a) Meaning of Actual Malice. [§ 778]

According to the Supreme Court, actual malice requires that the defendant know the statement to be false or that she actually entertained serious doubts as to the veracity of the statement. Thus, the simple failure to investigate alone is not enough to show actual malice.

> **(b) Example. [§ 779]** Mayor Parker sues the Daily Diatribe because it falsely reported that Mayor Parker accepted a bribe. The reporter for the Daily Diatribe based the story on one source, and did not verify the veracity of the charge. Provided that the reporter did not question the truth of the statement (i.e., believed it to be true) Parker will lose because she cannot prove actual malice. This is so even if the reporter was unreasonable (i.e., negligent) in relying on only one source.

(c) Burden of Proof. [§ 780]

In addition to requiring the plaintiff to prove actual malice, *New York Times v. Sullivan* increased the burden of proof on the plaintiff. Accordingly, in any case where a plaintiff has to prove actual malice, the Constitution requires that the plaintiff prove this by "clear and convincing" evidence (which, though ill defined, is higher than the usual tort preponderance standard).

e. Public Figures. [§ 781]

Shortly after *New York Times*, the actual malice qualified privilege was expanded to include those accused of defaming **public figures** (i.e., a public figure must prove actual malice in order to recover for defamation).

(1) Who Is a Public Figure? [§ 782]

A public figure is someone who has **special prominence in affairs of society or who is prominent in the controversy about which the defamation was published.** The Supreme Court has identified several classes of such persons. The first category consists of persons so famous that they have considerable power or influence and are thus an "all-purpose public figure" (e.g., a former President or an extremely well-known athlete or entertainer). The second category consists of so-called "limited public figures," heretofore anonymous persons who voluntarily thrust themselves into the limelight for some specific public controversy (e.g., a consumer advocate who publicly attacks a major corporation). The final category involves "involuntary public figures," who get drawn into a particular controversy (e.g., a victim of a plane hijacking).

(2) Limited Public Figure Factors. [§ 783]

To determine whether the plaintiff is a limited public figure consider: 1) whether there is a real public dispute that expands beyond the parties to the defamation suit; 2) whether the plaintiff voluntarily injected himself into the controversy (or otherwise got dragged in); and 3) whether the defamation grew out of or was related to the controversy.

(3) Scope of Privilege. [§ 784]

The qualified privilege relating to well-known persons applies to virtually all phases of the public figure's life (they are sometimes referred to as "all-purpose" public figures). With regard to the limited voluntary figure, however, the privilege relates only to those matters for which the plaintiff has voluntarily cast herself into the public eye. Thus, in *Time, Inc. v. Firestone*, 424 U.S. 448, 96 S.Ct. 958 (1976), the Supreme Court held that a socialite who generally sought publicity was not a public figure and, thus, did not have to prove *New York Times* malice when a news magazine chose to write about her divorce. The Supreme Court has defined narrowly who is a public figure.

f. Private Persons. [§ 785]

If the plaintiff is neither a public official or a public figure, he is a private figure. In order to determine the amount of fault a private plaintiff must prove in a defamation action, it is now critical to consider the subject matter of the defamation (i.e., is it a matter of public or private concern).

(1) Public Concern. [§ 786]

If the subject matter of the defamation affects a substantial number of people or involves an issue of societal importance it is a matter of public concern. The Supreme Court has defined public concern broadly, though it has not provided a test for determining "public concern" beyond noting that one must consider the "form, context, and content" of the statement (See *Dun & Bradstreet, Inc. v. Greenmoss Builders, Inc.*, 472 U.S. 749, 105 S.Ct. 2939 (1985)).

(2) Fault—At Least Negligence Required. [§ 787]

Although a private person need not prove *New York Times* malice, the common law rule imposing strict liability is an unconstitutional chill on the defendant's freedom of expression. **Thus, a private-person plaintiff must prove at least negligence with regard to falsity in order to maintain successfully his action—at least where the subject matter is of "public concern."** (See *Gertz v. Robert Welch, Inc.*, 418 U.S. 323, 94 S.Ct. 2997 (1974))

(3) Distinction Between Recklessness (Malice) and Negligence. [§ 788]

Recklessness, the minimum amount of fault necessary to establish "actual malice," requires proof that the defendant **in fact** had serious doubts as to the truth of the statement (i.e., a subjective standard). **Negligence merely requires that a reasonable** person in the position of the defendant would have questioned the truth of the statement (i.e., an objective standard). Thus, for example, a mere failure to check sources or confirm information received which appears to be reliable may be negligence, but would not be recklessness.

(4) Limitation of Damages. [§ 789]

A further limitation imposed on a private person's suit relates to damages. Whereas the common law often assumed damages so that the plaintiff could obtain a substantial recovery without introducing any evidence of injury, First Amendment interests require that the plaintiff recover only for damages **actually proven with**

reasonable certainty unless "actual malice" is proven. In other words, even if the defamation is slander per se or libel on its face, such that no special damages need be proven as part of the plaintiff's prima facie case, no recovery can be allowed without **proof** of some financial loss or injury to reputation or feelings. Even then, **punitive** damages (non-compensatory damages designed to punish the defendant) may be awarded only if the defendant had malice both in the ordinary sense (spite or ill will is generally required to be shown whenever punitive damages are sought) **and** in the constitutional sense (that the defendant knew that the statement was false or proceeded in reckless disregard of the truth). In addition, a plaintiff who is seeking presumed damages (because she is unwilling to prove harm to reputation) must meet the actual malice standard.

(5) Private Plaintiffs and Matters of Private Concern. [§ 790]

While this area remains in flux to some degree, the Court held that where there is a matter of private concern, a private plaintiff could recover presumed damages without proof of actual malice. The amount of fault required, however, was unstated and could be either negligence or possibly even strict liability (which would be a return to the common law). Ultimately, it appears that each state may define its own standards where there is a private plaintiff and a matter of private concern. (See Case, *Dun & Bradstreet v. Greenmoss Builders, Inc.*, 472 U.S. 749, 105 S.Ct. 2939 (1985).

g. Status of the Defendant—Media versus Private Defendants. [§ 791]

Since all of the Supreme Court cases have dealt primarily or exclusively with media defendants, the exact impact of the cases mentioned above is somewhat unclear when the defendant is an ordinary person not connected with the news gathering and disseminating media. It appears, however, that a majority of the Court would not distinguish between public and private defendants. Indeed, in the *N.Y. Times v. Sullivan* case, several members of the clergy were sued along with the newspaper, and the Court treated all defendants the same. This issue will surely be confronted by the Court in the future. The status of the defendant may be relevant to whether the subject matter is of public or private concern, however. Where there is a media defendant, it is harder to argue that the subject matter is of private concern.

(1) Public Officials and Public Figures. [§ 792]

The rationale of *New York Times* (the fear of chilling debate on the qualifications and acts of governmental agents), as well as the fact that co-defendants in the case were private citizens, makes it virtually certain that the private person has the same First Amendment qualified privilege to defame **public officials** as does the media. While slightly less clear, the same privilege would appear to apply to actions brought against a non-media defendant by **public figure** plaintiffs.

h. Falsity. [§ 793]

The Supreme Court has held that at least in cases where the plaintiff is a public official, public figure, or private figure and there is subject matter of public concern, the plaintiff must prove the falsity of the statement as well as the constitutionally required degree of fault. This marks another change from the common law where falsity was presumed and the defendant had to prove truth.

DEFAMATION

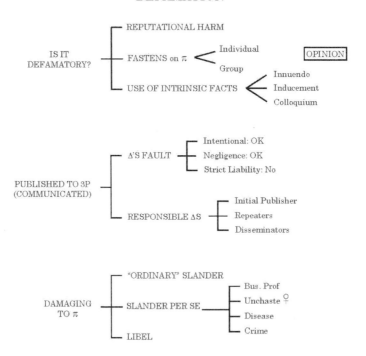

DEFENSES/PRIVILEGES

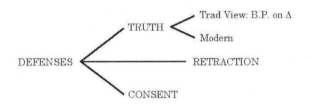

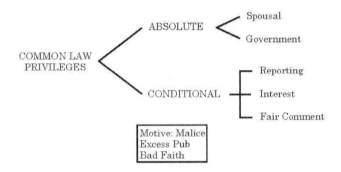

DEFAMATION CHART

STATUS OF π	SUBJECT MATTER	DAMAGES			BURDEN OF PROOF RE: FALSITY
		ACTUAL	PRESUMED	PUNITIVES	
PUBLIC OFFICIAL	Public	Actual Malice (A.M.)		A.M. + State Standard	π
PUBLIC FIGURE	Public	Actual Malice (A.M.)		A.M. + State Standard	π
PRIVATE FIGURE	Public	No Strict Liability	Actual Malice	A.M. + State Standard	π
PRIVATE FIGURE	Private	SL? Neg?	Actual Malice not required some fault?	State Standard	Open

Status of Δ?

Multiple Choice Questions 1–3 are based on the following fact situation.

Liz, a leading feminist spokesperson, having never been married, gives birth to a baby. Liz admits that she is proud to be a mother and refuses to identify the father. *Journal*, a news magazine, writes an article about Liz in which it is stated that it was rumored that Liz's father was not Liz's mother's husband, but was Star, who was a famous movie actor at the time of Liz's birth, but who has lived in quiet retirement for several years. The article also stated that it was surprising that Liz had had a baby as she was opposed to the act of sexual intercourse. This latter statement was in fact false, but could reasonably have been interpreted from public statements made by Liz.

1. Assume Liz's mother is dead. If the estate of Liz's mother sues *Journal*, *Journal* will win because

    (A) Liz's mother was a public figure.

    (B) Liz's mother is now dead.

    (C) it reported that the story was just a rumor.

    (D) Liz's mother was married at the time of Liz's birth.

2. If Star sues *Journal* for libel, he will lose even if the statement is false

    (A) provided that he is still considered a public figure.

    (B) because Liz is a public figure.

    (C) if he cannot show that *Journal* was at least negligent with regard to the truth of the rumor.

    (D) if he cannot show substantial damages.

3. If Liz sues *Journal* for libel due to the statement about her being homosexual, the probable result is that she will

    (A) lose because *Journal's* error was not reckless.

    (B) win because the statement was in fact false.

    (C) lose because she openly admitted giving birth to a child.

    (D) win because only statements made about her public life are protected.

ANSWERS TO THE MULTIPLE CHOICE QUESTIONS

Answer to Question 1.

(B) is correct.

Neither privacy nor defamation actions can be maintained if the subject was deceased at the time of publication. Thus, B is the correct answer. There are no facts to support the assertion in A, but her status as a public figure would be irrelevant due to the fact that she is deceased. C and D are clearly wrong since neither reason would preclude a defamation or privacy action.

Answer to Question 2.

(C) is correct.

A is not the best answer since it suggests that Star will lose only if he is a public figure. While it is true that Star would have a tougher time as a public figure who has to prove "actual malice," Star could still lose even if he is considered a private figure. Because the subject matter of the libel is of public concern, even if Star is a private figure, the First Amendment prohibits liability for defamation without some showing of fault. Thus, C is correct. Liz's status is irrelevant here so B is incorrect. D is wrong because there is no legal requirement in a libel action that the plaintiff establish "substantial damages."

Answer to Question 3.

(A) is correct.

B is wrong since falsity alone is not a sufficient basis for liability. C is wrong since truth as a defense requires truth of all defamatory statements. D is arguable, but it is dubious that statements about Liz's sex-related views fall outside the public figure privilege. If the statement does fall within the public figure privilege, the privilege can be defeated only by knowing falsity or reckless disregard of truth because Liz is a public figure. Thus, A is the best answer.

B. INVASION OF THE RIGHT OF PRIVACY. [§ 794]

There are four distinct torts encompassed by the label "invasion of privacy." They are (a) **intrusion;** (b) **misappropriation of personality;** (c) **disclosure of private facts;** and (d) **"false light" privacy.**

1. Intrusion. [§ 795]

The **intrusion** branch of privacy arises when the plaintiff's **right to solitude** is invaded by an unconsented and unwarranted act by defendant.

a. Nature of Intrusion. [§ 796]

The intrusion must actually violate the plaintiff's right to privacy or seclusion in a way that would be **objectionable to a person of reasonable sensibilities.** Thus, a person staring at another who is waiting for a bus might be annoying, but is not, without more, liable for intrusion.

b. Methods. [§ 797]

Normally, intrusion takes the form of improper surveillance, such as peeking through windows, listening at doors, rummaging through personal effects, or even electronic eavesdropping. However, **constant annoyances** (as by persistent and unwanted telephone calls) may suffice.

c. Need Not Discover Offensive Facts. [§ 798]

Since the essence of the tort is the psychological distress caused by the loss of the right to be left alone, it is not necessary that the defendant learn anything embarrassing or "private" about the plaintiff or disclose or publish information or private facts improperly acquired.

2. Commercial Misappropriation. [§ 799]

When the plaintiff's name, picture, or personality is used by another for some **commercial benefit** without consent, many jurisdictions will uphold an action for invasion of privacy. **In these cases the courts are not technically protecting privacy per se, but are instead protecting the commercial interest a person has in the use of his name and personality and the exclusive right to permit others to benefit from them.** In fact, in these cases the plaintiff is not complaining about the public exposure; rather she is seeking compensation for that exposure.

a. Use Must Be of Commercial Nature. [§ 800]

For purposes of this type of invasion of privacy, the name, picture, or personality of the plaintiff must be used by the defendant for a **primarily commercial purpose.** Thus, photographs and stories in newspapers and magazines as part of a news story are not actionable under this version of the tort even if they may indirectly help to sell newspapers and magazines.

> **(1) Example. [§ 801]** Flash, a photographer for Outside Sports Magazine, takes a picture of Reggie Slugger, a star baseball player, which is printed in the magazine. Since Reggie is drinking an Offbrand Cola, Offbrand uses the same picture in its advertisements. Even if Reggie did not consent, there was no misappropriation by Outside Sports if the picture merely illustrates an article on Reggie or his team or sport. Offbrand, however, is clearly liable for its use if the photo is being used to sell its soda.

b. Need Not Be a Celebrity. [§802]

While the name or likeness of a celebrity is normally of much greater commercial value than that of an "ordinary" person, the plaintiff does not need to be famous or even well-known to recover for commercial misappropriation.

3. Disclosure of Private Facts ("True Privacy"). [§ 803]

The **disclosure of private facts** version of invasion of privacy (often called "true privacy") consists of **disclosure** (usually in the mass media) of **non-public information** in such a way as to **offend a reasonable person's sensibilities.**

a. "Private" Facts. [§ 804]

Unlike intrusion, "true privacy" requires that the disclosure be of facts which a **reasonable person** would wish to keep private due to the embarrassment or other injury that disclosure would create. Further, the facts must have in fact been kept private by the plaintiff.

b. Publication and "Of and Concerning." [§ 805]

In true privacy actions (and in false light privacy actions (discussed in §§ 811–817, as well)), the plaintiff must show publication and that it is "of and concerning" the plaintiff. These elements seem to be handled by analogy to the law of defamation.

c. Defenses. [§ 806]

(1) Public Record and Public Acts. [§ 807]

As a general rule, the defendant has an absolute privilege to report matters of public record (e.g., conviction of a crime) or matters that happened in public.

(2) Newsworthiness. [§ 808]

The concept of **newsworthiness** is the rock on which most true privacy claims have foundered because the courts have been concerned with unduly interfering with the dissemination of ideas, thoughts, and news. Thus, where there is a legitimate public interest in the subject matter, no privacy action will lie. If information appeals solely to morbid curiosity, it is not newsworthy.

(a) Waiver or Consent Unnecessary. [§ 809]

Some cases have held that public figures waive the right of privacy by assuming public notoriety. The newsworthiness concept, however, does **not** rest upon waiver or consent, and even a private person involuntarily caught up in a newsworthy event has no cause of action based upon disclosure of his relationship to the matter.

(b) Persons and Events No Longer Newsworthy. [§ 810]

The issue that has most clearly split the courts is that presented when there is publicity given to a person who was clearly newsworthy in the past but who is no longer remembered. Courts allowing recovery have stressed the legitimacy of the plaintiff's desire for solitude, especially if the disclosure is harmful. Courts disallowing recovery have emphasized the difficulties involved in deciding when something is no longer within the sphere of legitimate public interest and the possible adverse impact on First Amendment rights.

4. False Light Privacy. [§ 811]

As indicated, publication of true and newsworthy facts is not actionable. However, even a newsworthy, technically true disclosure may be actionable if it puts the plaintiff in an objectionable **false light.**

> **a.   Example. [§ 812]** Dick uses a photograph of Pat to illustrate a newspaper article on Democrats. The article includes the caption "Pat, a typical Democrat, at a political rally." Pat has been placed in a false light if she is in fact not a Democrat and was merely walking by the site of the rally on her way to lunch; the fact that Pat was in fact at the scene of the rally is not enough to justify the misleading implication of the picture and caption.

b.   Objectionable to Reasonable Person. [§ 813]

As with all of the other torts which give redress for injury to feelings, the statement must be objectionable to a reasonable person who is not unduly sensitive.

c.   Nature of the Defendant's Fault. [§ 814]

As a matter of First Amendment privilege, the statement of the defendant must **deliberately** place the plaintiff in a false light or must be made with a **reckless disregard** of the truthfulness of the implication, at least when the plaintiff is a public official or public figure. It is likely the fault standard here parallels the law of defamation so that a lesser standard will be imposed when a private person's privacy has been invaded.

d. Relationship to Defamation. [§ 815]

The statement which places the defendant in a false light need not be defamatory, although it often is. Note that in the example about Pat in § 812, she would have no basis for a defamation action because being falsely called a Democrat is not defamatory. She may, however, have an action for false light if the statement can be construed as objectionable.

e. Statement Need Not Be False. [§ 816]

Unlike defamation, where the statement must be false, the statement which gives rise to the false light privacy action may be true. This distinction is not as crucial as it may seem, however, since truth with regard to defamation depends on the **thrust** of the statement which is closely related to the implication that creates a false light. Accordingly, there is often a blurry line between an action for defamation and false light privacy actions.

f. Injury Relates to Plaintiff, Not Third Parties. [§ 817]

As discussed above, the gist of defamation is the effect of the statement on third parties. In false light situations, on the other hand, the plaintiff need not show any adverse reaction by others so long as he, as a reasonable person, was offended by the statement complained of.

PRIVACY

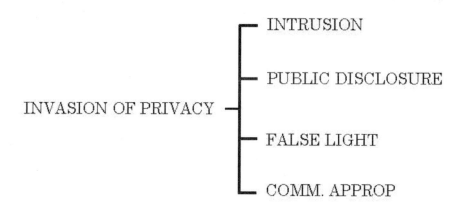

INVASION OF PRIVACY
- INTRUSION
- PUBLIC DISCLOSURE
- FALSE LIGHT
- COMM. APPROP

CHAPTER VI

OTHER BASES OF TORT LIABILITY

A. NUISANCE. [§ 818]

A person has a duty in the use of her land to avoid unreasonable interference with the use or enjoyment of the land of others. Violation of this duty is known as **nuisance.** Though a tort, this topic is often covered in the class on Property.

1. Nature of the Interference. [§ 819]

A nuisance does not require a trespass, since a variety of acts outside the land can interfere with the quiet enjoyment of land. Typically, a nuisance results from obnoxious noise, sights, or smells on the defendant's land which are easily perceived from the land of others. In addition, use of the land for certain objectionable purposes (e.g., operating a casino or house of prostitution) is generally defined as a nuisance.

2. Interference Must Be Unreasonable. [§ 820]

To be actionable, the interference must be **unreasonable.**

a. Determining "Unreasonableness"—Balancing of Interests. [§ 821]

When an action in nuisance is sustained, the **defendant's** right to use and enjoy his property is generally restricted. Consequently, **there must be some balancing of interests to determine whose interests should prevail.** Thus, the interference caused by the defendant must be "unreasonable" in the sense that the **plaintiff's harm outweighs any justification that the defendant may have in its creation.** A balancing of hardships is especially important in analyzing the propriety of injunctive relief (See §§ 822–826).

b. Plaintiff Must Be Reasonable Person. [§ 822]

Nuisance requires that the condition caused by the defendant be such that it would be offensive to a **reasonable person** (i.e., one who is not unduly sensitive).

3. **Intent. [§ 823]**

A nuisance is generally the result of intentional conduct, but negligent interference with use of the land in an abnormal or highly unusual manner may also suffice.

4. **Standing to Sue: Private versus Public Nuisance. [§ 824]**

   a. **Private Nuisance. [§ 825]**

   A **private nuisance** is an unreasonable interference by the defendant with the interests of the plaintiff in the use and enjoyment of the plaintiff's land. The tort is considered to be personal to the plaintiff, who must be either the owner or occupant of the realty disturbed by the defendant.

   b. **Public Nuisance. [§ 826]**

   A **public nuisance** relates to an act or a condition caused by the defendant which obstructs, inconveniences, or causes damage **to the public in general.** A public nuisance affects the community at large by affecting use of public property or offending the public sense of values.

   (1) **Proper Plaintiff. [§ 827]**

   Normally, an action based upon a public nuisance is brought by the state, but such an action may be brought by a **private individual** when the plaintiff has suffered special damages over and above the ordinary damage caused to the general public (i.e., he has standing to sue for a private nuisance). **Some** recent cases dealing with the issue of standing, stressing concern for environmental injury, suggest that a public nuisance action should be permitted by **any individual affected by the nuisance,** even if she cannot show actionable injury to her own property.

5. **Remedies. [§ 828]**

   a. **Damages. [§ 829]**

   The plaintiff may be awarded actual damages for the losses created by the defendant's nuisance.

   b. **Injunction. [§ 830]**

   When the nuisance is of a continuing nature, the plaintiff may seek **an injunction** to abate the nuisance. In order to obtain the equitable relief of an injunction, all the prerequisites for equitable jurisdiction must be established.

(1) **Inadequacy of Legal Remedy. [§ 831]**

The plaintiff's remedies at law must be inadequate. Legal remedies are normally inadequate in nuisance cases, however, because it is difficult to measure the degree of harm in such cases and the injury is frequently irreparable.

(2) **Continuing Nature. [§ 832]**

An injunction will not be granted unless the nuisance is of a continuing nature; it may not be merely an isolated or temporary nuisance. (The continuing nature of the nuisance creates an additional reason for finding the legal remedy inadequate, since a multiplicity of suits would be required to make the plaintiff whole.)

(3) **Balance the Equities. [§ 833]**

The equity court must balance the equities to ensure that the injunction will not cause an undue hardship upon the defendant. Included in this balance is whether the plaintiff "came to the nuisance" (i.e., were the defendant's acts that are now in issue going on at the time the plaintiff bought his land).

(4) **Significance of Trespass. [§ 834]**

Although, as mentioned above, a trespass is not necessary for there to be a nuisance, **an injunction is much more likely to be granted when the defendant's conduct constitutes a trespass.**

Multiple Choice Questions 1–3 are based on the following fact situation.

Dell recently moved into a neighborhood zoned for small business and residential use and opened up a hamburger stand. For many years, Mr. and Mrs. Poe had lived across the street from where Dell's stand now is located. Since Dell opened his stand, the traffic has been very heavy, forcing the Poes to keep their children away from the front yard. In addition, there is loud music being played until 2:00 a.m., and litter from Dell's stand is frequently blown onto their land.

The Poes sue to enjoin Dell's operation of his stand as a private nuisance.

1. The fact that the area was zoned for small businesses

   (A) requires the court to find for Dell.

   (B) requires the court to find for Dell if the ordinance is reasonable.

CHAPTER VI

(C) is relevant to resolving the dispute.

(D) is irrelevant to resolving the dispute.

2. The fact that the Poes lived in the area before Dell's stand was opened

    (A) requires the court to find for the Poes.

    (B) requires the court to find for the Poes if they could not have foreseen the opening of a hamburger stand.

    (C) is relevant to resolving the dispute.

    (D) is irrelevant to resolving the dispute.

3. Which of the following is Dell's best defense?

    (A) The Poes are not the only ones injured by his actions.

    (B) He is not responsible for the traffic, noise, or litter.

    (C) Commercial rights are to be favored over private domestic rights.

    (D) A complete injunction upon his operation of the ham burger stand would be unfair.

ANSWERS TO THE MULTIPLE CHOICE QUESTIONS

Answer to Question 1.

(C) is correct.

Zoning laws are relevant to the determination of nuisance. Conformity of the alleged nuisance to zoning is neither irrelevant nor conclusive. Thus, A, B and D are incorrect statements of law.

Answer to Question 2.

(C) is correct.

No longer is so-called "coming to the nuisance" determinative. That the plaintiff's ownership preceded the alleged nuisance is neither irrelevant nor conclusive. Thus, A, B and D are incorrect statements of current law. The use of land prior to the alleged nuisance is relevant, however.

Answer to Question 3.

(D) is correct.

A is wrong since a private nuisance may be actionable even if there are other plaintiffs who have standing to complain of the nuisance. B is both factually and legally incorrect. C is an inaccurate statement of law. While the defense may not succeed, D is the only plausible answer.

B. TORTS TO ECONOMIC INTERESTS. [§ 835]

1. Disparagement (or Injurious Falsehood). [§ 836]

An injured person or business may maintain an action for **disparagement** (also known as **injurious falsehood**) when another's false statements cause an interference with the plaintiff's economic interests. Disparagement is defined as: (a) the **publication** (b) of a **false assertion of fact** (c) injuring the plaintiff's **economic interests** (d) with **improper intent**.

a. Act. [§ 837]

The necessary act consists of publishing a false assertion of fact.

(1) Publication. [§ 838]

"Publication," as in the defamation context, is a term of art meaning that a third party must hear and understand the statement.

(2) Falsity. [§ 839]

Proof of falsity is an element of the prima facie case and must always be proven **by the plaintiff.**

(3) Assertion of Fact. [§ 840]

The false statement must be an **assertion of fact. Opinions** and **advertising "puffing"** are thus **not actionable.**

(4) Protected Interests. [§ 841]

Normally, the falsehood relates to the quality of the plaintiff's goods or other property, or to his ownership of property. However, statements which allege that the owner of a business is dead or that his employees are incompetent, or even statements causing such non-commercial loss as being subjected to deportation, are actionable as disparagement.

b. Intent: At Least Reckless as to Truth and Injury. [§ 842]

The Restatement Second now makes it clear that disparagement is not a strict liability tort. Generally, the defendant must know that her statement is false or act with reckless disregard for the truth **and** she must intend to harm the plaintiff's economic interest or be reckless with regard to the damage that may result.

c. **Injury: Special Damages Required. [§ 843]**

In **every** disparagement action the plaintiff must prove **special** damages—actual pecuniary injury resulting from the response of third parties to the false statement.

d. **Defenses. [§ 844]**

The absolute and qualified privileges discussed in the Defamation section of this outline (See §§ 729–762) are all applicable to an action in disparagement. **Note, however, that truth is not a defense, but rather falsity is an element of the plaintiff's cause of action.**

> **(1) Example. [§ 845]** Connie Customer asks Drew, owner of Drew's Record Emporium, if they have a certain compact disk in stock. When Drew responds that they do not, Connie asks if Paul's Music Hut down the street might have it. Drew knows Paul does have the CD, but, because Paul is a competitor, tells Connie that Paul does not carry it. Paul could recover against Drew for disparagement.

2. **Interference with Contractual Relations. [§ 846]**

The plaintiff may recover in tort if the defendant intentionally interferes with an existing contractual relationship involving the plaintiff. The tort requires: (a) an **act by the defendant** (b) **with knowledge** of a contract (c) for the **purpose of interference** with (d) the **contractual rights of the plaintiff.**

a. **Act. [§ 847]**

In order to be liable for interfering with contractual relations, the defendant must perform an act which prevents completion of a contract **or** creates difficulties, making the contract less capable or likely of being performed.

b. **Intent: Knowledge and Purpose. [§ 848]**

The defendant must have **actual knowledge** of the existing contractual relationship **and** he must have acted with the **purpose** to interfere with that relationship. If the defendant did not know there was an existing contract, there is no liability.

c. **Injury: Substantial Difficulties. [§ 849]**

The conduct of the defendant must be effective at least insofar as it creates **some substantial difficulties** with regard to an actual contractual relationship to which the plaintiff is a party; **it is not required that the contract actually be breached, however.** Note that it is the relationship, not the contract, which is being protected. Thus, an action lies even when the defendant interferes with a contract which could not have been enforced anyway because of **technical defect** (e.g., it failed to comply with the Statute of Frauds). The defendant will not be liable where the contract is illegal, against public policy, or is a contract to marry, however.

d. **Defenses: Proper Means to Attain Justifiable End. [§ 850]**

(1) **Act in Public Interest. [§ 851]**

The defendant's interference with contractual rights is privileged when she acts in the public interest. Of course, the defendant is only privileged to use proper means— persuasion is proper but fraud or threat of violence is not.

> **(a) Example. [§ 852]** Ponti owns a beautiful movie house that is losing money. Ponti contracts with Leveler to tear the building down. De Mille may be privileged to interfere with this contract if the theater is a legitimate public landmark and he is merely seeking a delay so that he can try to convince the city to acquire the theater by eminent domain.

(2) **Protection of Defendant's Own Interests. [§ 853]**

The defendant may also defend by showing that the plaintiff's contract would interfere with a legitimate interest of the defendant. That the defendant was acting with a purely competitive purpose will not be a defense.

> **(a) Example. [§ 854]** Dino needs widgets and contacts XenaCo knowing that XenaCo is contractually bound to provide all widgets to Porti. Dino offers XenaCo double the contract price and XenaCo breaches. Porti may bring a successful action against Dino even though Dino was acting out of his own competitive interests.

> **(b) Example. [§ 855]** Puff contracts with a wrecking company to tear down a building. Dough is privileged to interfere with the contract if he has a colorable claim to title in the building.

e. **Remedies. [§ 856]**

A wide range of remedies is available for this tort. Under a proper showing, an **injunction** against the intentional and future conduct of the defendant may be granted, even without a showing of actual pecuniary damages. Also, damages— including **consequential damages**—unforeseen expenses, mental suffering, damage to reputation, and even punitive damages—may be awarded in appropriate cases.

3. Interference with Prospective Economic Advantage. [§ 857]

Under certain circumstances, prospective economic advantages may be protected even in the absence of a contract. This tort is closely akin to the action for interference with contractual rights, and the basic elements are the same. Because there is no existing contract to protect, the defendant will be afforded far greater leeway in conduct, which ultimately interferes with the plaintiff's **prospective** advantages than when the plaintiff has an existing contract.

a. Not Limited to Commercial Prospects. [§ 858]

Historically, recovery in tort for interference with prospective advantage was limited to purely commercial prospects. Recently, however, courts have allowed recovery in non-commercial areas as well, as when the defendant has interfered with the plaintiff's expected receipt of a gift or inheritance; in the non-commercial area, however, the expectation must be highly probable.

b. Malicious Intent. [§ 859]

In most cases, the defendant must not only have intended to interfere with the plaintiff's known prospective advantage, but must have a **malicious or spiteful intent** to justify recovery. The defendant is not liable if he acts solely for competitive purposes. When there is some **special relationship** between the parties (such as a lawyer-client relationship or when the defendant is a common carrier), however, negligence **may** be enough.

C. MALICIOUS PROSECUTION AND ABUSE OF PROCESS. [§ 860]

Malicious prosecution and abuse of process are related, yet distinct, torts.

1. Malicious Prosecution. [§ 861]

Malicious prosecution requires: (a) **initiation of a criminal or civil proceeding by the defendant;** (b) **without probable cause** and (c) **with malicious intent** which (d) **terminates in favor of the defendant therein** (i.e., the plaintiff in the malicious prosecution action) (e) **resulting in actual damage.**

a. **Act. [§ 862]**

The defendant must **initiate** or **cause the initiation** of criminal or civil proceedings.

(1) Criminal Proceedings. [§ 863]

There can be no malicious prosecution if no official action is taken. If the decision to prosecute is made by someone other than the defendant, the defendant is liable only if he **knew** that the information that he supplied to the authorities was false **and the authorities conducted no independent investigation.**

(2) Civil Proceedings. [§ 864]

Originally, malicious prosecution was inapplicable to civil proceedings, but a majority of courts have extended the tort to institution of such actions.

b. **Intent: Improper Motive and No Probable Cause. [§ 865]**

For malicious prosecution, the defendant must act **both** with malice and without probable cause.

(1) Improper Motive. [§ 866]

The act must be done for an improper motive. Thus, in this sense, "malice" exists if a criminal proceeding is instituted with some purpose other than bringing the offender to justice, or if a civil proceeding is instituted for some reason other than adjudication of the controversy. **Actual ill will or spite is unnecessary.**

(2) Lack of Probable Cause. [§ 867]

An action for malicious prosecution based upon a prior **criminal** charge may be successfully maintained only if the defendant acted without probable cause to believe that the present plaintiff is guilty of the charges filed (i.e., that it is more likely than not that she was guilty); **if the defendant acted with probable cause, there can be no cause of action for malicious prosecution even if she acted solely for spite.** Lesser grounds for belief that the action was justified will be a defense when the earlier action was **civil** in character, but there still must be some belief that the suit had a reasonable chance of succeeding.

c. **Result: Termination in Favor of Present Plaintiff. [§ 868]**

The previous proceeding **must** have been resolved in favor of the malicious prosecution plaintiff in a manner consistent **with his innocence** (i.e., not solely due to a procedural technicality).

(1) **Criminal Proceedings. [§ 869]**

Conviction in the criminal proceeding is a bar to the action, **even if obtained by perjury or fraud**. Similarly, termination of the previous action which leaves open the issue of guilt, such as a **negotiated plea**, is insufficient to permit a subsequent action for malicious prosecution.

(2) **Civil Proceedings. [§ 870]**

When the allegedly improper prior action was civil, termination in favor of the present plaintiff in the malicious prosecution suit must be shown unless the proceedings were ex parte (i.e., there was no opportunity to contest the facts). Again, termination by settlement or compromise prevents one from maintaining an action for malicious prosecution.

d. **Actual Injury. [§ 871]**

In theory, an action for malicious prosecution cannot be maintained in the absence of proof of damage. In practice, however, in the case of malicious abuse of **criminal** process, the action may be maintained without pleading or proof of any particular damage, as it is presumed that damages necessarily follow. Once the action is maintainable, damages recoverable include both pecuniary loss (e.g., attorney's fees) and injury to reputation and feelings. Punitive damages may also be awarded.

e. **Defenses. [§ 872]**

(1) **Actual Guilt or Liability. [§ 873]**

Proof to the court adjudicating the malicious prosecution action of the actual guilt or fault of the plaintiff for the offense or civil wrong charged in the prior proceeding is a complete defense, even if the present plaintiff was found not guilty or free from liability in the prior action.

(2) **Separation of Powers and Immunity. [§ 874]**

Prosecuting attorneys and other law enforcement officers have broad discretion with regard to acts within their official capacity and courts are extremely reluctant to interfere with the manner in which a co-equal branch of government carries out its duties. In addition, the doctrine of sovereign (or governmental) immunity (See § 938) may effectively bar an action for malicious prosecution against governmental officials.

2. Abuse of Process. [§ 875]

Abuse of process requires: (a) **a misuse of legal process** (b) **for an ulterior purpose** (c) **which causes actual injury.**

a. Act. [§ 876]

Like malicious prosecution, the act necessary to support an action for abuse of process is the initiation or causing the initiation of a civil or criminal proceeding.

b. Intent: Ulterior Motive. [§ 877]

Abuse of process is the civil equivalent of extortion in the criminal law. **The gist of the action is use of legal proceedings for an ulterior purpose.** This is similar to the notion of malice in malicious prosecution.

Since the tort is for misuse of otherwise legitimate process, there is no requirement of termination in the accused's favor.

c. Injury. [§ 878]

Actual injury will not be presumed and must be proven with reasonable certainty.

d. Defenses. [§ 879]

As stated above, the fact that the party now suing for abuse of process lost in the prior action is not a defense to this cause of action.

D. DECEIT (OR FRAUD). [§ 880]

To maintain an action based on a claim of **deceit** (also known as fraud or misrepresentation) the following elements must be established: (a) there must be a **misrepresentation by the defendant of a past or present material fact;** (b) the defendant must be acting either with **knowledge of the falsity or with reckless disregard as to the falsity of the representation (called "scienter");** (c) the defendant must have the **specific intent to induce reliance** on the part of the plaintiff; (d) **the plaintiff must, in fact, have relied upon the misrepresentation;** (e) the plaintiff's **reliance must have been justifiable under the circumstances;** and (f) **the plaintiff must have been damaged** by his reliance on the misrepresentation.

1. Act. [§ 881]

Not every misrepresentation of fact is actionable.

a. Materiality. [§ 882]

The misrepresentation must be of a **material** fact—a fact which a reasonable person would have considered in making the relevant decision.

b. Past or Present Fact. [§ 883]

The defendant must misrepresent a **past or present fact.**

c. Promise with No Intent to Perform. [§ 884]

Deceit may be predicated upon a **promise to act in the future** only if the promise is accompanied by **a present intention not to perform.** The defendant's misrepresentation of his state of mind is sufficient to warrant an action in fraud. On the other hand, if the defendant plans on performing when he makes the promise, he is not liable for deceit if he subsequently changes his mind (although he may be liable for conversion or some other tort).

d. Problem of Omissions. [§ 885]

As a general rule, a failure to disclose a pertinent and material fact is **not** sufficient to show fraud.

(1) Exception 1: Duty to Disclose. [§ 886]

When the defendant is under an **affirmative duty** to make a disclosure, as when he is **specifically asked** about the matter or there is a **special relationship** between the parties, his failure to disclose will be actionable in deceit.

(2) Exception 2: Active Concealment. [§ 887]

If the defendant **actively conceals** a material fact, his concealment may be construed as an affirmative misrepresentation and not a non-disclosure.

(3) Opinions. [§ 888]

An expression of an opinion, general recommendation, or "seller's talk" may not be held to be a statement of fact. Usually, however, these factors are analyzed as an issue of whether the plaintiff's reliance was reasonable.

2. Intent: Scienter. [§ 889]

Deceit may be committed only if the defendant **knows** of the falsity of his representation or acts in **reckless disregard** for the truth or falsity of that representation **and** when he has the specific intent to have the plaintiff act upon the facts as he represents them. (For negligent misrepresentation, see § 242.)

> **a.   Example. [§ 890]** Dinah tells Prince that the corn she is selling is Grade A when it is really Grade B. Dinah, in a hurry, misread a form and believed that she was telling the truth. She is not liable for misrepresentation because she lacked scienter. She may have been negligent, but she did not know of the falsity of her statement, nor did she consciously disregard the risk of falsity.

3. Result: Reasonable Reliance. [§ 891]

The plaintiff must have **reasonably relied** upon the misrepresentation.

a.   Fact versus Opinion. [§ 892]

In determining whether the plaintiff's reliance upon a misrepresentation of fact was reasonable, courts distinguish between **misrepresentation of fact** and **opinions**. Normally, representations made in opinion form (e.g., "This is the best car on the road," "In my opinion you will have no problem with this car for five years," etc.) may not be the basis for reasonable reliance. **An exception to this rule is if the defendant has superior knowledge, skill, or expertise in the area which would induce a reasonable person to rely upon the defendant's opinion.** Thus, while an opinion regarding the state of the law by a salesperson is an opinion upon which the plaintiff could not reasonably rely, the same statement may be an actionable deceit if made by a judge, lawyer, or public official who ought to have knowledge of the law.

4. Injury. [§ 893]

In order to support a claim for deceit the plaintiff must prove with reasonable certainty that his reliance caused **actual injury;** nominal damages will not be awarded. Whether the plaintiff recovers out-of-pocket loss or the loss of his bargain depends on the jurisdiction and the equities of the case.

5. Defenses. [§ 894]

There are no special defenses to an action for deceit—the ordinary defense is an attempt to negate any or all of the required elements of the action. Attempts to waive liability by a contractual provision, such as "defendant disclaims all liability for misrepresentations," are generally deemed to be void and have no effect.

CHAPTER VII

CONCEPTS RELEVANT TO ALL TORTS

A. VICARIOUS LIABILITY. [§ 895]

In certain contexts, a person will be held liable in tort for the wrongful conduct of another simply because of the relationship.

1. Vicarious Liability in the Family. [§ 896]

a. Husband No Longer Liable for Wife's Torts. [§ 897]

At common law a **husband** was liable for the torts of his wife committed either before or during marriage, but this liability is no longer recognized today.

b. Parental Liability for Child's Torts. [§ 898]

In general, parents are not liable for the torts of their child merely because of their parenthood (although many states have adopted statutes which impose vicarious liability for torts of the child, with a liability limitation). Nevertheless, virtually all jurisdictions will impose liability when (a) the parent **entrusts the child with an instrumentality** which, because of the child's lack of age and judgment, may become a source of danger to others, (b) if the child committing the tort is **acting in a relationship of servant** of the parent, (c) the parent **knows of the child's wrongdoing and consents to it or sanctions it,** or (d) the parent **fails to exercise control** over the child although he knows, or in the exercise of due care should have known, injury to another was a probable consequence. In these instances the parent is directly, not vicariously, liable.

> **(1) Example. [§ 899]** Sal, a four-year-old boy, had a well-known tendency to attack strangers. D'Angelo, Sal's father, hired Ellis to babysit for Sal, but did not warn her of Sal's habits. Sal knocked Ellis down, breaking several bones. D'Angelo was negligent in failing to warn Ellis or otherwise protect her from Sal and is thus liable for the injuries suffered by Ellis. *Ellis v. D'Angelo*, 253 P.2d 675 (Cal. 1953).

2. Ownership of a Vehicle. [§ 900]

a. Negligent Entrustment. [§ 901]

An owner of a vehicle is liable for injuries caused by a person to whom he has entrusted the vehicle when the owner **knows or should know of the negligent propensities** of the one he has allowed to use his vehicle.

> **(1) Example. [§ 902]** Owner lends his automobile to Driver. Owner is aware that Driver has a habit of drinking before driving. Owner will be held liable for injuries caused by Driver's intoxication. Note that Owner would not be liable without negligent conduct by **both** himself (in entrusting) and Driver (in driving).

b. Family Purpose Doctrine. [§ 903]

An owner of an automobile is not only liable for the negligent acts of those he negligently entrusts with his vehicle, but he is also liable for the negligent acts of members of his family when such person is using the automobile for **family purposes**, including any use for pleasure or enjoyment.

c. Owner Consent Statutes. [§ 904]

Many states have adopted **owner's consent statutes** which impose liability on an owner of an automobile for the negligence of **any person** who is driving that automobile with the owner's consent.

(1) Presumptions. [§ 905]

There is a rebuttable presumption that the vehicle was driven with the consent of the owner, and substantial evidence is required to overcome this presumption. There is also a **conclusive** presumption that the person whose name is on the registration certificate is the owner of the vehicle.

(2) Restrictions on Use and Manner of Operation. [§ 906]

Problems arise when the owner has put some restriction on the use or manner of operation of the vehicle by the driver, and the driver violates these restrictions.

(a) Restrictions as to Use. [§ 907]

Restrictions as to the **use** of the automobile will relieve the owner from liability for injuries resulting from the unauthorized conduct, as such conduct is not "with permission."

> **(i) Example. [§ 908]** Dawn allows Friend to drive Dawn's car only during daylight and only within the city limits. Dawn will not be liable for injuries caused by Friend's operation of the vehicle at night or when Friend was driving to a distant city. Insignificant variations, however, will not shield the owner from liability.

(b) Restrictions as to Manner of Operation. [§ 909]

Restrictions as to the **manner of operation** (e.g., "Don't drive more than 35 miles per hour"), however, will not relieve the owner from liability.

3. Vicarious Liability in the Employment Setting. [§ 910]

a. Preliminary Definitions. [§ 911]

(1) Master. [§ 912]

The **master** is the person who hires another to do a specific task or series of tasks. This odd term still is used as a master will not always be an employer.

(2) Servant or Independent Contractor. [§ 913]

(a) Servant. [§ 914]

A **servant** is a person employed by the master and who is obligated to follow the instructions of the master as to his **physical actions.** A servant is usually, but not always, an employee.

(b) Independent Contractor. [§ 915]

An **independent contractor** is hired by the master to accomplish specific goals, but who is free to determine the manner of performance.

(c) Distinction. [§ 916]

The key distinction between the servant and the independent contractor is the master's **right** to control the physical acts or manner of performance of the employee, not whether she in fact exercises such control.

(d) Relevant Factors. [§ 917]

In determining whether an employee is a servant or an independent contractor, courts will consider the following factors:

(i) Supervision. [§ 918]

If the work is of a type which is customarily closely supervised, the requisite right to control is presumed to exist and the employee is a servant. If no supervision by the master is normally given, the employee is an independent contractor.

(ii) Continuity of Service. [§ 919]

If the person serves on a **continuous basis** so that the compensation can be viewed as a salary or wages, the employee is likely to be held to be a servant. On the other hand, if the person performs work intermittently and is paid by the job, the relationship is usually considered one with an independent contractor.

(iii) Employer's Facilities and Instruments. [§ 920]

A presumption of right to control arises whenever the employer supplies the facilities and the instruments for the work performed. On the other hand, if the worker uses his own tools and the work is performed away from the employer's place of business, the relationship is most likely a non-servant one.

(iv) Employee's Service to Others. [§ 921]

If the employee makes himself available to provide the service or skill to many unrelated parties, he will not be deemed a servant unless one of the other indicia of control are present.

(v) Level of Skill. [§ 922]

The more menial the skill involved in performing the task, the more likely that the court will find there is a master-servant relationship. Individuals performing tasks requiring a particular skill or professional expertise are generally deemed to be independent contractors.

b.   **Liability of Master for Acts of Servants: Respondeat Superior. [§ 923]**

The master is vicariously liable for the torts of his servant committed within the scope of the employment. This is known as the doctrine of **respondeat superior.** The policy behind respondeat superior liability is that the employer should bear the risks of the enterprise and is in a position to spread the losses of the activities.

c.   **Scope of Employment. [§ 924]**

The master is only liable for the torts committed by his servant **in the scope of the servant's employment.**

(1) **Intentional Torts. [§ 925]**

Generally, the commission of intentional torts is held to be outside the scope of authority. The most important exceptions appear below.

(a) **Assault and Battery. [§ 926]**

An assault or battery committed by the servant is within the scope of his employment if the servant's duties are such that the behavior could be expected. Thus, the master will be liable for the assault or battery committed by a servant employed as a bar bouncer, repossession agent, or security guard since the use of force can be expected by these types of employees.

(b) **Fraudulent Representations. [§ 927]**

Whether the agent's fraudulent representation may be asserted against his master depends upon the type of relief the plaintiff seeks. When the plaintiff seeks to recover **damages** from the master for the servant's fraudulent representations, the plaintiff must establish that the servant was authorized to make the representation. On the other hand, when the plaintiff seeks **rescission** of a contract entered into on the basis of the agent's fraudulent representations, relief is typically granted regardless of whether the agent was acting within the scope of his employment and regardless of whether the agent was authorized to make those representations.

(2) Geographical Departures: Frolic or Detour. [§ 928]

No coherent approach has been developed to resolve whether a tort committed by a servant while departing from the natural or customary geographical course for performing his master's work takes the tort outside of the scope of employment. The tendency among courts has been to deem the tort committed within the scope of employment if the departure was a mere **detour** which could be expected, but outside the scope of employment if the departure was so unforeseeable that it could be considered a **frolic** on the part of the servant. Considerations include time and space—the duration and distance of the deviation from the assigned route or task. Some courts use an enterprise liability theory considering whether the servant's tortious conduct was an inherent risk of the enterprise.

(3) Incidental Acts. [§ 929]

The master generally will not be liable for torts committed by the servant's incidental acts (i.e., those not directly related to performing the assigned task). However, if the incidental act is so dangerous given the nature of the required performance that the master should have prohibited the act entirely, that act is within the scope of employment.

d. Liability of Master for Acts of Independent Contractors. [§ 930]

The general rule is that an employer is not liable for the torts committed by independent contractors even if they arise within the scope of employment. **The employer will be liable, however, if he had a non-delegable duty.**

(1) Inherently Dangerous Work. [§ 931]

An owner or general contractor may be liable for injuries sustained by third persons as the result of **excavation, demolition,** or **other inherently dangerous work** even though such work has been delegated to an independent contractor.

(2) Streets and Highways. [§ 932]

The obligation of governmental agencies to properly maintain their streets and highways is non-delegable. Thus, the government is liable for injuries caused by improper maintenance even if the work was done by an independent contractor. (Note, as discussed below, **governmental immunity** normally will not apply as such activities are ministerial, not decisional policy-making.)

(3) Other Obligations. [§ 933]

Duties of **landowners** and **manufacturers and sellers of goods** and those imposed by **contract** are non-delegable.

B. JOINT ENTERPRISES. [§ 934]

When two or more people undertake to act in concert to carry out a certain objective, they are said to be engaging in a **joint enterprise** (or joint venture). As such an arrangement is very much like a business partnership (albeit for a more limited time and/or purpose), each actor is considered an agent for the others and, as a consequence, **each is thus vicariously liable for the torts of the others committed within the scope of the enterprise.**

1. Common Purpose. [§ 935]

To be vicariously liable under the doctrine of joint enterprise, there must be some **common purpose**. While the purpose need not be for financial gain, a mere agreement to travel together to some destination is not enough.

2. Mutual Right of Control. [§ 936]

The key to the joint enterprise doctrine is that all members have an **equal right to control the manner in which the joint activities are conducted.** Thus, for example, a passenger in an automobile normally has no right to control the actions of the driver, and thus the passenger is not vicariously liable for the negligence of the driver.

C. IMMUNITY. [§ 937]

1. Governmental Immunity. [§ 938]

At common law, federal, state and local governments were immune from tort liability. Modernly, to determine whether a governmental entity is subject to liability it is important to look at what the governmental entity was doing. Where the governmental entity is engaged in an activity traditionally done by private actors (a **proprietary function**), such as running an apartment complex, it is treated the same as a private actor. Where the government entity is involved in what is typically a public sector activity that involves judgment, discretion and resource allocations (a **discretionary function**), such as determining where to place a stoplight, immunity is most commonly found. Finally, where the government entity is negligent in executing a decision that has already been made and funded (a **ministerial function**), such as negligently putting up a traffic sign backwards, tort liability will follow.

2. Charitable Immunity. [§ 939]

At common law, tort immunity was recognized for non-governmental, charitable organizations (e.g., churches, hospitals, etc.). The rationale of this rule was that since the charitable organization was working for the public good, it should be treated as a public agency. **Charitable immunity is no longer recognized in most jurisdictions;** in the others, it has been riddled with exceptions.

3. Inter-Family Immunities. [§ 940]

a. Inter-Spousal Immunity. [§ 941]

(1) Common Law. [§ 942]

At common law, a husband and wife were regarded as a single legal entity. The rule, therefore, was that neither party to the marriage could sue the other for torts committed by the other, whether the tort occurred before, during, or after the marriage.

(2) Modern View. [§ 943]

Today, either spouse may sue the other for **torts to property** (i.e., trespass, conversion, fraud, etc.). The common law rule as to **personal** torts is still followed in some jurisdictions; **in recent years, however, many states have begun to allow interspousal recovery, at least to the extent of liability insurance.**

b. Rationale. [§ 944]

The chief reason relied on by jurisdictions which retain immunity between husband and wife is that legal disputes would disrupt, and possibly destroy, the marital tranquility; also, in cases where insurance is involved, there is a possibility of collusion between the "adversary" spouses. Jurisdictions which have abolished this immunity stress that insurance is paid for and the insurance company should not avoid liability simply because the insured and the victim are married.

c. Torts Between Parent and Child. [§ 945]

At common law, actions could not be maintained for **personal** torts by a parent against his child, or by a child against his parent, during the child's minority. While **the trend** is beginning to allow actions between parent and child, at least to the extent of liability insurance, the majority still deny the action. Even at common law, **property** actions could be maintained by either.

d. **No Bar to Actions Between Siblings. [§ 946]**

The doctrine of inter-family immunity has never extended to siblings (i.e., brothers and sisters **may sue each other on** any type of claim or cause of action).

4. **Immunities in the Employment Setting. [§ 947]**

The flip side of strict liability imposed on an employer by virtue of the worker's compensation acts for employment connected injuries to the employee is an absolute immunity from a common law suit for an injury which is compensable under the act. **Note that this immunity is complete, and protects an employer from suit even if the injury is caused by wanton misconduct.** Likewise, an employee is immune from liability to his co-employee for work-connected injuries under the same act.

5. **No-Fault Automobile Insurance. [§ 948]**

In jurisdictions which have no-fault insurance systems providing for relatively full compensation of victims of automobile accidents, the common law suit against negligent drivers is generally barred except in cases of very serious injury.

D. DAMAGES. [§ 949]

While many courses in torts pay little attention to damage rules (other than the question of whether a certain type of injury must be proven as part of the prima facie case or is protected by the particular tort action in question), the following general rules apply except when this summary has pointed out special damage rules in regard to specific torts.

1. **Compensatory Damages. [§ 950]**

a. **Personal Injury. [§ 951]**

When the plaintiff is personally injured, whether or not the extent of the injury was foreseeable (See § 43 on the Egg Shell Skull Rule), he can recover for the following losses proximately caused by the defendant's tortious conduct.

b.   Loss of Earnings. [§ 952]

The plaintiff may recover for lost wages and may also recover for loss of future income when the defendant's conduct prevented the plaintiff from working.

c.   Medical Services. [§ 953]

If the plaintiff can show that medical services were made reasonably necessary because of the defendant's conduct, he may recover for: (a) **services rendered** by doctors, nurses, and hospitals; (b) **medicine, x-rays,** and similar expenses required to diagnose his injuries or effectuate a cure; and (c) **miscellaneous expenses** such as travel costs to the doctor or to places recommended by the doctor as part of treatment (e.g., the doctor sends Pam to the desert as the hot, dry air will help Pam regain her health).

d.   The Collateral Source Rule. [§ 954]

Under the collateral source rule, the fact that a plaintiff has received compensation from an outside source, such as an insurance policy, does not relieve the tortious defendant of her obligation to pay those damages. While this raises the potential for double-recovery, many insurance companies have subrogation provisions by which they can be repaid for expenditures should the insurer recover damages in a tort action. Further, many jurisdictions have limited the reach of the collateral source rule.

e.   Pain and Suffering. [§ 955]

Pain and suffering constitutes an important element of damages for which recovery is allowed in an action for personal injuries. Also, an award for **future** pain and suffering on the part of the injured person as a consequence of the injury is allowed if there is the requisite probability that such pain and suffering will result.

f.   Real Property Damages. [§ 956]

There are two alternative rules measuring damages in cases involving injury to a person's interest in **real property.** Which of these rules will be applied depends upon the jurisdiction and the equities of the particular case.

(1)   Diminution in Value. [§ 957]

The **diminution in value rule** entitles the injured party to recover the difference between the value of the real property immediately before and immediately after the injury.

(2) Cost of Repair. [§ 958]

The **cost of repair rule** entitles the injured party to recover the cost of restoring the realty to its condition immediately prior to the injury.

g. Personal Property Damages. [§ 959]

The ordinary measure of damages for **injury to personal property** is the difference between its market value immediately before and after the injury, although some courts use the "cost of repair" measure of damages. In cases of **destruction of the property,** its market value at the time of destruction is the measure of damages.

2. Punitive Damages. [§ 960]

Punitive damages are money awarded in addition to compensatory or nominal damages as a **punishment for particularly aggravated misconduct on the part of the defendant.**

a. Defendant's Mental State Is Key. [§ 961]

It is the defendant's **mental state,** rather than her outward conduct, that justifies punitive damages. Courts have developed terms to describe this kind of mental state such as **"malicious," "oppressive," "evil,"** or the conduct as **"wanton"** or **"morally culpable."** Thus, anything that negates an improper state of mind will preclude punitive damages, as when the defendant has acted in good faith or due to a material mistake.

b. Amount of Damages Awarded. [§ 962]

While the U.S. Supreme Court has held that there must be some reasonable relation between the punitive award and the amount of compensatory damages awarded, courts recognize that a **punitive award may properly vary with the defendant's financial circumstances and the nature of his misconduct,** since the purpose of punitive damages is to punish the defendant and deter him from acting in the same manner in the future.

c. Vicarious Liability. [§ 963]

The majority of courts hold an employer liable for punitive damages for malicious acts of her employee. The **Restatement Second** view is that an employer is not liable unless she or her managerial officers order, participate in, or ratify the employee's aggravated misconduct.

d. Punitive Damage Reforms. [§ 964]

Many jurisdictions have adopted provisions making it more difficult for plaintiffs to recover punitive damages, such as increasing the burden of proof from a preponderance to "clear and convincing."

E. JOINT AND SEVERAL TORT LIABILITY. [§ 965]

1. Several Liability. [§ 966]

Liability is **several** when some logical basis can be found for distributing damages among the different defendants. Thus, if Alpha shoots Pi in the arm, and Beta concurrently shoots Pi in the leg, each is liable only for the injury he caused—Alpha for the arm, and Beta for the leg. Several judgments impose liability on each defendant for his share of the plaintiff's injury.

2. Joint Liability. [§ 967]

The defendants are **jointly liable** when there is no reasonable way to apportion damages.

3. Instances of Joint Liability. [§ 968]

There is joint liability in the following instances:

a. Acts in Concert. [§ 969]

Each of two or more defendants will be jointly liable when they are engaged in a **common endeavor** which results in injury. It does not matter whether the independent acts of one caused the entire harm, or the acts of all of the defendants combined to produce the injury so long as it can be shown that there was an express or implied agreement to act in concert and it is clear that the acts of at least one of them caused the injury.

b. Successive or Indivisible Injuries. [§ 970]

There may be joint liability when there are **successive injuries** to a plaintiff, but it is **impossible to determine which tortfeasor caused which injury.** Similarly, when the actions of two or more tortfeasors each constitute a **substantial factor in causing a single, indivisible injury,** the preferable rule is to hold the defendants jointly liable unless each defendant can adequately prove the limit of his liability.

> **(1) Example. [§ 971]** Pry is harmed by drinking water polluted due to the negligence of Ann's company and of Ben's company. Because each was a substantial factor in causing her indivisible harm, Ann and Ben are jointly and severally liable. Thus, Pry could recover full damages from Ann alone or from Ben alone (giving rise to a contribution claim against the joint tortfeasor not sued), or Pry could sue both Ann and Ben.

c. Vicarious Liability Situations. [§ 972]

A tortfeasor and all persons vicariously liable for the acts of that tortfeasor are jointly liable to the plaintiff.

4. Joint Judgment. [§ 973]

If the defendants are jointly liable, a **joint judgment** will be entered. While the plaintiff can collect only once, he can collect the full amount from any one defendant or any combination of defendants.

a. Contribution. [§ 974]

If the plaintiff collects the entire amount against one of several defendants, the defendant who paid may seek contribution from the others. At common law, the amount paid was a pro rata share (e.g., if there are three defendants, each is liable for 1/3). The modern trend is to have equitable contribution based on each defendant's amount of fault.

b. Indemnity. [§ 975]

As between the tortfeasors, the entire loss can be shifted from one joint tortfeasor to another if there is a right of **indemnity**. In addition to indemnity rights provided by contract, a right of indemnity exists in **one vicariously liable** against the defendant who actually committed the tort; against a **supplier of goods** when a seller incurs liability for the sale of a product which was defective when the seller received it; and against one with a **"primary duty"** by one who is **"secondarily liable"** (as when a landowner is held liable for failing to remedy a dangerous condition on her land which was created by another). **Rights of indemnification in no way affect the rights of the plaintiff to collect all or any part of his judgment from either defendant, however.**

Multiple Choice Question 1

As Pam walked across the street, she was hit by two negligently driven cars. It is impossible to discern which defendant caused which harm. One car was driven by Dale and the other by Dinah. Pam sues Dale only. A jury finds her to have suffered $10,000 in damages and finds Dale 40%

at fault, Dinah 40% at fault, and Pam 20% at fault. How much can Pam recover from Dale? Assume that action is brought in a pure comparative fault jurisdiction that has retained joint and several liability.

(A) $10,000

(B) $8,000

(C) $5,000

(D) $4,000

ANSWER TO THE MULTIPLE CHOICE QUESTION

Answer to Question 1.

(B) is correct.

B is the correct answer because joint and several liability survives the adoption of comparative fault in the jurisdiction. Accordingly, Pam may sue either defendant (or both) and recover for her injuries, less her percent of fault. Thus, A, C, and D are incorrect. [See Text §§ 479, 480].

PRACTICE ESSAY QUESTIONS

Question 1

Defendant bought a car for $50,000. The car had interior gold fixtures, genuine leopard fur on the seats, a slideout bar, a TV set, and other like accessories. In order to protect the car from vandalism and theft, Defendant equipped it himself with a system, which, if a door was opened, caused an alarm to sound and induced a severe electric shock to a person touching the handle of the door as it opened.

Baker, a commercial photographer, seeing the car parked on the street, induced his friend, Art Archer, to get into the car as a gag for the purpose of taking a picture of Art at the wheel. Art was reluctant but finally agreed. Art took hold of the handle of the door on the sidewalk side. The door was unlocked. As he started to open the door, he received a shock. Such a shock ordinarily would not seriously injure a healthy person, but because of his pre-existing heart condition, the shock caused Art to stagger back, collapse on the sidewalk and die shortly thereafter.

As he fell, his wife Sue Archer, who witnessed the incident, ran to help him but was knocked down when he fell against her. As a result of this experience, she was unable to sleep, and frequently experienced headaches, nausea and vomiting.

Neither Art nor Baker knew that the car was wired to induce electrical shocks. Neither had seen a sign on the front windshield which could be read from the sidewalk and which stated, "Beware, this car is equipped with a protective device—DO NOT TOUCH!" Suit is brought against the Defendant for damages for the death of Art and the injury to Sue Archer. What result? Discuss.

Question 2

The manager of defendant's store, in order to deter shoplifters, adopted a policy of stopping people at random as they were leaving the store and asking them whether they had taken certain items which were commonly pilfered. Plaintiff was stopped and questioned in this manner and when she appeared to be flustered, the manager ordered her to go back to his office. When she hesitated, he placed his hand on her shoulder and turned her in that direction. She then proceeded to the office without any further assistance from him. When they arrived there, he told her to sit down and wait until he returned with the police.

Instead of going for the police, the manager closed, but did not lock, the office door and stepped into an adjoining office where he watched plaintiff through a one-way mirror to see if she would try to hide anything she might be carrying on her person. Plaintiff could not see the manager and after a few moments went to the mirror, fixed her makeup, unbuttoned her blouse, adjusted her bra, and returned to the chair.

When the manager saw that plaintiff was not trying to hide anything, he returned to the office, apologized for having detained her, said he had decided not to call the police but that so many items were being stolen that a person couldn't be too careful and escorted her to the door. What are the plaintiff's tort claims against the defendant and the defenses thereto? Discuss.

Question 3

Plaintiff, a married man of 30 with two children, became mentally ill. He was receiving psychiatric treatment on an outpatient basis at a local clinic. One day, suffering from a severe psychotic episode, he appeared on a public street some blocks from his home in the nude. He was found by his wife, who had been called to the scene by a friend. She covered him with a raincoat which she had brought along and returned home with him, but not before a local reporter had photographed him.

The wife discovered the identity of the reporter, called him up, and told the reporter not to publish the picture as her husband was mentally ill and couldn't be responsible for his acts. The defendant newspaper, however, published the nude picture of the plaintiff over a caption reading, "A neighbor goes for a mid-morning stroll. This mild weather we are having brings out all kinds." No other comment or explanation appeared in the paper. After the plaintiff recovered from his illness and within the period required by the local statute of limitations, he commenced an action against the newspaper. Assume that no issue of retraction is involved in the case. Discuss the issues involved in the suit and any possible defenses.

Question 4

D, out hunting with a high-powered rifle equipped with a scope sight, sighted F sitting in a train window some 400 yards away. D pointed the rifle at F, not planning to shoot, but only to take aim at F for practice. T, a passerby hidden from D, saw the weapon pointed at the train and, thinking D was about to shoot, ran out and hit D's arm, deflecting the weapon and discharging it.

The bullet entered the engine, killing the engineer who had just started the train. The engine was not equipped with a "dead-man" device (as required by federal law), which would have automatically brought the train to a stop. No such device was required by state law and the engine was not so equipped because it was never used outside the state although it was pulling a train carrying passengers coast to coast. The federal law imposed a penalty on any railroad that operated a train in interstate commerce without such equipment.

Before the engine could be stopped, it had gathered momentum and the train had proceeded around a curve, hitting a car driven by X at a crossing one-half mile from the station. X was unaware of the approach of the train because it appeared around the bend at high speed and without any warning signal. The crossing was protected by a simple crossbuck railroad warning sign. The impact threw X's car into a ditch beside the road on the side from which he had been coming and killed him instantly. Who can sue whom for what? Discuss and decide all issues.

Question 5

Julio (J), an employee of GasCo Oil, Inc. (G), was driving his big-rig with 8,000 gallons of gasoline on Old Oaks Road through downtown en route to one of the gas stations he services. This was the only available route to the gas station. It was 3:00 a.m., and this was J's usual time and route for delivery of gasoline to gas stations. The big-rig was specially built for the transportation of gasoline and was as secure as possible.

Old Oaks has a sharp 90-degree curve. J was aware of the need to slow while making this curve and did so. He had never had any problems at this intersection before nor had he ever been in an accident with his big-rig.

As he was slowly making the turn, J saw a large dog standing about twenty feet away in the road in front of him. He immediately began braking and honking the horn, but it was clear that the dog was not going to move. To avoid hitting the dog, he turned the steering wheel to the left. Although he used all due care, the big-rig ran off the road, rolled over and ruptured, spilling most of the gasoline into the street. Some of the gasoline spilled into the sewer system. Several minutes later, a person from the neighborhood, Al, hearing the commotion, came onto the scene. He was smoking a cigarette. After briefly surveying the situation, en route to his home to call the police, he dropped his lit cigarette into the sewer. The gasoline ignited at once, completely destroying Pol's house nearby.

Evidence reveals that the dog J encountered was owned by Ernestine (E). The dog had bitten strangers on several occasions and was ordinarily kept locked in E's yard. On this occasion, however, E had inadvertently left the gate unlocked when she left hurriedly for a nearby hospital upon learning that her father had been seriously injured in a car accident.

Pol sues E and G seeking to recover damages. What causes of action should she plead, and how will the issues likely be resolved?

Question 6

Pauline was driving her five-year-old U.S. Motors Astro on the highway. As she drove underneath a pedestrian over-crossing, an unidentified youth dropped a brick from the over-crossing with the apparent intention of hitting Pauline's car. This conduct violated both state and federal criminal laws. The brick crashed through the car's sunroof, which was closed, and struck Pauline in the head.

The shock and surprise of the incident caused Pauline to lose control of the car, and she crashed into the center divider, causing additional personal injuries and damages to the car. Pauline was not wearing her seat belt at the time of the accident. Although she was not required by law to wear the seat belt, the seat belt would have prevented the additional injuries she suffered when the car hit the center divider.

The sunroof was approximately 1/4 inch thick and was made of plexiglass, a relatively light plastic that is structurally weak. At the time Pauline's car was manufactured, an alternative material, lexan polycarbonate sheeting (LPS), was being tested by the research and development division of the Bavarian Motor Works, a German car manufacturer, for use in sunroofs.

LPS is both stronger and heavier than plexiglass, and the evidence establishes that if LPS had been used in Pauline's car, the brick would simply have bounced off. LPS is about twice as expensive as plexiglass. As a result of consumer testing, U.S. Motors asserts that given a choice between the lightweight plexiglass and the heavier LPS, consumers manifested an overwhelming preference for the plexiglass. U.S. Motors arrived at this conclusion because consumers have expressed concerns about cost and about fuel efficiency. The extra weight of LPS would decrease the fuel efficiency of the Astro considerably. The Astro is advertised as U.S Motors' most fuel efficient car. At the time of Pauline's injury, only the Bavarian Motors Works used LPS in the sunroofs of its luxury sedans.

Discuss all issues that would arise in a **strict products liability** suit by Pauline against U.S. Motors.

SUGGESTED ANALYSIS TO THE ESSAY QUESTIONS

Answer to Question No. 1

This situation presents interesting analogies to the celebrated spring gun cases in which the intentional tort liability of one who sets a trap gun designed to hit intruders is considered. As in those cases, the defendant's conduct can be characterized as the intentional infliction of an electric shock on anyone who opened a door (even though injury to no particular person was intended), and hence a battery unless justified. The issue, as in the spring gun cases, is one of justification.

The spring gun cases have permitted recovery when a trespasser is injured by a spring gun, set to wound intruders on the defendant's real property. It may be argued that these cases are inapplicable because a spring gun represents the use of deadly force, and ordinary privilege rules do not permit the use of deadly force in defense of property. The force exerted by the protective device is much less, and was such as would not seriously injure a healthy person. It may well be that in some situations defendant could use analogous force had he been present to keep intruders out of his car. However, the protective device, like the spring gun, is unable to discriminate. For example, if defendant had been present when Art entered his car, by analogy to the rules relating to defense of real property, he would have been required to request that Art leave before being privileged to use any force at all. Defendant may counter that a warning had been given—the sign on the windshield— and, again, given the non-deadly nature of the force, it should be privileged. The difficulty with the argument is that there was one sign on the windshield—one that might well be missed (as it was) by a person dazzled by defendant's opulent vehicle. Whether the shock device would have been privileged, given more adequate, prominent, and pointed warnings, is a question which need not be pursued: it was not privileged here.

Assuming defendant has committed a battery, he is liable for all consequences, including the death due to Art's peculiar susceptibility, under the rule that the defendant takes the plaintiff as he finds him. Further, since the tort is battery, any argument that Art was contributorily negligent in not noticing the sign is unavailing, since contributory negligence is no defense to battery.

If defendant is liable for Art's death, is he also liable for Sue's injuries? While the tortious conduct as to Art is intentional—a battery—the relevant analogy is to negligent infliction of emotional distress. Defendant did not intend emotional distress, nor was he reckless in causing it. A transferred intent argument seems strained. Sue's claim might qualify under an impact theory, as Art fell against her before he died and as he recoiled from the shock. There is no requirement that the trivial impact be that which caused plaintiff's distress, and even in jurisdictions which have extended liability beyond impact, impact may still be a significant theory of recovery. In those jurisdictions which limit recovery for shock due to injury of a relative in situations where the plaintiff is in the "zone of danger," it may be argued that Sue was sufficiently close to Art although she was not apparently endangered. Sue, however, was not endangered at the moment Art received his shock. It may be argued that Sue is a "rescuer," and, as in other "rescue" cases, should be treated as one within the "zone of danger." Finally, under the California view, a close relative who actually views serious injury may recover for emotional distress. A requirement in many jurisdictions for recovery for negligent infliction of emotional distress is that the plaintiff suffer physical injury. Since the cases which impose the physical injury requirement deal with pleadings and jury instructions, it is unclear what constitutes physical injury. It may well be that the combination of sleeplessness, headache, nausea, and vomiting will, in combination, qualify. If plaintiff has suffered physical injury, she will also recover general damages for pain and suffering. (Note that plaintiff **cannot** recover damages for grief in the wrongful death action that she is permitted to bring, but can recover for grief, if at all, as a parasitic element of damages in her cause of action for negligent infliction of emotional distress.)

Answer to Question No. 2

Battery and Assault. D intentionally placed his hand on P's shoulder and turned her in the direction of his office. Arguably, this may be an offensive touching. P may have an assault claim too if she saw D about to touch her.

False Imprisonment. The issue will be whether there has been an imprisonment. D will argue that P followed him to the office, he closed but did not lock the door, and he merely "asked" P to wait while he called the police. Yet, in that context, P may have believed that she had to follow D and that she had to remain in the room. She did not know the door to the office was unlocked and even if she did, she may well have concluded she had to stay until the police arrived.

False Arrest. This is a variant on the imprisonment theory, although it is arguable that when D said he was going to call the police, and P thereafter stayed, she was acquiescing in a citizen's arrest for a misdemeanor. An advantage of this theory to P over false imprisonment generally is that traditionally such an arrest for a misdemeanor was not privileged by probable cause, but was privileged only if a misdemeanor had, in fact, been committed by the arrestee. Courts which have developed the broader merchant's privilege discussed below, however, would probably apply it here as well.

Invasion of Privacy. This theory has been applied beyond mass media publication to cases of physical intrusions into privacy. D did observe P through a one-way mirror in a situation in which P obviously supposed no one was observing her. In the absence of trespass, the physical invasion of privacy theory bases liability on conduct that is excessively invasive of the plaintiff's sphere of privacy. Finding an invasion of privacy may well depend on the same kind of conclusions which will be discussed with reference to intentional infliction of emotional distress, below.

Slander. If other people saw the incident, there may be publication of a non-verbal accusation of theft, which is slander per se if the jurisdiction includes charges of petty theft within that category. However, it is questionable whether other people observing the incident, unless they also overheard the questioning, would conclude that P was being so accused.

Intentional Infliction of Emotional Distress. The Restatement of Torts permits recovery for intentional infliction of emotional distress when there is intentional (or reckless) "extreme and outrageous" conduct resulting in the infliction of severe emotional distress. The total course of D's conduct can be characterized as extreme and outrageous, particularly in light of the discussion of lack of probable cause below. D may have been reckless as to P's emotional distress but probably not as he seemed to think his conduct appropriate. Nor is there evidence that P suffered severe emotional distress.

Privileges—The Shopkeeper's Privilege. Many courts permit a merchant to escape tort liability when the merchant has reasonable suspicion that a customer has stolen an item, and the detention is done for a reasonable amount of time and in a reasonable manner. Even under the most generous interpretation of this privilege, it would not apply here since it is stated that D stopped people at random and not upon probable cause. Given a strong policy not to permit detention and interrogation except with probable cause, the fact that P became flustered when stopped and questioned without cause should not justify D's subsequent conduct if it can be classified as tortious. Because of the lack of "reasonable suspicion" the privilege will fail and the defendant will be liable.

Answer to Question No. 3

(1) **"True" Privacy.** The Warren and Brandeis article on privacy (*The Right to Privacy*, 4 Harv.L.Rev. 193 (1890)) argued for an actionable right of privacy when the mass media went beyond the bounds of decency in publicizing current events. Nevertheless, in the case of true privacy, the concept of newsworthiness (whether non-newsworthiness is viewed as an essential element of the prima facie tort or newsworthiness is an affirmative defense) has arguably swallowed the tort. Despite some dicta to the contrary, defendant's rights to print the picture and a true

news report do not depend on a newsworthy figure's voluntary waiver of privacy but on the public's interest in the news, thus weakening the argument that there was no waiver here because of plaintiff's incompetence. Nor are there any cases which have been able to limit the privilege to print true stories about current happenings with reference to notions of the kind of news it is "decent" to print. None of the cases which have found privacy violations with reference to the printing of a picture have gone so far as to provide protection to a newsworthy plaintiff photographed in a public place. Probably, then, there is not a "true" privacy case by P against D.

(2) **"False Light" Privacy.** The bulk of privacy cases which have sustained P's right to "privacy" have been so-called false light privacy cases. Even if the event is newsworthy, P may recover if the picture and story distort the truth. The nature of the falsity required under this theory is not certain, but if this story can be characterized as false, it can arguably be one of those which damages P in the eyes of others more than a true story would. It is clear that the falsity need not be defamatory in the narrow sense of reflecting on P's "character." Was the story false? D will argue that all statements it made were true—P was out for a mid-morning stroll—and that at most, D omitted facts which would put P's conduct in a different light. P will argue that the omission of the additional facts made the statement false. Assuming that P prevails on the issue of falsity, under the United States Constitution, D retains the newsworthiness privilege unless it knew of the falsity, or acted with reckless disregard of the truth. Since P's wife had told the reporter about the background facts, if omission of those facts caused the story to be false, P may demonstrate that the "falsity" was at least reckless. Probably, P can recover on a false light privacy theory.

(3) **Defamation.** P has little advantage in proceeding on a defamation theory as opposed to a false-light privacy case. First, the defense of truth will require the same inquiry as to whether or not the story is false that is required under false light. In addition, since this case involves a media defendant, it is likely that it involves an issue of "public concern." Accordingly, P would have to show actual malice to recover punitive damages or presumed damages, and would have to prove "actual damages" to recover at a lesser standard. On a defamation theory, P will have the additional problem of showing that, to the extent the statement is false, it is defamatory. Again, whatever the overlap between false-light privacy and defamation, probably the false innuendo that P is strolling in the nude for a lark will go sufficiently to his character to be defamatory even in jurisdictions with a narrow view of that concept.

(4) **Intentional Infliction of Emotional Distress.** There are few cases applying this tort—"extreme and outrageous conduct likely to cause emotional distress"—to mass media publications. Probably that is because of the more relevant defamation and privacy theories. Even if

the theory is applicable, however, constitutional free speech considerations probably require application of the truth and newsworthiness defenses, as in privacy or defamation. P may not make an "end run" around the safeguards in defamation and privacy actions by calling it intentional infliction of emotional distress. If P can recover for defamation of privacy, he can recover for intentional infliction of emotional distress provided he proves the elements of that tort.

Answer to Question No. 4

F v. D. Unless F was aware of D's conduct in aiming the rifle at him, there is no tort of assault. If F was so aware (which is unlikely on the facts), D is liable to F for assault—i.e., D created in F an apprehension that he would be subjected to an imminent battery.

Engineer v. D. The engineer may recover from D, whether the theory is negligence or an intentional tort of battery in the context of transferred intent. The issue of which is the correct theory will be most significant in the case of **X v. D.**

X v. D. D may claim he owed no duty to X as X was not endangered by his conduct. X's survivors may argue that D's tort was intentional as to the engineer, and that a tortfeasor guilty of intentional misconduct is responsible for wider consequences than a negligent tortfeasor would be. If F was unaware of D's conduct, however, D's conduct was not even tortious, and even if it was, it is not clear whether D's intent to assault F can be transferred to constitute a battery on E, and then transferred farther to justify recovery by X. D's argument is, basically, that harm to X required violation of the deadman statute by the railroad—intervening wrongful conduct—required the intervention of T, and resulted in harm a considerable distance away. At a purely formal level, X's survivors may counter the intervening wrongful conduct argument by arguing that D acted on a "set stage" and that the railroad's failure to have the device was not "independent" or "intervening." Given the serious nature of D's conduct—pointing a loaded gun—a court might be unimpressed by D's argument of lack of foreseeability and impose liability for a wide range of consequences, even if D's conduct may be characterized only as negligence. Judge Cardozo's theory in the *Palsgraf* case—that a negligent tortfeasor is never responsible to plaintiffs at such a distance that they are not foreseeably endangered by his conduct—has been rejected by most courts despite the prominence of that opinion.

D v. T. T's conduct was a battery as to D unless it can be justified. There is a privilege to use reasonable force, even to protect a complete stranger, and most courts would reject limitations on the defense to protect others from harm to members of the defender's family and the like.

Engineer v. T. If T's conduct were unreasonable, it would not only cause his defense to D's battery claim to fail, it would impose liability for injury to engineer on a negligence theory.

X v. T. The lack-of-foreseeability, *Palsgraf*—type defense, discussed under **X v. D**, should be more available to T than it was to D, since T's conduct, even if unreasonable, was considerably less blameworthy than D's. Note the anomaly, however, that T's tort as to D is intentional if his defense-of-others privilege fails because his conduct is unreasonable. It is arguable that this demonstrates the unreliability of the well-worn concept that an intentional tortfeasor is responsible for a wider range of consequences than one who is merely negligent, since in many cases of technically intentional torts, the defendant's real fault lies in negligence in conduct which would have been justified if reasonable.

X v. Railroad. Railroad's violation of a federal safety statute should be negligence even though the statute is federal and the tort action will be based on state law. The relevance of the statute lies in imposing a standard of reasonable conduct on the railroad and not in creating a federal cause of action. The railroad should not be able to defend on the basis of the intervening wrongful conduct of D, since the purpose of the statute was to guard against the disablement of the engineer from any cause, and the particular cause should be irrelevant. (It is not inconceivable, though, that a court impressed by the overwhelming nature of D's wrongdoing would characterize it as an independent intervening act, relieving the railroad of responsibility. If that kind of decision is ever proper, however, it ought to be reserved for the case where D deliberately shoots the engineer.) The statute is not the kind of paternalistic measure which makes the defense of contributory negligence irrelevant. However, X's alleged contributory negligence should be, at most, a question for the jury. Holmes's position in *Baltimore & Ohio Railroad Co. v. Goodman*, 275 U.S. 66 (1927)—that a motorist who fails to stop, look, listen and if necessary, get out of his vehicle if he can't see approaching trains is contributory negligence as a matter of law—has been moribund for decades.

Answer to Question No. 5

P v. G.

Cause of action—Strict liability for abnormally dangerous activity (ADA) of transporting gas. Pol has to prove cause in fact, proximate cause & ADA. One who engages in an ADA is liable to others for loss of land, chattels, or person, even though utmost care is used. The liability is limited to the type of harm the risk of which makes it abnormally dangerous. Here it is arguable that a house burning down is not within the risk that makes transporting gasoline abnormally dangerous, but the better argument is that the flammability of gasoline is much of the reason for its potential as abnormally dangerous.

To determine whether a certain activity is "abnormally dangerous," the best approach is to focus on the Restatement (Second) of Torts, section 590 factors. These factors are for the court to consider and balance in making its determination of whether liability without fault is appropriate.

Is transporting gas an ADA?

1. High degree of risk to land, chattels, person? P argues that transporting gas is high risk because gas is explosive, and even at 3 a.m. is highly flammable.

2. Gravity of harm likely to be great? 8,000 gallons of gas, if spilled or exploded, can cause a great deal of damage to anyone in the vicinity.

3. Extent to which harm can be lessened by use of utmost (due) care? Here, "rig" was specially built, and the driver used all care around a curve, yet harm occurred. Apparently cannot be lessened.

4. Common usage? Common to gas companies, but not all people. Analogous to *Langan v. Valicopter, Inc.*, 567 P.2d 218 (Wash. 1977), where crop dusters were used by "only" 274 people. Gas is carried every day and may be more common than crop dusting, but clearly not as common as driving a car.

5. Whether inappropriate to place? Here, Pol has a problem. It is 3 a.m. and this is probably a good time to carry on this activity. In Pol's favor, however, G had to go through downtown. While this is a problem for G, this is the **only** route available. May be inappropriate but than we would never have gas in cities.

6. Value to the community? People love their cars. There is a high value on having gas available. But to the extent that strict liability focuses on who best should bear the cost of the accident, G is best positioned to absorb the injury costs as a cost of doing business.

While there is room for debate, a judge balancing these Restatement factors probably would find that activity here to be abnormally dangerous.

Some courts have rejected the balancing approach of the Restatement, claiming it is too close to a negligence standard. These courts would look at the activity involved and simply determine if it is appropriate for strict liability treatment.

Cause in fact

It cannot be stated that but for the transportation of the gas, Pol's house would not have burned, because there are two (or three) potential defendants here. Each, though, was a substantial factor in the burning of the house. The dog and the truck could and did not independently cause the harm; they joined together to cause indivisible harm to Pol.

Proximate cause

The dog and rig only caused the rig to rupture and pour down the sewer. Then, Al came on the scene. The risk created by transporting gas is injury to persons and property, particularly by fire, Pol will note, and that is just what happened here. G will argue the risk is limited to spilled gas. Further, G will contend that Al's conduct was so grossly negligent as to be superseding. The facts state that Al "surveyed" the situation and then dropped his cigarette. If he smelled gas, or saw gas, or even saw the truck, he probably was aware of the risks of dropping the cigarette. However, it was 3 a.m., presumably dark, and it is unlikely, in such an emergency situation, that Al's conduct was so extreme as to be superseding.

P v. G—negligence.

Because J was acting in the scope of employment at the time of the harm, G is vicariously liable for his tortious conduct. In addition to liability based on ADA, P could contend that J acted negligently (unreasonably). While J drove generally without fault, he did, however, choose to turn the truck to avoid running over the dog. Although he was acting in an emergency not of his own making, the burden of hitting the dog and not tipping the truck (while morally repugnant), is not high. Probability of harm is substantial as it was a large truck and the potential magnitude of harm is also significant since gasoline is so flammable.

P v. E

P can sue E for letting her animal loose, knowing it had a propensity to cause harm. This is the oldest rule of strict liability—liability for animals. This rule, of liability without fault, has been preserved since days of wandering cattle.

P can also sue for E's negligence in letting the dog run loose and cause harm. E has a duty to her neighbors because the animal is hers and has caused harm in the past. Letting out the troublesome dog is probably a breach of duty. A reasonably prudent person would know that the burden of closing a gate is less that the probability of harm and magnitude of such harm. P may contend, however, that the "emergency doctrine" should apply here. While this doesn't change the standard of care, the determination of reasonableness would take into account the fact that E was rushing to the hospital. Cause in fact—E's negligence was a substantial factor in causing P's harm. Proximate Cause—E will contend that her breach was not the proximate cause of E's injury because the risk created by her negligent conduct was harm to persons by her "vicious" dog. Because risk to property—certainly by fire—is not one of the foreseeable risks, E would argue she should escape liability. P has a tough time here, though she could try to define the potential risk as generalized harm.

Answer to Question No. 6

The first question is whether Pauline (P) is a proper plaintiff for purposes of strict products liability (SPL). Under Restatement section 402A, any user or consumer is a proper plaintiff. Here P is clearly a user of the product and is, thus, a proper plaintiff.

Is U.S Motors (USM) a proper defendant? One who is in the business of dealing with the product in question and who is part of the marketing chain is a proper defendant. As the manufacturer, USM is clearly a proper defendant.

Is there anything preventing recovery under SPL? There is no indication that the product was altered. While USM may try to argue that P misused the product by not wearing the seat belt, this is at best foreseeable misuse (particularly since there was no law requiring use of the seat belts). Further, it is doubtful that the failure to wear a seat belt is relevant to the defect involved—here the plexiglass being used instead of LPS. P would have been shocked and would have lost control of the car even if she had a seat belt on. Finally, this product does not fall under Restatement section 402A comment (k) because there are alternatives and it does not possess the extraordinary utility normally associated with unavoidably unsafe products.

The key issue is whether the Astro's sunroof is defective in design. The focus is on a design defect because the product is in the condition intended by the manufacturer. Some jurisdictions require (under 402A) that the plaintiff prove that the product was unreasonably dangerous (so as to fail to meet the ordinary consumer expectation test). Many jurisdictions have followed the lead of California and have gotten rid of the "unreasonably dangerous" requirement because it tends to inject too much negligence into a strict liability analysis. Under the ordinary consumer expectation test, P will argue that an ordinary consumer would not expect a closed sunroof to break when an object hits it. USM more likely will argue successfully that the ordinary consumer has no real expectation or understanding of the composition of sunroofs.

Most jurisdictions have provided an alternative test to determine design defectiveness: the risk-utility balancing test. Under this test, the risk of harm is weighed against the utility of the product as designed. In many jurisdictions, knowledge of the risk is imputed; in many states, then, U.S. Motors would be assumed to know that the sunroof may break under certain circumstances. Here the gravity of potential harm is very high-personal injury including possibly even death, harm to the eyes, etc. The likelihood of the harm is less clear. While no statistics are given, since the plexiglass is structurally weak, it is likely to break upon a certain impact. It is unclear how much pressure is needed. It is rare for things to be intentionally dropped from over-crossings. It is less rare that other things are dropped or that cars are in collisions. There is a feasible alternative that was knowable at the time of manufacture—

LPS. There may be other knowable alternatives too. The cost of alternatives is relevant, however.

While the facts are vague, USM will try to show that LPS is expensive. Since the cost of the Astro would increase, it is logical to assume that LPS is expensive. Further proof is the fact that LPS is used only in BMW luxury cars. P will respond that the sunroof is a small part of the car so the increase would be minor. USM will further argue that use of LPS will negatively affect the Astro and society as a whole as LPS will lessen the fuel efficiency of the Astro. It is likely that the primary reason consumers choose the Astro is because if its excellent fuel efficiency. P will contend that safety concerns are more important than relatively unimportant things like sunroofs. Much of the rationale of SPL is based on the desire to create incentives toward safer products. Further, if USM wishes to continue to market this sunroof on the Astro, it may do so and simply pay for the harm caused. Under enterprise liability notions, USM is best positioned to pass along the costs associated with this accident. Based on these facts, a jury could, but is not likely to, find the risk created by the plexiglass outweighs its value.

Cause in fact. It is clear that the lack of LPS was a substantial factor in P's harm. Had USM used LPS, the brick would have simply bounced off.

Proximate cause. The risk created by using a structurally weaker product is that property damage and personal injury will ensue when it breaks. USM, however, will argue that there was unforeseeable intervening conduct that should relieve it of liability. While it may be foreseeable the sunroof would break, it is not foreseeable that a person would intentionally throw a rock on the car. Since the conduct was intentional and criminal, the act may be deemed superseding. Just because the conduct is criminal, however, does not make it superseding and a jury could find USM liable. Proximate cause may be interpreted generously in the context of SPL, and USM is profiting from marketing the Astro with the cheaper and more dangerous sunroof.

Defenses. Under 402A, P's contributory negligence is not a defense to a SPL action unless P has assumed the risk. It is unlikely that she has the requisite **subjective** understanding to have assumed the risk. There is no suggestion that she was aware of the breakability of the sunroof at all. Thus, in a jurisdiction following 402A, there would be no defense. [Nor would her failure to wear the seat belt be assumption of the risk. It may have other effects, however, as discussed below.]

Most jurisdictions that have adopted comparative fault have imported those principles into the strict liability context, reducing a plaintiff's recovery by her percentage of fault. Here, if USM is found strictly liable, they will contend that P was unreasonable for not wearing a seat belt. USM would note the tiny burden involved with fastening the seat belt and that there were foreseeable risks of significant harm for failing to do so. P would correctly respond that her failure to wear the seat belt was not causally related to the defective product causing injury—the shattering of the sunroof. Many courts, nonetheless, would permit a reduction of plaintiff's recovery under the guise of a failure to mitigate damages ("anticipatory avoidable consequences") or as part of general notions of comparative fault. Some courts would not reduce plaintiff's recovery.

TABLE OF CASES

References are to Pages

INDEX

247